AN ENGLISH RURAL COMMUNITY:

BATHEASTON WITH S. CATHERINE

by

B. M. WILLMOTT DOBBIE

Colligite fragmenta ne pereant

Bath University Press

Notes: (1)   The motto on the title page is that of the Scottish Historical Society.

(2)   Dates mentioned in text except in verbatim quotations, are expressed in New Style.

© B. M. Willmott Dobbie, 1969

SBN 900843 06 3

Printed by Coward & Gerrish Ltd.,
Larkhall, Bath, Somerset, England.

Contents

List of illustrations

Preface

THE village of Batheaston, with the associated hamlet of S. Catherine, comprise an ancient community with a continuous history at least from Saxon times. Though S. Catherine is now for most purposes regarded as a separate parish, it has evolved from a chapelry of Bath Abbey annexed to Batheaston. As late as 1840 the Tithe Award denotes it a "Chapelry and Hamlet", and it has always been served by the vicar of Batheaston. However, it had its own churchwardens by the end of the sixteenth century and levied its own rates from the middle of the seventeenth.

From a standpoint which is frankly amateur I have tried to study as many aspects of their past as I could profitably touch upon, keeping always in mind the prime purpose of the enterprise, the interest and pleasure of the inhabitants; and I have tried to make for them especially a useful book of reference. Nevertheless the work contains material illuminating English social history beyond a single parish, and so, I venture to hope, may interest a wider public than the purely local one.

W. G. Hoskins, in his *Local History in England*, wrote: "Some of the best documented local histories betray not the slightest sign that the author has looked over the hedges of his chosen place, or walked its boundaries, or explored its streets, or noticed its buildings and what they mean in terms of the history he is trying to write." Truly, the task requires the use of both head and feet, and besides scrutinising every relevant document I could lay my hands upon, I have travelled many miles in search of "treasure". One consequence is the necessary assumption of topographical familiarity which may repel possible readers who are strangers to the place. This I have held to be inevitable, and I hope that the maps may serve to make the matter intelligible.

Learned societies of the past have published accounts of their visits and the expositions of scholarly amateur historians and naturalists who so adorned them. I have made full use of these important sources. Documentary material is rich, and I have mined it

deeply. We are fortunate to possess in Batheaston an exceptionally complete set of parish records, embalming, as it were, all aspects of village life from the seventeenth century. Little remains of records kept at S. Catherine; a late register and fragmentary churchwardens' accounts. The Tithe Maps and Awards of 1840 are sources of great value, especially for field names and agricultural history. From all these records I have used extensive quotation, believing that *ipsissima verba* evoke a far more vivid picture than words of mine could do; for the same reason I have retained the spelling. Readers who find quotations boring have only to omit them. Some may be irritated by what may appear excessive use of references and lists. These I have included to ease the task of any scholar who may pass this way in the future. This consideration accounts for the use of appendices to publish some transcriptions not otherwise required in full.

Much that is written here is trivial in itself, and much commonplace; but were an account confined to the peculiar or even the unusual it would be a grotesque distortion of village history. The book describes this little world at length, and is crammed with fact. Where I have tried to excise I have often spared, fearful lest the withdrawal of one glow-worm power should injure the scene I was trying to illuminate. It may seem that excessive attention is devoted to the Church and the Poor; but this prominence only reflects the truth that throughout most of the historical period the focus of community life was the Church, to which everyone of necessity and by law belonged, and which touched his life at every point from birth to death. As for the Poor, disablement and destitution were evils which no one could ignore, never out of sight or mind, ever liable to strike, always a care of the Church, for nearly four centuries also a constant and increasing burden on the communal purse.

I owe a huge debt to all those who have patiently endured my questioning, whose personal recollection and knowledge, so gladly bestowed, have added to field and documentary sources yet another reservoir of local history. I am very grateful also to the Vicar, Prebendary R. A. Evans, who granted full access to the parish records in his custody, provided facilities for working and a sea of coffee, and permitted the reproduction of material; to Major Strutt, who allowed me to study the documents in his possession and thereby greatly added to the value of my work on S. Catherine; and to Mr. Christopher Blathwayt, who made available that notable source, the diaries of the Blathwayt family of Eagle House. For the use of documents in their archives I am indebted to the Dean and Chapter of Christ Church, Oxford. Mr. Peter Coard generously allowed me to draw upon his profound knowledge of the vernacular architecture, and for this I warmly thank him. With pleasure I record my gratitude to Mr. J. H. Lamble, of Bath University Press, to whose reassuring patience I owe so much.

"Of making many books there is no end; and much study is a weariness of the flesh." With diffidence I have made yet another book. If it gives pleasure to only a few the weariness of much study will be amply recompensed.

Batheaston
October 1969

Chapter 1

Setting the scene

Bath-Easton. This is a small town, of one tolerable street in length, and the appearance of the houses is very neat and clean.
                                    PIERCE EGAN 1819

(Numbers in the text refer to Map 1)

BATHEASTON and S. Catherine are in the extreme north-west of Somerset; immediately to the north is Gloucestershire, part of the eastern boundary adjoins Wiltshire. Situated on the north side of the valley of the Bristol Avon, some three miles from Bath, the river forms a natural southern boundary. S. Catherine's valley, renowned for its beauty, runs from north to south, its brook falling into the Avon a few yards after crossing the line of the Fosse Way, now the London Road, at Stambridge; the name implies an early stone bridge at this important crossing. The lower end of the valley is the site of the Saxon settlement, marked by the parish church (23). A main source of S. Catherine's brook rises at 600 feet above sea level (46); at its junction with the Avon it is less than 100.

In three places the land rises to more than 600 feet, in each case to a plateau: Charmy Down and Little Solsbury to the west, Banner Down to the east. These eminences are the southern tip of the Cotswolds; in fact, the land immediately to the north is typical Cotswold country, and there Batheaston can shew the familiar stone walls bounding the fields.

Geologically the area consists of middle and upper lias, overlain by the oolite on the high ground. An ample supply of springs provides a great part of the water supply of Bath. The soil is a calcareous clay, in the valley fertile and good for market gardening. The slopes are steep, and quite large patches of wood and scrub persist, probably primeval. On the high ground the soil is thin, and two large areas have never been enclosed, Banner Down (60 acres) and Little Solsbury (25 acres). The summit of Little Solsbury, with an Iron Age camp, includes an additional 22½ acres of National Trust property. To-day dairying and cattle raising predominate over arable farming, but at one time far more land was under the plough (Figs. 15 and 16). There are about 97 acres of market garden. The cloth trade, important in the past, has long come to an end. Many, perhaps the majority, of present inhabitants, however, earn their living in Bath. There is also a large number of retired persons, enjoying the dual pleasures of rural surroundings and the amenities of Bath. For the present, the Green

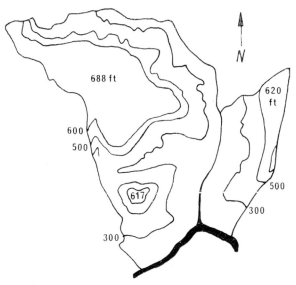

Fig. 1.   Contours

Belt protects the whole of S. Catherine, and that part of Batheaston—by far the greater part—not already "developed".

The boundary is for the most part certainly ancient, and largely pre-Conquest. On the east it is the Roman

Fosse Way, described in a charter relating to the adjacent parish of Bathford, and recording a grant by King Eadwig of land to Bath Abbey in 957.[1] The relevant part runs:

> Aarest of Afene andlang Straet on thane anne Stan. Of than stane on Beonnan Lehe.

> First from the Avon along the Street to the one Stone. From the stone to Banner Legh.

The designation Street was customarily given to a road of Roman origin. There is doubt about the exact course which the Fosse Way took as it climbed from the Avon valley up the slope of Banner Down; though tradition holds that it was the Fosse Lane, there is reason to believe that the present parish boundary follows its line.[2] If the line is correctly identified, the short walled driftway, once known as Henyard Lane, which leads on to Banner Down to the west of the present road (28), and the wall which continues its direction across the down, perpetuate the ancient course. From the point where the "one stone" presumably stood (41) the Fosse Way separates Batheaston from Colerne (and Wiltshire). The Three

Shires Stones (42) have been mistaken for the rebuilt burial chamber of a long barrow, but were, in fact, a new construction erected in 1859 by a subscription among neighbouring gentry, to make a more conspicuous landmark than the earlier stones. These at the present time stand little more than a foot above ground, arranged in the form of a triangle, the letters G,W, and S cut into them, the Gloucestershire stone bearing also the date 1736.

Good evidence of the antiquity of the boundary between Batheaston and Marshfield (also the county boundary), from the Fosse Way to S. Catherine's Brook, resides in the name Mercombe (Old English: mearc cumb: boundary valley) which belongs to a field on the Marshfield side of the boundary; and the name was used, too, of land on the Batheaston side in 1625.

Thence, travelling northward, the brook is a natural line of demarcation. From the point where the parishes of Marshfield, Cold Ashton and Batheaston meet the boundary is recognisably defined in a charter of the tenth century, shortly after 931.[3, 4] The

Pl. 1.   The Street, Batheaston, 1868
(drawing by J. T. Irvine in the Bath City Libraries Collection)

Pl. 2.   King's Watermeet 1969
(a pier of the bridge divides Cold Ashton Brook)

charter records a grant made by King Athelstan to Bath Abbey of land in Cold Ashton:

> Andlang Broces to thaes Cinges Gemythan Of thann Gemythan west be Broce to Linleg Wylle Of thaere Wylle on tha Hyle Thonne be thaere Hyle upp andlang Slaedes to Hafoc Wylle Of Hafoc Wylle on Heort Leage westweardre.

> Along the Brook to the King's Watermeet From the Watermeet west by the Brook to the Spring at Flax Lea From the Spring to the Bend Then by the Bend up along the Slade to Hawk Spring From Hawk Spring again to Hart Lea westwards.

The translation is Grundy's, as are the topographical identifications. The watermeet is the junction of S. Catherine's Brook with Cold Ashton Brook (49). The spring may have been on the site of Monkswood Reservoir. The bend was probably where the boundary turns south-west beneath the reservoir. The name of the spring survives in the modern Hawkswell (46), where the spring still bubbles out of the ground, a thousand years after the Saxon surveyors defined the boundary. The old name of the Lea survives in Hartley Farm (45).

What determined the course of the western boundary with Swainswick is unknown. At 39, where the line crosses a field, it is plainly marked by a bank of stones, evidently cleared off the ground and dumped on the no-man's-land of the boundary. In about its middle third the parish boundary follows a very ancient line, the track of the eastern branch of the prehistoric Jurassic Way, winding round Little Solsbury towards a crossing of the Avon.[5] For a short distance the modern Gloucester Road (A46) takes the line of this track, which used to be called Slaughter (Sloe Tree) Lane. The boundary then runs along Swainswick Lane, which probably perpetuates the Jurassic Way, deeply sunk between high banks. Then it turns to the south along a course the history of which is obscure, and after crossing the Fosse Way (London Road, A4) follows the line of a wet ditch to the Avon, which forms the entire southern boundary.

A tantalising little mystery lies at 15, where the boundary diverges for a short distance to the west of the lane, isolating a small sliver of land. Steep banks prove that the lane has not changed its course. Melmoth Walters, in his notes on a perambulation of the bounds in 1823 (p. 66) describes without expressing surprise or opinion how they went through the hedge and followed the line, ordering that stones, one of which remains, be placed where the boundary leaves and rejoins the lane.

Nothing is known of how the boundary between Batheaston and S. Catherine came to be drawn, but it is probably related to the old manorial extents if not to those of Domesday which preceded them. It is very complex; at an enquiry in 1816 it was held to bisect two fields, and one (Map 2, C28a) is an island of S. Catherine territory in Batheaston.

The present village of Batheaston is of four parts: the ancient nucleus now called Northend, having the parish church (23) as its focus; next, the High Street, still known to old residents as "The Street". Here the habitations have long spread to the west

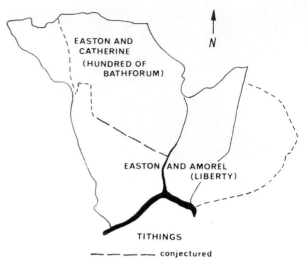

Fig. 3.   Tithings

beyond the old Townsend (Map 2, B12) towards Bath, at first elegant villas, later dwellings of less pretension. Batheaston is now nearly joined to Bath and in 1965 narrowly escaped being engulfed altogether, Bailbrook and the south-west corner of the parish falling to the strong neighbour as trophies of the fight. The third portion of the village is an "estate" of Rural District Council houses, built on the east side of the valley after 1945 on previously agricultural land. The fourth part consists of a somewhat aloof residential nexus, also modern, on the lower slopes of Banner Down, at the east end of the parish.

The hamlet of S. Catherine remains small, remote and scattered—its focal point the little church. The inhabitants in 1961 numbered only 90, while Batheaston had 3,307. Hilly as it is, there is little arable land, and only one market garden.

The position of the ancient farmhouses clearly indicates the nucleated type of settlement, the farmers having shares in the common fields. Several farmhouses date from the seventeenth century or earlier. Some fine houses owe their existence to the cloth trade. These subjects are developed in later pages.

In the part still rural the lanes, with their high banks, especially on steep ground, indicate a pattern of great age; they probably date from the early centuries of occupation, and may well be in part prehistoric. Grimes finds evidence that a very ancient track crossed Charmy Down and descended

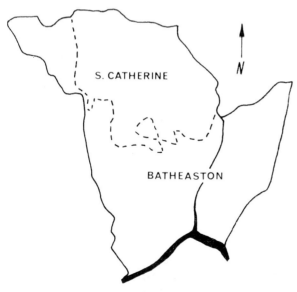

Fig. 2.   Parish boundaries
(Batheaston/S.Catherine simiplified)

into the valley by the line of the present Hollies (previously Hollows) Lane.

The Fosse Way, running from Exeter to Lincoln, traverses Batheaston along the Avon valley, here part of the ancient highway which for nearly two thousand years has linked London with the west, before turning north-east to climb Banner Down. The famous Bath Road has carried countless passengers of all kinds, from kings and queens to "poore travilers" and sick folk seeking the healing waters of Bath, a fact which has its bearing on the history of the place.

From its Saxon origins, Batheaston grew slowly, and at the end of the seventeenth century consisted of dwellings along Northend, the most closely inhabited part; a cluster of houses at Stambridge, others strung along the Street as far as Townsend, and the ancient mill on the Avon. Thorpe's map of 1742, the earliest to shew detail, gives a similar distribution.

Under the ancient system which divided counties into hundreds, and hundreds into tithings, our area consisted of the tithings of Easton and Catherine, in the hundred of Bathforum; and Easton and Amorel, part of the liberty i.e. land not in a hundred, of Hampton and Claverton, and including also Shockerwick, part of the parish of Bathford. For the historian this is inconvenient, requiring, for example, two lists of those liable for king's taxes where most parishes have only one. It has not proved possible to identify exactly the line dividing the tithings, but the one suggested in Fig. 3, deduced from taxation and jury lists, is approximately correct.

Chapter 2

Early days

We are part of the great social current formed of a multitude of intermingling streams that have come down from remote ages and distant lands.

G. ELLIOT SMITH

THIS chapter, necessarily compiled from published material, merely outlines the archaeological history of Batheaston, but includes references to all the sources quoted, so that any interested reader may easily pursue the subject. I am especially indebted to the work of Professor Grimes,[1] whose report is exhaustive for the Charmy Down area, and contains much besides of local interest (Fig. 4).

The story of human occupation of the Batheaston valley can be traced for about four thousand years, since men of the Neolithic Age made and used the flint instruments found in hundreds by J. P. E. Falconer; scrapers, knives, and the leaf-shaped arrowheads characteristic of their culture.[2] In the damp climate that was their lot the flat tops would be attractive sites for occupation. The north-western part of Charmy Down was the richest area for flint collection, and scraps of pottery of the Neolithic A. type have been found on the Down. Neolithic men may well have used the Jurassic Way (p. 3). They may have used the River Avon, too, for though the route taken by those amazing visionaries who brought the Blue Stones from the Prescelly Mountains in Pembrokeshire to Stonehenge is not certainly known, the likeliest is considered to be by way of the Bristol Avon; if so, the Blue Stones came by in the course of one of the most extraordinary exploits of early man.

There is plenty of evidence, too, of occupation in the Early and Middle Bronze Age. There were characteristic tanged arrows among the flints collected by Falconer; flint cores on Little Solsbury indicate that the material was worked there, though there was no local supply of flint. Pieces of polished axes have been found, and articles of bronze, among them a spearhead or dagger on Banner Down,[3] a bronze palstave on Little Solsbury and a flat bronze axe in S. Catherine.[4] During the making of the Monkswood Reservoir, just in Gloucestershire was uncovered an important "hoard" of bronze objects, and two bronze armlets and two fibulae were found at Cherrywell in 1857[5] (Map 1, 38).

The most conspicuous relics of the Bronze Age, however, were the round barrows on Charmy Down, finally and completely destroyed in the making of the airfield in 1940. [G.R. 31/756704, 31/762703] (John Aubrey noted a barrow on Banner Down, but it has quite disappeared. Banner Down is relatively poor in archaeological evidence, the only remaining visible object being a field bank). The Charmy Down barrows excited curiosity long ago. John Skinner, rector of Camerton, relates in his diary[6] how he and a Mr. Conybeare, probably the vicar of Batheaston, made an expedition in 1822 to explore some of the mounds, the largest of which had already been disturbed. Their trophies, which included a skeleton, were otherwise scanty.

The final examination of the barrows is recorded by Grimes, who was in charge of the archaeological survey of the site before the making of the airfield. Two barrows on Hartley Farm belonged to the Early Bronze Age; the main group, of five barrows, three in a composite mound, were of the Middle Bronze (Fig. 4). They had suffered much from the previous disturbances. The large mound as Grimes found it was 150 feet in length, including what remained of the surrounding ditch, and he demonstrated rings of stones forming the foundations of the individual barrows.

The remains of an important Iron Age camp crown Little Solsbury, which probably takes its name from Sul, the deity of Bath. The defences, though, have been largely destroyed by quarrying, and by wanton damage. Two excavations on the site by the University of Bristol Speleological Society were fully reported.[7, 8] In archaeological terms, it was a pure Iron Age A site and large numbers of sherds of that

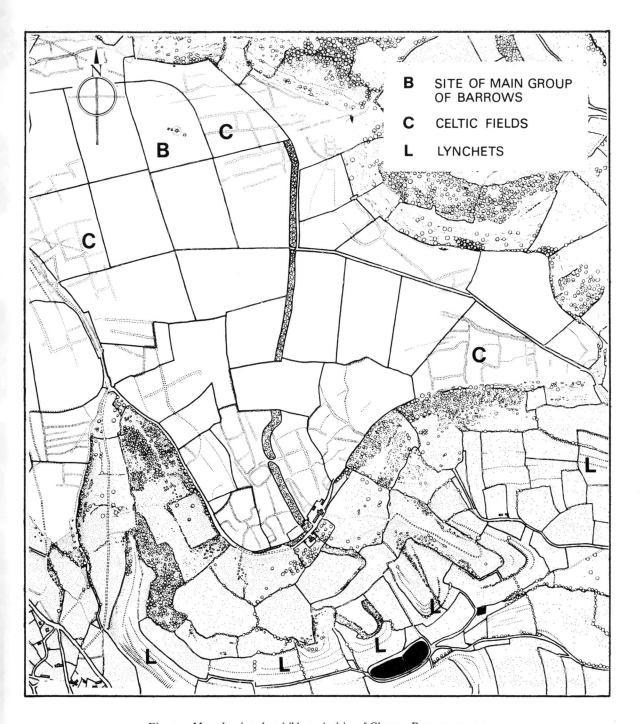

B SITE OF MAIN GROUP OF BARROWS
C CELTIC FIELDS
L LYNCHETS

Fig. 4.   Map showing the visible antiquities of Charmy Down as at 1940

Based upon the Ordnance Survey Map with the sanction of the Controller of H.M. Stationery Office, Crown copyright reserved

type were found. The camp was advantageously placed, with plenty of good springs just below the plateau. The occupation was in two phases, and the evidence indicates that the rampart was thrown down, or fell down, between the two phases. Within the rampart were rectangular huts built with large posts and walls of wattle and daub. What occasioned the change in occupation is not known; the second phase was relatively long, and may not be earlier than the second century B.C. The cause of the abandonment of the site is not known either. The excavators found no Roman remains whatever, so the occupation probably ended before or shortly after the Roman invasion.

The Bronze Age barrows were not the only relics left by early man in Charmy Down, for until the construction of the airfield it bore four groups of the small squarish fields, bounded by banks, known to archaeologists as celtic fields. Fields of this type may date from the last centuries B.C., and into the Christian era. Grimes suggests that the Charmy Down fields may have been made by the settlers on Little Solsbury, and he thinks it probable that the whole of the plateau was covered by these fields until the banks were destroyed by ploughing in historic times. Some of the fields have so far escaped obliteration; the banks are shewn up well by a low sun, or when a fall of snow is melting. They are clearly seen also in air photographs. Bathampton Down has a fine set of celtic fields, and they exist in large numbers on the Marlborough Downs, notably at Fifield.

Of the Roman occupation, the main relic in Batheaston is the road they made, the Fosse Way.

Pl. 3.   Roman coffin at Batheaston

In a district so amply supplied with Roman remains it is perhaps surprising that so little has come to light. The known settlement sites hereabouts are mostly eastward of the Fosse Way. A Roman coffin, unearthed during the building of the Elmhurst Estate, rests at the foot of the church tower. Another one was found at Millway Gardens[9] (Map 2, B30). An important find was recorded by Prebendary Scarth[10] in these words:

"In 1875 a hoard was found in the suburb of Easton, on the line of the Roman road leading to Bath. This hoard amounted to many thousands; only 732 were saved and examined. Six hundred are of the reign of Constantius Clorus and Constantine the Great, 70 and 530. Also coins of Crispus, Licinius, Diocletian etc. They seem to have been hidden about the middle of the fourth century." It is regrettable that the present whereabouts of this hoard cannot be discovered.

Chapter 3

Saxons and Normans

Domesday Book is a record of unique value for
English village life.

G. G. Coulton

OF THE years between the end of Roman domination and the coming of the Saxons, during which Bath fell into ruin, no scrap of evidence relating to the land that was to become Batheaston is known; probably it was scantily inhabited by descendants of the Romano-Britons.

Soon after their victory at Dyrham in 577 the invading Saxons took Bath, found the situation propitious, and colonised it. Subsequent strife between their warring tribes does not concern this study. It may safely be inferred that some time after the foundation of this new Bath S. Catherine's valley found favour with a group based upon it, and there they settled, calling it the *East tun*, "the settlement to the east", obviously looking from Bath as headquarters; the origin of Weston was surely similar. The prospect must have been attractive—a secluded, fertile valley, its western side well exposed to the sun, many springs for an ample supply of water. The first settlement was doubtless near where the church now stands; these people were not Christians, but when they were converted they would build the church at the heart of the village. Certainly in later centuries a demesne farm was situated there (p. 13), and that, too, is a pointer.

These settlers left no documentary evidence, and no archaeological trace of them other than scraps of pottery has been found. The first certain knowledge is no earlier than the period shortly before the Norman Conquest, and it comes from the Domesday Book, which put on record facts about land ownership in the time of Edward the Confessor.

THE DOMESDAY RECORD

The counties of Somerset, Devon and Cornwall are uniquely fortunate that their records of the Domesday survey of 1086 include not only the Domesday Book itself, but also a considerable amplification of it, the Exeter Domesday. It is thought to be a draft of the record ultimately presented to the King, and contains, what is rarely preserved, the numbers and kinds of livestock on the demesne farms. The Exeter text of the entries concerning Batheaston is given here:

The King holds Estone. There are 2 hides there and it paid geld for 1 hide. There is land for 10 ploughs. In demesne there is 1 hide and 1 plough, and 2 serfs and 7 coliberts, and 13 villeins and 3 bordars and 3 cottars with 5 ploughs and 1 hide. There are 150 sheep and 24 she-goats. There are 2 mills paying 100 pence, and 50 acres of meadow and of underwood 2 leagues in length and breadth. These 2 hides were and are of the demesne farm of the burgh of Bath.

Land of the Church of Bath. Walter Hosatus holds of the Church Estone. Ulward the abbot held it to T.R.E. (in the time of King Edward) and paid geld for 1½ hides. There is land for 2 ploughs. In demesne there are 1 hide and 1 virgate and 1 plough with 1 villein and 8 bordars with 1 plough and 1 virgate. There are 250 sheep. There are 2 mills paying 6s 8d. There are 2 acres of meadow. It was worth 30s, now 40s. This estate cannot be separated from the abbey.

Hugolin holds Estone. Ingulf held it T.R.E. and paid geld for 3 hides. There is land for 5 ploughs. There are 3 ploughs and 3 villeins and 6 bordars and 2 serfs and a mill paying 5s. In demesne are 1½ hides and 1 plough and the villeins have 1½ hides and 2 ploughs. It was formerly worth 40s. Now worth 60s.

The existence of three estates in one community, or vill, is rather unusual in the Bath district, though Bathwick had four, and Weston and some others two. The King's had come to him in 1074, on the death of Queen Edith, the widow of Edward the Confessor, and was already firmly associated with the parent town of Bath. The evidence lies not only in the statement

"These 2 hides were and are of the demesne farm of the burgh of Bath", but Estona was added in with Bath in computing payments by Bath in Domesday Book, thus: *Cum predicta Estona reddit per annum Burgum istud 60 libras ad numerum et unum marcam auri——* That Burgh, with the aforesaid Estone, pays annually 60 pounds and a gold mark. (Land of Queen Edith in Somerset). It may be for this reason that Batheaston usually appears with its prefix from

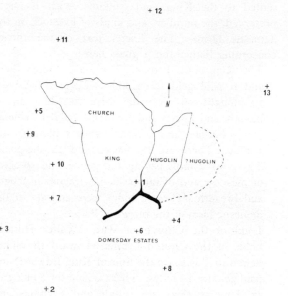

Fig. 5. Domesday estates and neighbouring vills

Pl. 4. Facsimile of entry of King's land

the thirteenth century, while its neighbours continued as Ford and Hampton until modern times.

Walter Hosatus, the sub-tenant of the Church's estate, held other lands, both from Bath Abbey and from Glastonbury Abbey. He was probably one of a family whose name gradually changed into Husse, or Hussey, who were large landowners in the district in succeeding centuries.

Hugolin, the tenant-in-chief of the third estate, appears variously as "interpres" (interpreter) and "legatus" (officer). He held nine hides in all in Batheaston, Woolley and Claverton, as well as three in Bathampton under the abbot of Bath.

The exact significance of the information preserved in Domesday is for the wrangles of professional scholars, and long and well have they fought over the ground. For this study the monumental Domesday Geography of England, has been an invaluable aid.[1,2]

The presence of three estates, or manors, in Batheaston does not mean that they were necessarily entirely separate on the ground. A system of common field agriculture was established before the manorial organisation was imposed upon it and the strips

Table 1. Some figures from the Domesday Survey

Domesday Name	Modern Name	Hides	Ploughs	Mills	Villeins	Total workers	Estimated population	Value
1 Estona	Batheaston	6½	11	5	17	48	216	£5[1]
2 Lincuma	Lyncombe	10	6	–	4	22	99	£8
3 Westona	Weston	20	13	2	13	41	184	£18
4 Forda	Bathford	10	8	1	5	18	81	£10
5 Tatewica	Tadwick	1½	4	–	1	13	58	£1 7s.
6 Hantona	Bathampton	5	6	–	3	12	54	£5 10s.
7 Cerlacuma	Charlcombe	5	4	–	5	12	54	£6
8 Clafertura	Claverton	4	6	1	4	15	68	£7
9 Lancheris	Langridge	2½	5	1	5	15	68	£3
10 Wilege	Woolley	1	3	2	–	15	68	£3
11 Escetone	Cold Ashton	5	4	1	3	8	36	£4
12 Meresfelde	Marshfield	13	35	–	36	67	301	£47
13 Colerne	Colerne	10	11	1	13	28	126	£10

[1]Value of King's manor returned with Bath.

belonging to the several manors, like those of the men who worked them, were probably mingled in the common fields. The evidence enables the main lands of the three manors to be located with some confidence. The land set aside for mowing was always that near the water, and the fifty acres of the King's meadow can scarcely have been other than the Avonlands lying between the river Avon and the Roman road which was the east–west highway. The Avonlands were common meadow until recent centuries. Evidently the greater part of the land, as yet small woodland scrub, remained in the King's hands; the entry usually gave, it seems, what was of course a rough estimate, the greatest length and breadth of a tract of woodland, and the Domesday league is thought to be one and a half miles. The only place where a woodland of anything like the size given could lie is the uplands which include Little Solsbury, the col between it and Charmy Down, and part, at least, of the down, where there is still an outlier of Batheaston parish. If this were so, the fertile land of the lower slopes would remain to be cultivated by the eleven ploughs. The demesne farm of one of the manors was undoubtedly the site of the present Church Farm (p. 13), and the situation of the church close to it indicates an important estate.

If that identification is provisionally accepted, the probable sites of the other manors may be considered. That of the Church included only one villein and eight bordars, and two ploughs, but supported 250 sheep, nearly twice as many as the royal manor. Other evidence apart, this strongly suggests S. Catherine—rugged, steep, mostly quite unsuitable for the plough, but always in later times providing grazing for a large flock of sheep, the "ewe flock of Charmy Down". Bath Abbey at least from the early Middle Ages had a grange at S. Catherine, and maintained a chapel there, and it is quite likely that they were established before 1086.

Hugolin, of the third manor, was lord also of Hampton and Claverton, a fact which suggests a clue to the whereabouts of his Batheaston property, for that part of Batheaston which formed the liberty of Easton and Amorel in later times was often associated with the liberty of Hampton and Claverton, while the rest of Batheaston, with S. Catherine, are in the hundred of Bathforum. The former

association must have historical significance, and though doubt attaches to the precise extent of Amorel, a place-name now obsolete and lost to memory, the liberty (sometimes counted a tithing), certainly included that part of Batheaston to the east of Stambrook, or S. Catherine's brook, as eighteenth century maps shew. If we look at the entry for the third manor, we find that, while inferior in arable to that of the King, it easily exceeded that of the Church, and was worth half as much again. This would well fit the area suggested. While it would be rash to claim certainty, these identifications accord with the known facts.

A sketch of a community requires in order to give it life some estimate of its size and prosperity in relation to comparable neighbours. Fig. 5 shews the settlements which were recorded in Domesday. Though reasons have been given for believing the bounds of Batheaston to have been more or less determined from Saxon times (p. 2), it would be wrong to assume that the same is generally true. However, as all the immediately surrounding settlements except Swainswick, which was probably one of the two manors comprising Tadwick, appear in Domesday, and no others, it is likely that the pattern was much what we know to-day. A little farther afield, Weston contained two manors, but neither Kelston nor North Stoke appears, so they were probably included in Weston.

It must be observed that the system of recording was not uniform. The terms used vary, and equivalents are not always certain; this is particularly the case from region to region, and even in neighbouring counties, which adds to the difficulties, since we have to consider vills in Somerset, Gloucestershire and Wiltshire. Nevertheless, Domesday is an astonishing achievement, for the data were all collected and arranged in the course of eight months. Table 1 is a simple summary of comparable figures.

Excluding Bath, which was, of course, a burgh, with an estimated population of about a thousand, the most populous, prosperous and valuable settlement in the district was Marshfield, followed by Batheaston and Weston. It is unfortunate for our purpose that the King's manor of Batheaston was assessed with Bath and not recorded separately, so we do not know what value was put upon it, and are ignorant of the total value of the place. The recorded

12

AN ENGLISH RURAL COMMUNITY

workers may not all represent family units, and some adult males, a steward on the demesne farm, perhaps, and probably a priest, were not counted at all. However, if the number of workers is multiplied by four and a half, an estimate of average family size, the result may be not far from the truth. It is noteworthy that the villeins, the highest class of manorial tenants, were relatively numerous in the larger and more valuable settlements.

With five mills, Batheaston was exceptionally well supplied; there were 371 in the whole of Somerset, and only nine settlements with five or more. Sheep farming was an important industry, 450 being returned for Batheaston, 450 for Weston, fewer elsewhere; the size of Marshfield's flock is not known, as in Gloucestershire farm animals were not enumerated.

The conclusion is inescapable that shortly after the Norman Conquest Batheaston was a thriving little community.

Chapter 4

The Manors

The peasant cultivators, in relation to each other were a self-governing community, but in relation to the lord of the manor they were serfs.

G. M. TREVELYAN

SOON, all the Batheaston of Domesday was to belong to the Church. In 1090, William II sold for 500 marks to the bishop of the diocese, John de Villula, Bath, city and abbey, *"cum omnibus appendi-tiis tam in villis quam in civitate"*, that is, including estates outside the city but linked with it, such as Batheaston. The explicit purpose of the transaction was to increase the revenues of the diocese of Somerset.[1, 1a]

In 1106, de Villula gave this property to Bath Abbey, and with the gift was the land of "Hugolin with the beard", including the estate at Batheaston, which land, he says, he had bought. The abbey thus acquired the revenues of Batheaston, which it enjoyed until the suppression of the monastery, but the bishop reserved to himself the overlordship, so lordship of the manors is always said to be held "of the bishop of Bath", later, "of Bath and Wells". To the man working on the land, though, whoever had the grant of his manor was his lord, and to him he owed fealty; what happened between his lord and the bishop was no business of his.

There were three manors in the feudal period, and there is no reason to doubt that they represent the three estates of Edward the Confessor's time and of Domesday. Two of them, the King's and that of Hugolin, were called the manor of Batheaston without distinction between them, and this fact has caused a confusion which began with Collinson who based his account of the descent of a single supposed manor on such records of the two as were available to him; and his view does not seem to have been challenged. In the account and follows the terms Batheaston and Batheaston and Amorel are used, the latter chosen arbitrarily because Amorel was certainly included in that estate, as will appear.

THE MANOR OF BATHEASTON

It is probable that the lands of the manor were approximately the present parish of Batheaston, except part or all of the land to the east of S. Catherine's brook. Such sites as can be more or less accurately determined from the court rolls bear this out. The desmesne (lord's) farm lay, as would be expected, near the church; in fact, the present Church Farm derives from it. Until at least the end of the eighteenth century it invariably appears in the parish records as The Farm, the name preserving its original exceptional status. It is also surely not coincidence that the Robert Townsende to whom "the site of the

Fig. 6.   The Manors
(– – – – conjectural)

manor" was leased in 1580 was followed by one Anthony Townsend, a prominent inhabitant whose initials as churchwarden appear on the 1634 bells, and who certainly occupied The Farm, as records shew.

Most of the evidence for the descent of this manor is contained in the Button manuscripts at the County Record Office. Some transactions are recorded in the Feet of Fines, and the final conveyance of 1670 is a chance find among the manuscripts in Bath Reference Library. What is known of the descent is as follows:

1342. Two parts of the manor of Batheaston conveyed from John de Sobbury (Sodbury) to James Husee of Hampton.

1349. James Husee recorded as lord of the manor.

1379. Quitclaim by John Gylemyn, chaplain, of lands granted by James Husee, Knight, to his (Husee's) heir, Thomas de Berle.

1395. The manor conveyed by Thomas and Alice Berlegh to Richard Godefelagh, cleric.

1419. John Blount lord of the manor.

1470. Edward Blunt, lord of the manor, died, leaving his son Simon heir (This date and the following one are quoted from Collinson, but his source has not been found.)

1478. Simon Blunt died, leaving his daughter Margery heiress.

1530. The manor conveyed to William Button from the Hussey family.

1550. The manor leased for life to Thomas Wryghte, of Wilton, at the annual rent of £5 6s 8d.

1580. "The site of the manor of Batheaston manor late in the occupation of one Richard Writt" leased to Robert Townsende, yeoman, at the same rent.

1656. Sir William Button conveyed the manor to trustees to sell.

1667. Sir Robert Button, William Duckett, and Thomas Blanchard of North Wraxall sold the manor for £600 to James Lancashire of Manchester.

1670. Sir Robert Button, Knight, William Duckett, Esq., and James Lancashire and Anne his wife sold the manor "with the appurtenances, and twenty messuages, ten cottages, one watermill, one dovecot, twenty gardens, twenty orchards, one hundred and fifty acres of arable land . . ." All this, and more, was sold and quitclaimed to Charles Stewart, Esq., and John Fisher, Senior, Gent, and the heirs of Charles Stewart for ever, for the sum of £40 sterling! Whatever this transaction may have been it was obviously largely fictitious.

The story is certainly incomplete, and at times seems contradictory. One explanation lies in the practice of fragmenting manors, more than one lord seeming to be in possession at a time, and of letting them out on lease, while retaining ultimate possession.

Of the procession of lords and lordlings, important in their time to the villagers whom they ruled, usually through their stewards, little knowledge has survived the passage of the centuries. There is no evidence to tell whether Matilda, "the lady of Batheaston" of the thirteenth century (p. 20) held this manor or not. In 1291 the Prior of Bath was himself granting land in this lordship to one Ralph the Cornmonger.[2] (Pl. 5.) The Husseys were large landowners in the district, lords of a number of manors. They perhaps derived from the Hosatus of Domesday. John Gylemyn inherited from his mother, Edith; her name heads the list of a rent roll of 1359.[3] Whether Richard Godefelagh is to be identified with the Richard Goudfalewe who was fined three pence at the Michaelmas Court of the manor of Catherine in 1388, or the Richard Godffelowe who was in trouble for appropriating land at Yarngrove in 1422 it is not possible to say. Thomas Wryghte was a wealthy man who held much land, especially at Barford S. Martin near Salisbury, and who set down in his will anxious and particular directions to guide his widow in the upbringing of his children.

The transaction of 1667 came at a time when the feudal system had decayed, and all that remained was a financial interest in land. Money troubles beset Sir William Button, lord also of the manor of Bathampton, who arranged for the sale of his property by trustees to pay his debts. The tenants who held their land by lease or by copy of court roll bought their freeholds (some of the conveyances are in the County Record Office), and the now empty title Lord of the Manor fell into disuse.

Of a Great House and resident "Squire" in Batheaston there is no trace deriving from the manorial period. Rather, the picture is of the steward travelling from place to place to hold the lord's courts, collecting dues and imposing fines, and certainly from the early seventeenth century of a vigorous community of farmers and smallholders, largely conducting

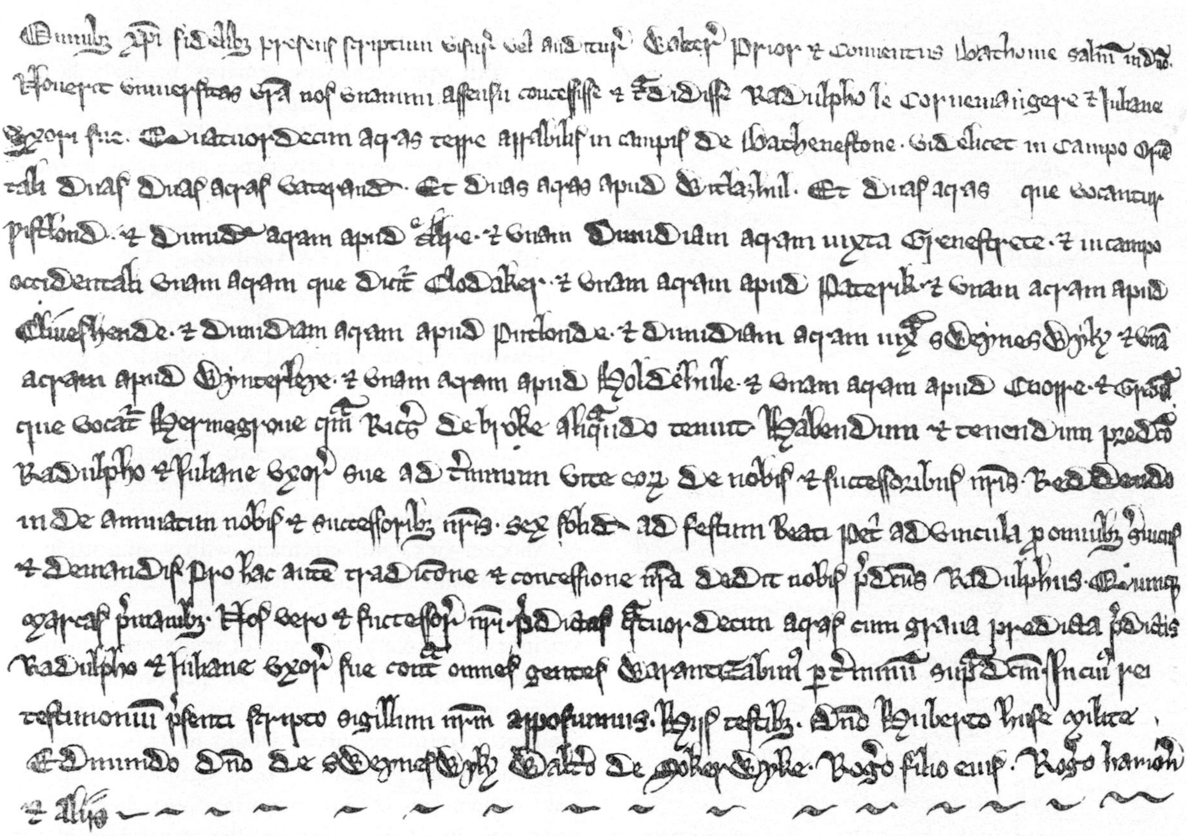

[facsimile of medieval Latin manuscript]

Grant by Thomas, Prior of Bath to Ralph le Cornmangere and Julian his wife of fourteen acres of arable land in the fields of Batheaston; that is to say: in the east field two acres at Gaterand and two acres at Witlazhul, and two acres called Thistlond and half an acre at Alre and half an acre next Grenestrete, and in the west field one acre called Clodaker and one acre at Paterik and one acre at Cliveshende and half an acre at Pitlonde and half an acre next Sweyneswyk and one acre at Wynterleye and one acre at Holdehule and one acre at Cuorre called Hermegrove which Richard de Broke previously held.

About 1291, Lincoln's Inn, Hale LXXXVII,
The Bath Abbey Cartulary

Pl. 5. Facsimile and translation of land grant to Ralph le Cornmangere
(reproduced by permission of the Lincoln's Inn Library)

their own affairs and regulating their agricultural practices according to the common will (p. 132).

Court rolls are in the County Record Office for certain courts held between 1418 and 1431, and one of 1565. They are written in mediaeval Latin, and follow the usual pattern of manorial custom and discipline, their special interest for the local historian being their record of place names, some of them still identifiable. A few illustrative items are here presented:

At the court of 10 November 1422 several tenants were fined—two or three pence—for failing to mend their houses. Grazing their sheep "above Banward" without leave cost John Herewest and John Stryng six pence apiece. Thomas Wiltshire was in trouble for letting his pigs stray, and William Broke fined for pursuing his quarrel against him, a suggestive juxtaposition!

The Prior of Bath was distrained for keeping his sheep in the pasture called Langrowe between the Feast of the Purification of Blessed Mary (2 Feb.) and the Feast of the Exaltation of the Holy Cross (14 Sept.), at which time the said pasture was common for all other animals, but not for sheep; and he

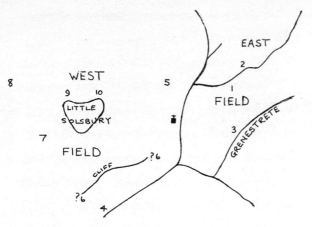

Fig. 7.   Grant to Ralph le Cornmangere 1291

Key to Fig. 7
1. Gaterand (Gattrell)
2. Witlazhul (Whitley Hill)
3. Grenestrete (Fosse Lane)
4. Clodaken (Map 2, B3)
5. Patrik (P. 11/7)
6. Cliveshende (Cliff's End)
7. Pitlond (Pitland)
8. Next Sweyneswyk (Swainswick)
9. Wynterleye (Winterley)
10. Hermegrove (Groves)

had overgrazed with sheep the common pasture at Lez Leyes. The distraint reappears at successive courts, and there is no record that the Prior complied!

At the court of 16 November 1425 William atte Broke and William Wyles were fined three pence each for allowing their closes at Shortewode (Map 2, B133) to lie open and waste to the harm of the manor, and they were to mend them by the next court on penalty of twelve pence. (The Wyles family may have given their name to the field called Willis' (Map 2, C27) not far from Shortwood.) Henry Guyse was fined five pence for not mending his close "between Monkemede and Horteley", in the extreme north of the manor.

The seemingly cruel custom whereby on a tenant's death his best beast went to the lord as a heriot is instanced several times: a sheep, a goat, a mare, a calf worth forty pence. An entry at the court of 20 November 1431 is typical:

"Item they (the homage) present that John Bygge, who holds of the lord one messuage five acres of land and appurtenances adjacent has died, by whose death there falls to the lord as heriot

one ox worth eighteen pence, and the said messuage with appurtenances remains to Isabella his widow, and she does homage".

Usually, there was a "fine" (fee) for entry of a new tenant, from twelve to forty pence appearing in these rolls.

After a gap of 134 years we have the last surviving record of a court, that of 6 April 1565. Tenants were still being ordered to repair their houses, and John Gorsseledd was to build a wall between the tithing of Batheaston and the tithing of Marshfield, on pain of a fine of forty shillings.

THE MANOR OF BATHEASTON AND AMOREL

It is evident that this manor was from early times a financial investment, always associated with the manor of Shockerwick, and gradually with a multitude of other holdings in many parts of the country. The history of it is particularly complex, for the conveyance of a moiety of it and of many other manors associated with it, to a list of persons obviously acting in partnership occurs again and again; to attempt a complete survey would be tedious indeed and doubtfully profitable. It is significant that the only known roll of this manorial court, held in the year 1485 by Robert Horner, the steward, is at the West Suffolk County Record Office in Bury S. Edmunds. It records a few rents for Batheaston and Shockerwick.

Exactly what was the extent of this manor is uncertain. It included Amorel, for John de Salso Marisco during his lordship paid two shillings for Aumerle (obviously an early form of Amorel) to the Lay Subsidy of 1325–1326, and after the lapse of 334 years the Earl of Northumberland, also lord of the manor, paid tax in 1650 for the tithing of Easton and Amerill. Eighteenth century maps shew Amorel to the east of S. Catherine's Brook, and a note by the vicar, J. J. Conybeare, written in the Poor Book in 1818, clearly indicates a similar site adding that it included Shockerwick, in Bathford parish; but the name has passed from memory, and its precise situation and extent are unknown. There is little doubt that it is to be identified with the estate of Hugolin in 1087 (pp. 9, 11). Cold Bath Farm, on the site where Elmhurst now stands (Map 1, 18), seems to have been the only ancient settlement in this part of the parish, and was probably the demesne farm.

Transactions relating to this manor are recorded in the Feet of Fines and the Patent Rolls. Dates of the fourteenth century are quoted from Collinson, who, however, does not give his sources.

1328–9. The manors of Shockerwick and Batheaston passed from Giles, son of John de Salso Marisco, to William de Whitefeld.

1361. Ralph Fitzurse died, and the manor passed from him to Maud, eldest daughter of Sir Hugh Durborough, and from her to the Brien family.

1396. William Brien died, leaving Phillipa Devereux and Elizabeth Lovell co-heiresses. Phillipa married Sir Henry de Scroop, afterwards Lord Scroop, who held the manors of Shockerwick and Batheaston.

1436. A moiety of the manor conveyed from Ralph Durborough to Edward Grevyll, who in his will of 1436, ordered "I will that the lordship of Batheaston shall be sold to have mass in the parish church of Cherdelynche."

1456. It was found by inquisition post mortem that Avicia, wife of James Boteler, Earl of Wiltshire, lately attainted for treason, held the manor of John Newton. She died the same year, and Humphrey Stafford succeeded.

1461. The manor, with many others, granted to the King's uncle, William Neville.

1463–75. The manor in the hands of the King's brother, George, Duke of Clarence. This was he who was reputed to have been drowned in a butt of Malmsey in 1478 while a prisoner in the Tower.

1478. The manor granted to John Sayntlo, Knight, for life, which he had for life of the late Duke of Clarence.

1553. The manors of Shockerwick and Batheaston, which were leased to John Saynt John at a rent of £22 9s 2d now leased to Edward Courtney, Earl of Devon, at the same rent.

1557. The manors of Shockerwick and Batheaston, with many others, conveyed to Thomas, Earl of Northumberland.

The history of the manor of Batheaston with Amorel ends here, save for a last echo in the letter of Henry Walters (p. 19).

THE MANOR OF EASTON, (BATHEASTON) AND CATHERINE

This was the Church's estate of Domesday, and it is noteworthy that in feudal times it always appeared with the double title: Easton, Estone, Batheneston, Kateryn, Katerin, Cattern, Catherine, are among the many renderings, in later centuries often with Courte subjoined. How much of the present parish of Batheaston was in this manor it is not possible to say; Partrygges (p. 19) was certainly in it. The inhabitants had rights in the west field of Batheaston. It seems a likely guess that its original extent was that of the tithing of the same name.

Whether Bath Abbey was used to retain this manor in its own hands is uncertain; it undoubtedly built the church. A line of three fishponds can still be traced (Map 2, C41). Not later than 1490 the manor was leased to the family of Herford, and from them passed to a Thomas Lieuwelyn, who married Isabel Herford. A deed of 1534 granting the reversion of the manor to the sons of Alice and Thomas Lieuwelyn contains matters of interest (Appendix 4).

At the dissolution of the monastery in 1539 the manor came into the hands of Henry VIII, Thomas Llwellin collecting the rents for him until in 1546 the King granted it to John Malte, his tailor, and Etheldreda Malte, otherwise Dyngley, the bastard daughter of Malte by Joan Dyngley for £13110 0s 2d[4] The grant reads "one capital messuage and farm called Katerinscourte" and 400 ewes, "the Yowe Flocke of Charmerdon".

There is a story that Etheldreda was the King's own daughter, but the source of it I have not been able to trace.

At this time the value of the rents was:[5]

Rents of freeholders		8s 0d
Rents of copyholders	£13	0s 11¾d
Rents of tenements called Martyn's Yewe		17s 8¾d
Rent of a dovecote, now or late in the tenure of Alice Herford		6s 8d

The whereabouts of Martyn's Yewe, and why it appears separately have defied discovery.

In 1548 Etheldreda married John Harington of London. She died about 1551 and her child also died. Harington married again, and his son John inherited the property. This John, a godson of Queen Elizabeth, and the reputed inventor of the water-closet, who had his headquarters at Kelston, was banished from court because his somewhat rabelaisian essay, *The Metamorphosis of Ajax* (*a jakes*) offended the Queen!

In 1591, Harington leased the manor and Court to John Blanchard, of Marshfield, gentleman. The fee was £1250, with rent of £20 a year, and a couple of capons at the Feast of the Circumcision. Blanchard was to keep the property in repair, taking sufficient "housebote, haybote, firebote, gatebote, stilebote, cartbote, foldbote, frith, fuel, and hedgebote". The meaning of this is that he was entitled to sufficient wood and timber.

Three years later, in 1594, John Harington sold the manor house and demesne farm to William Blanchard, the son of John, now dead. The property included, besides the capital messuage, that is, the Court, with the lands belonging, tithes from the whole parish of Catherine, and common of pasture for 400 wether sheep on Holts Down. Harington reserved to himself the chief rent of £20 and certain of the tenants' rents. At the same time he sold the freehold of the northern part of the property to one of the tenants, Thomas Sallmon, for £120, and other tenants bought their freeholds. The feudal system was breaking up, and from this time the manor, as an entity having rights and duties, practically disappears.

S. Catherine's Court and the demesne farm continued in the ownership of the Blanchard family through the lifetimes of two more Williams (died 1644, 1686), then by marriage of Querina Blanchard to Thomas Parry, who rebuilt the church tower in 1704. When Holts Down was enclosed by agreement in 1748, the Thomas Parry of that time was allotted nearly half of it, but by virtue of the number of sheep he was entitled to pasture; neither manor nor lordship is mentioned.

In 1841, Colonel J. H. Strutt bought S. Catherine's Court and farm and the property has been in the family from that time. Manorial rights are long extinct, and Major Strutt, the present owner, has no knowledge of a right to claim the lordship.

There was trouble in the time of the first William Blanchard about his rights, especially his right of common in Holts Down. By a Bill in Chancery of

3 May 1620, the late copyholders of the manor, now freeholders, Benedicte Horsington, Thomas Sallmon, Robert Chewar, Thomas Biggs, Martin Ballmon, William Dyer, Ellen Ballmon, widow, and Maude Dyer, widow, complained that Blanchard, whose right in the soil and inheritance of Holts Down was in respect of 400 sheep, all the rest having common for 650, had claimed the whole down as his freehold, and forbidden them to put their sheep thereon. Blanchard answered that the customary tenants had enclosed most of the land of the common fields, and by so doing had extinguished their common rights. He did not intend to deny rights in Holts Down except to such as had enclosed. He claimed right of common for 700 sheep, but said he put in only 400 as the down was not sufficient for all his sheep "until the copyhold estates be ended". He lost his case, and found the quarrel an expensive one. However, in 1632, he was claiming the rents of the remaining small tenants, which had been paid to Harington. Both sides took evidence from chosen inhabitants, and these survive in Chancery Depositions, the information they contain being perhaps more interesting for the light they throw on agricultural practice than for the arguments of the quarrel. Again, Blanchard lost. (Much of the material from which this account is drawn is from papers in the collection of Major Strutt.)

The known court rolls of the manor of Easton and Catherine are in the Public Record Office. There is one of 1311, others of various dates 1377–1397, 1422–1452, 1492–1502.

The court of 23 April 1310 records a long list of tenants paying for their stock grazing in the pasture or in the enclosures (*in defensis*), evidently a fee rather than a forfeit. The total paid was 8s 9d. The list of names, some of them obviously of local origin, appears in Appendix 1.

The inference from the court of 23 April 1378 (Appendix 2) is that the men tied to the soil were rebelling against their servitude, and making off. Maybe it was fairly easy to get "lost" in the city of Bath nearby. It may be noted that the whole community had paid a fine for their escape. "The lordship of the lord" probably means the whole of the church's estates in and around Bath. Why we have details of the families of Walter Wodeward, John Wyltshure, and John Stybbe we do not know.

From 1377 to 1443 the total of rents rose from 9s 7d to 10s 10d. In addition there appears from time to time an amount of from eight to twelve pence "for works of the vineyard" (*de operibus vinee*). The site of the vineyard is still known (Map 2, C43). What is not known is when the cultivation of grapes ceased in the valley.

An entry of the court of 23 April 1446 is worth quoting in full, as detailing the kind of agreement that was made, and a wayleave still identifiable: (Map 2, B109, C31):

> To the same court came Walter Cole and gives to the lord a 20s fine to have ingress to a parcel of land lying at Charmbury containing 2 acres and 1 rood, to hold to the said Walter for the term of his life according to the custom of the manor, paying however annually 2s at two yearly terms viz. at the Feast of the Annunciation of the Blessed Mary and of S. Michael the Archangel in equal portions. And it is granted to him that he shall have a way to the said parcel of land over the lord's land there called Gaterad and over the lord's land called Sixacres and so descending by the lord's stalls there to the said parcel of land.

Here is an agreement for the renewal of a copyhold, from the court of 17 April 1451:

> To the same came Thomas Balman son of John Balman and gives to the lord a fine of eight marks sterling for the reversion of one messuage and one cottage called Partrygges with its appurtenances which John Balman his father now holds, to hold to the said Thomas for the term of his life according to the custom of the manor.

The unravelling of the whereabouts of Partrygges illustrates the fascination of an enquiry into local history. Obviously it was to be identified with the Patrik of a deed of 1291, whereby the Prior of Bath conveyed certain land to Ralph the Cornmonger (Pl. 5). Patrik was in the west (later called Solsbury) field. The name reappears in the highway accounts of the seventeenth and eighteenth centuries as Partridges Lane and occurs from time to time until 1835. The places from which stones were brought to repair it suggest that it was probably the late Waterworks Lane, now Sevenacres Lane. Finally an old resident volunteered that he remembered hearing it called "Parsonage" Lane—obviously a corruption, for it is nowhere near the parsonage—and the problem

was solved: Patrik, Partrygges, Partridge, Parsonage.

Finally, some records of a court of 1502 are interesting for rustic details and human perversity:

Elena Roger fined 2d for not repairing a wall of wattle, John Peynton 2d for the roof of his barn, John Southwood 2d for the wattle of the lord's bakehouse, as ordered at the last court. John Dondy must well and sufficiently repair the roofs of his houses called Arnolds, and John Herford the gate of his house called Gyse, or each be fined 5d. And it is ordered to John Stybbe to remove and fix in the proper place a fence not long since built by him between his holding and the holding of William Stybbe his brother, by which he has unjustly encroached on ground belonging to the said William, and this to be reported at the next court on penalty of 3s 4d.

It is evident, then, that in Batheaston the feudal system, with its intricacies of rights and duties, was by the seventeenth century reduced almost to a memory, and had practically lost all meaning. The final echoes come from the eighteenth century, and provide a useful summary of the utter confusion that accompanied the end of feudalism. The papers are among the parish archives.

A letter from Henry Walters to Ralph Allen relating to his right to the manor of Batheaston:

20 October 1746.

Sir

On hearing that you have sent your servants to enquire about some Cottage houses and Wastlands in this parish I think proper to let you know some things that possibly you may not have heard off. Mr. Holder and his father has been talking of this thing long ago and it was moved in the Court Leet at Hampton fifteen years ago and a presentment made by the Jury in pursuance thereof a true Copy of which I now enclose you.

There were three Mannors in this parish Viz. The Mannor of Easton and Catterne which was Abby Lands and Seized and granted by K. Henry ye 8th to one of his favourites and there is still a considerable reserved Rent pd out of it to the Crown besides this Mannor is in Bathforum Hundred. Consequently you can have no Claim there and a great part of it is in this p'ish. The Earl of Northumberland had the Mannor of Shockerwick part of which is in this p'ish also. And the Buttons had another Mannor in this p'ish. Now Sir these three Mannors are so mixed togrther that tho' you had a Right it would be impossible to find it out in many cases. I have Lands of all three of these Mannors in one Ground now thrown together which cannot be distinguished one from another and where there is Wastland in the Highway and the Ground on one side of it is in Easton and Cattern and on the other side Ground in Easton and Amorell who does that Waste Land belong to. The Lords of the Court Leet of Bathforum Hundred have never demanded or had as I know of any WastLand in the said Hundred of Bathforum in other Gent's Mannor and the Mr. Holders or ye Bassets never had a foot of land in this p'ish and the Cottages have been disposed of time out of mind by the parish Officers to such poor people as wanted it most and have been repaired by the p'ish.

The house that Beale now lives in was as I have heard inhabited by a Man who had some dispute with the p'ish Officers and then went to Sir W. Basset and desired him to grant him a Lease but I believe no Chief Rent was ever paid or demanded.

I am Sir yr. very humble Servt

Henry Walters

At the Court Leet and Court Baron of Charles Holder Esq. for the Manour aforesaid held the 19 day of October 1731 Before Andrew Imrys gentleman steward of the said Manour.

Whereas Charles Holder Esq. Lord of the Manour of Hampton claimes a Right to the Waste Ground and several Cottages within the parish of Batheaston in the County of Somerset We the Jury sworn to inquire amongst other things what Lands and Tenements belong to the said Charles Holder Esq. as Lord of the Manour aforesaid Do here present that the said Charles Holder Esq. hath no right or title to any Cottages or to any Waste Ground or Common Right or to any other Lands or Tenements whatsover within the said parish of Batheaston.

The last word on the subject was written about 1852 by Melmoth Walters, descendant of Henry

Walters, on the occasion of some dispute about the right to cut turf:

About the year 1656 Sir William Button then Lord of the manors of Batheaston and Bathampton and owner of considerable estates in each of these parishes conveyed the same to trustees to sell and in consequence thereof the estates at Hampton or greatest part thereof were sold together with the manor. But in Batheaston the estates were sold off separately and those who held by leases or copies of court roll purchased the reversions in fee and from that time no court has been held at Batheaston nor any other manorial rights exercised there. But the courts being continued at Hampton the Parishioners of Batheaston attended there for the appointment of their officers to save the trouble and expense of going to the Quarter Sessions and about the year 1750 Mr. Allen, then Lord of the Manor at Hampton pretended to be Lord also of the Manor of Batheaston, and privately attempted to prevail on the occupiers of the above mentioned parish houses to take leases thereof from him at his expense and to execute counterparts thereof which being discovered a Vestry was held at Batheaston 11 Feb. 1750 when an entry was made.

MATILDA, LADY OF BATHEASTON

This appealing figure appears mysteriously on the local stage, dominates it for a few years, and disappears from the scene, probably removed by death. This is known: she was a member of the family of Champflower, written variously Chamfleur, Campo Florido, who were important landowners in Somerset in the early middle ages, and whose name survives in Huish Champflower and Wyke Champflower.

In her transactions with the monks of Bath she is always spoken of as 'domina de Batheneston', and the agreement of 1262 implies that she held that manor, but no evidence to account for her status has been found in records of manorial descent and grants. One small clue there is to landownership by the family: in the Exchequer Lay Subsidies of 1325–1326 the Hundred of Bath forensecum (Bath Forum) includes lists of names for Stone (Estone) and for Aumarle Chaumflour. The latter must surely be an early form of Amorel (p. 16), doubtless corrupted from Albemarle, and the family name linked with it indicates that the family at one time owned the manor which included that part of the parish.

Matilda appears first in the deed of 1258 granting the advowson to the Prior and Convent of Bath[6] (also, Liber Albus, I, f. 104.)[7] She is described as daughter and heiress of William, Knight, late of Batheaston, and in free and lawful widowhood. For her generosity she was honoured by the concession translated thus:

Concession by Thomas, Prior etc. to the lady Matilda of Batheneston, that on account of her devotion to their house a perpetual mass should be celebrated for her either by a monk or a chaplain at the newly erected altar in their church near the altar of the Holy Cross, on the north side, in honour the Blessed Virgin Mary and S. Catherine; that in her lifetime the mass should be in honour of the Blessed Virgin Mary, and S. Catherine, and for all the faithful departed, and after her death for the soul of her, her parents, friends etc. with Dirige and Placebo; that on the day of her death the convent bell should be tolled, and that its anniversary should be kept for ever by feeding one hundred poor, each with bread, relish, and a dish of food, as on the anniversaries of kings and pontiffs; that each monk in priest's orders should sing five masses for her, and those of a lower order sing three psalms, and that her name should be written in their Martyrology. Moreover, that an arch should be made for her tomb near the new altar, so that all might see it from within and without (the choir), and be reminded to pray for her; that the anniversary of her father should be kept on the day of S.S. Simon and Jude, and of her mother on that of the Conversion of S. Paul, each by feeding one hundred poor as above. They submit themselves to the jurisdiction of the bishop of Bath and Wells, and to his censure if they fail in the above, and renounce all legal or other means of escaping their obligation.[8]

In 1262 she forgave a debt of fifty marks which the monks owed her,[9] and in the same year made an agreement with them about her rights of common on Charmy Down. The deed stands at the head of their cartulary[10] but is written in a much later hand. It is of interest to justify quoting it in translation.

In the year of our Lord 1263 this agreement was made between Walter the Prior and the Convent of Bath on the one part and the Lady Matilda of Batheaston on the other; namely that the said Lady Matilda admitted and quitclaimed on behalf of herself and her heirs to the said Prior and Convent all the rights she had . . . in common of Pasturage of six acres on La Holtes in two closes near the sheepfold of the said Prior and Convent on the east and on the west, and in a certain pasture below the hill which is called Haldebrech, to the extent of four acres, between the road leading to S. Katerine and the wood of William Stubbe, and in a half acre in Sobbelegh next to the land of William de Teldelegh, that the whole of the said right of pasture should be held by the said Prior and Convent for ever. In consideration of this remission and quitclaim the Prior and Convent gave to the Lady Matilda her heirs or assignees the right of common for six beasts free from all custom beyond the number that she had on Chermerdune and in all places and at all times that she should have and was wont to have rights of common, and thus in all the Lady Matilda will have thirty beasts and three horses free and quit all custom as aforesaid.

Below: The said Lady had to the end of her life from the Prior and Convent the common pasture for two hundred sheep on Chermerdoon until the said hill, according to old custom, was enclosed.

One other transaction of Lady Matilda's is recorded in the Feet of Fines 1262–1263, when she bought fourteen acres of land in Batheaston from William and Isabella de Okeford, situated in fields named le Leys, Empnete, Remmescumb, Wydertherecumb (Widercombe), Naruretherecumb (Narrowercombe). The last two lie in order westward from Ramscombe (Map 1).

No more is known of Lady Matilda. The vanity of her human wishes was manifest at the Reformation; indeed before, for the monks for their own purposes tried to deny her gift (p. 23). She apparently left no descendants. There is one mysterious echo: at the court held at S. Catherine on 23 April 1310 a fine of sixpence was levied on "the shepherd of the Lady of Bathenestone for his sheep in the pasture". While it is certainly possible that she was alive in 1310, she would be of a great age. Perhaps the likeliest explanation is that her shepherd, still living and in prosperity, was himself an owner of sheep.

Chapter 5

The Church

Se maegh eal fela   *Hoc possunt universi*
Singhan and secghan   *Canere et prædicare*
Tham bith snyttru-cræft   *Quibus est solertia*
Bifolen on ferthe   *Insita in animo*

So may the wiser sons of earth proclaim
In speech and measured song, the glories of his name.

Anglo-Saxon Hymn of Thanksgiving. J. J. Conybeare's
translations.

THAT part of the Domesday Survey relating to Somerset did not usually record the existence of a church, so the absence of any reference to a church in Batheaston has no significance; but the greater part of the land being divided between the Church and the King there can be little doubt that the church of Batheaston was in being before the Norman Conquest. For as it was quite usual for lesser lords in Saxon times to endow a church to serve their estates, so it is almost certain that powers royal and ecclesiastic would do as much.

The earliest documentary evidence of the church of Batheaston, found in a charter of Theobald, Archbishop of Canterbury, confirms to Robert, Bishop of Bath, sundry possessions, including "ecclesia de Eston".[1] The date is 1136, and from the context there can be no doubt of the identification. The word "ecclesia" implies a rectory, not a chapel.

In 1258, Matilda, "the Lady of Batheaston" (p. 20), gave the advowson to the Prior and Convent of Bath, together with the chantry chapel of S. Catherine.[2] This is the earliest reference to a chapel of S. Catherine.

The first vicar of Batheaston whose name is certainly known was Richard le Gist, who was instituted in 1260. Two years later there was an agreement between the Prior and Convent and the vicar, defining the duties of the latter.[3] The translation given below is that of Collinson in his *History and antiquities of Somersetshire*.

The vicar for the time being should in future receive all oblations and small obventions, tithes of horses, colts, heifers, swine, flax, wool, milk, honey, gardens, pigeons, and mills of the said parish, except in certain lands belonging to the prior and convent. That the said vicar should have a dwelling-house situated near to the church, with a competent garden and curtilage, and the grass of the churchyard; together with the tithes of all the hay of the fields contiguous to the Avon within this parish, and likewise all mortuaries whatsoever. That the said vicar should sustain all ordinary vicarial burdens, together with the chantry of the chapel of S. Catherine within the said parish, the vicar for the time being to provide at his own expense a chaplain for the daily service thereof, who shall every day, except the Lord's day and solemn festivals, celebrate mass, with the full service for the deceased, viz: the Dirige and Placebo, and especial commendations for the souls of all the bishops that have filled the cathedral see of Bath and Wells; and for the souls of the father and mother of lady Maud of Batheaston, lady of the said vill, their ancestors and successors; and for the souls of all the priors and monks of Bath, and canons and vicars of Wells; and also for the souls of all the parishioners of Bath-Easton, and all the faithful deceased throughout the realm. And for the better support of the said chantry, the prior and convent of Bath agree to give up a certain area with curtilage to the vicar of the said church of Bath-Easton, to be built on at his expense for the residence of the said chaplain, and allow seven bushells of wheat from their grange, to be paid every year on the next Sunday after the feast of S. Michael the Archangel. All other burdens usually belonging to the rector, the said prior and convent covenant to sustain.

From this time onwards it seems that the vicar of Batheaston has always been responsible for duty at S. Catherine. Nothing is known of the land and house provided, presumably near the chapelry, for the chaplain who served it. The grass of the church-yard remained a perquisite of the vicar; indeed, he is probably entitled to it to this day, should he care to take it. He retained the right to some of the tithe of hay of the Avonland to the end of the tithe era.

The status of the church of S. Catherine was continued as a chapel of Batheaston. For example, the Chantry Return of 1548 records:

Bathe Eston wth the Chapell of Caterne annexed. The Chapel situate in Horteley within the sayde paryshe. The rent of the same Chapell wherein an Armyte sometyme dwelled and nowe in the occupying of William Lewys   2s 8d

The same William Lewys hathe occupied the saide Chapell or Armitage by the space of XII yeres last past without eny thinge paying therfore.

The chapel at Hartley where the hermit dwelt has disappeared without trace. The other provisions of the agreement of 1262 of course lapsed at the Reformation.

THE ADVOWSON

The convent was not to remain in unchallenged enjoyment of the advowson, for in 1343 the King issued a writ to Bishop Ralph, thus:

"We wish to be certified concerning the name of the last person presented by us or our predecessors to the church of Batheneston, of your diocese."

"We cannot find that any person was presented by you."

Whereupon, the King presented John de Houton.[4]

There is no record of de Houton's institution in Bishop Ralph's register. In 1346 the King formally claimed the advowson.[5]

The King brought a Quare Impedit against the Prior of Bath, and counted, by Notton, that it belonged to him to present for the reason that one Maud Chaumflour was seised of the advowson, and held the advowson of King Edward the grand-father of the present King in capite, and presented her clerk, one Martin Chaumflour, in the time of the same King, and that this Maud aliened the advowson to one Walter, the Prior's predecessor, which Walter appropriated the same church

without license, and therefore the right to present accrued to King Edward the grandfather.

To which the mendacious monks replied:

As to that we tell you that Maud never had anything in the advowson, and that Martin Chaumflour was not admitted on her presentation, and that she did not aliene the advowson to our predecessor, but that we and our predecessors have held the church *in proprios usus* from the time of the Conquest to the present.

The King's representative retorted:

A fine was levied in the time of King Henry between Maud and your predecessor Walter, by which fine Maud acknowledged the advowson to be the right of your predecessor, as that which he had of her gift.

At a previous hearing the Prior "shewed that before the conquest there was an Abbot of Bath who then purchased the advowson from the King, and appropriated it, and he shewed the King's charter, and a papal bull for the appropriation". The Norman French reads: "*Et donque il moustra qe devant le conqueste y avoir Abbe de Baaz qe adonque du Roi purchacea lavoeson, et lappropria, et moustra chartre le Roi et bulle del appropriacion*". This was, of course, a flat contradiction of their own cartulary, already quoted. Significantly, the convent was at the time heavily in debt, and John de Iford, the prior, was in 1346 convicted of adultery with Agnes Cubbel.[6] There is no evidence that he resigned or was deprived. The convent was in a bad way.

The case was adjourned at successive hearings until 1364, when it ends without a decision, and the advowson remained with the monks.

It is not possible to say whether Martin Chaumflour was ever vicar of Batheaston.

THE RECTORY

By a deed of 1522, the oldest document in the parish archives, the Prior (William Byrde) and Convent of Bath granted the rectory to Richard Herforde of Batheaston and Agnes his wife, for the longer of their lives, "*utriusque eorum diutius vivent*". The rent was £12 a year, to be paid at Michaelmas and Lady Day in equal parts, and heriot and mortuary. They were to receive all such tithes of grain and hay as William Stybbes and other farmers were used to receive, and perform all such customary works as they were used to do. The suggestion is that the farmers were acting during a vacancy. A second deed, dated 1535, granted the reversion of the rectory to Richard and John, sons of Richard and Agnes Herforde.

(Though parish property, this deed was given to the British Museum by Melmoth Walters.)[7]

The Herfords (sometimes spelt Harvord, later Harford, corrupted to Harrod as a field name (Map 2 B.80) were a family prominent in Batheaston in this and succeeding centuries, and at one time held the manor of Easton and Catherine.

At the dissolution of the monastery its property came to the King. In 1546 is recorded[8] the grant to the Dean and Chapter of the Cathedral of Christ, Oxford, of the King's foundation, of the rectory and advowson of the vicarage of Batheaston. The following account is drawn from deeds and papers, some at Christ Church, some among the parish records.

Following an arbitration in 1555, the Dean and Chapter granted the parsonage (that is, the rectory) and advowson to John Harington of London Esq. and Awdry, his wife (p. 17) for 99 years, for £500 and an annual rent of £10, and the right "when place shall be void to nominate one scholar being sufficiently learned which being so named shall be by the said Dean and Chapter admitted and established in the roome of a Scholar of the same Church having and taking all such allowances as other Scholars there shalle use to have and soe from time to time as the same scholars place shall be void the said John Harington shall and may nominate and present another Scholar to succeed continually during the natural life of John Harington". By a deed executed a month later, and part of the same transaction, the Dean and Chapter quitclaimed "all the lands and tenements glebe lands closes meadows feedings and pastures woods underwoods commons and hereditaments whatsoever to John Harington".

In 1560, Harington demised the parsonage and advowson for 29 years to William Blanchard of Batheaston. Harington died intestate, and in 1585, his son John, of Kelston, let the property to William Blanchard, he, after the expiration of the 29 years to pay "two cople of good and fatt capons yearly at the feast of the birth of our Saviour Christ for 24 years". The substantial part of the rent was presumably the £10.

The rectory and advowson continued with the Blanchard family until in 1692 the Dean and Chapter leased for 21 years "the parsonage and advowson and patronage of the Vicaridge and the presentation of a Clarke to be Vicar there when and so often as the same vicaridge shall happen to become void to Anne, Joyce and Rebecca Blanchard". The rent was still £10, £6 13s 4d to be paid in money, and £3 6s 8d "as 4 quarters of good, clean, dry and sweet wheat being after the rate of 6s 8d the quarter, and 8 quarters of good, sweet clean dry and seasonable barley mault after the rate of 5s the quarter; or in lieu thereof pay at the rate paid in Oxford market. They shall so often as need shall require well and sufficiently repair the Chancell belonging to the Parish Church of Batheaston and the Parsonage house". They were to allow the Dean and Chapter "at or in the Parsonage house as often as they shall come thither sufficient Meat, Drink, Fire and Lodging fitt for men of their Degree and calling, and also Hay, provender, litter and Stable room for their horses by the Space of two Day and two nights so as thay do not exceed the Number of four persons and four horses and come above once in two years."

Two years later, in 1694, these ladies assigned their lease to Eldad Walters, clothier, who married Rebecca as his third wife. Repeated renewals of the lease, continuing the provision for payment in money, wheat, and malt but reserving the advowson, maintained the rectory in possession of the Walters family until 1856, when Melmoth Walters, a bachelor, and the last of the family to reside in Batheaston, declined to renew the lease. The tithe redemption charge, then worth £233 10s 1d, was applied by the Dean and Chapter to augment the income of the vicar.

Thus the rectory of Batheaston was held by one family for almost 300 years.

Turning now to consider the extent of the rectory, several terriers exist to define the property and the rights belonging to it. The first is of the sixteenth century, in the collection of Christ Church, and is endorsed by an unknown hand "?1555". Most of it is legible without much difficulty:

House garden and lytle orchard A lytle closse lying on ye west side of the barn containing by estimacion 2 acres A great closse with a narrow entry from the house into the farme closse containing in all by estimacion 4 acres of pasture

... and lying ... on the west side next the ground of Mr. Button, on the north side next the ... southward towards the highway 4 acres of meade lying in dyvers parcells at the west end of yaverland (Avonland) meadow 1 acre at thest end and 1 acre in the myddest of the same in 2 partes.

In the West Feld 20 acres of arable ground and in est Feld 20 acres all lying in dyvers parcells throwht owe all the said Feldes

Other comodities and proffite none

And the tythes of all the corne and grayne and part of the haye viz. all except the tythe haye ... in orchard groundes and half the tythe hay ... all yeaverland except in 10 acres which the farmer hath ... to himself

He may keep 100 shepe for his glebe land.

Presumably the land sold by John Harington to William Blanchard in 1555 was the 40 acres of arable, and was either the precursor of the Hill Farm, or added to the already existing holding there, for in the next terrier we find the barn of the rectory attached to the barn of Thomas Blanchard, who held the property called Hill Farm; and the great barn is there to this day. (Map 1, 14).

Terror of Batheston dd to Mr. Deane and Treasurer at their visitation

1. To the houseinge belonginge to the Rectorie conteyneth 3 fields or bayse of barne roome att the north-end of the great barn (wch belongeth to the Messuage and Tenement of Thomas Blanchard) or thereabouts—and noe more Housinge or buildinge. And there belongeth to the Rectorie one Parcell of arrable land in the westfield called the Chancell Land conteyninge in Length three perche, and in bredth one perche and a half and there belongs noe more meadowes pastures or woods to the sd Rectorie, than is therein before sett downe.

2. To the Rectorie there belongs all tythe Corne and Grayne of Batheaston and Catherine (except what tithes Mr. William Blanchard of Catterne claymes due to him out of his Farme of Catterne and the Messuages and tenements there under a Pretense of the Letters Pattents of H. 8. I.) And all tythe Hay doeth belonge to the Rectorie (except such Tythe Hay as the Vicar there claymes by a composition) conteyninge about 3 or 4 loads per annum.

3. Customes none.

4. The Rector receaves tythes only in the Parishe and Hamlett of Batheston and Catterne and not elsewhere.

5. There belongs noe Mannor to the sd Rectorie neither are there any tenement or tenements that belongs to the sd Rectorie.

6. There is a Viccaridge belonginge to the Rectorie who hath all tythes (not menconed before) issuing forth of Batheston and Catterne.

August 3, 1640
Thomas Blanchard

Another terrier, in the same hand, but neither signed nor dated, is similar, but adds:

First the Chancell is in good and sufficient repayre [That the barn is in good repair]

There is a Viccaridge belonginge to ye said Rectorie and a Mansion house and some out Houses, thereunto adjoining, and Glebe lands viz. a Church Yard by estimacion 2 acres a meadow near the Viccaridge house by estimacion 2 acres with the Gardein adjoyning and there belongs to the Viccarr the Tythes of Hay of some particular grounds within the Rectorie ... to the value of three loads

And the Viccarr hath all other smale tythes as Wooll, Lamb, pigg, calve kyne white etc.

In this version the Chancel Land is "as much as a peck of Corne will sowe and noe more". This suggests an area rather than a defined piece of ground. Its revenue was evidently intended for the upkeep of the chancel, always the duty of the rector.

The next terrier to survive is dated 1709, and records the parsonage barn, 44 feet long, adjoining the barn of Henry Walters belonging to the Hill House (Farm). The Chancel Land amounted to 11 perches with the additional information that it was enclosed out of the common field with lands of Richard Harford 20 years before. In William Chapman's valuation of 1779 the 11 perches were bounded with stones at each corner, and worth two and sixpence a year; the land was pasture.

The later history of the Chancel Land is a good example of English conservatism. In 1892 a firm of solicitors wrote to Christ Church on behalf of a client who was acquiring the field in which it lay (Map 2, B7a), and asking to buy it. It was then 21 perches—evidently that peck of corn had been sown economically—and rented at thirteen shillings. The Tithe Map of 1840 allows exact identification. The reply has not been preserved, but to-day the owner of the field, now a market garden, pays thirteen shillings a year to the vicar!

THE VICARAGE

Among the parish archives is a terrier of the vicarage, pre-Reformation, but undated, and partly illegible. The Rev. John Higson transcribed it thus:

> . . . omnes Oblationes et minutas Obventiones Decimas Agnorum Pullorum Vitulorum Lini Lanae Lactis et Mellis Gardinorum Columbariorum Molendinorum totius Parochiae . . . Sustinebit interim Vicarius qui pro tempore fuerit omnia onera ordinaria quae solent Vicariae incumbere cum Capellae Sanctae Katharinae in praedicta Paroikia . . . Alia autem onera quae ad Rectorem pertinere solebant Prior et conventus plenarie sustinebunt.

It may be translated:

> . . . all Oblations and small Obventions Tithes of Lambs Chickens Calves Flax Wool Milk and Honey Gardens Dovecotes Mills of the whole Parish. . . . The Vicar for the time being will perform all the regular duties which usually fall to the Vicarage with (those of) the Chantry Chapel of Saint Katharine in the said Parish. . . . The Prior and convent will fully carry out the other duties which customarily belong to the Rector.

At a visitation in 1623 Thomas Blanchard and Richard Ponting reported "that the chancel windows and the church porch are out of repaire and that they have not 'a booke of homilies' (Every parish was required to possess one). That they have no terrier of their glebe land belonging to their vicarage." Before the end of their year of office the omission was made good, and the terrier is in the County Record Office. Its special interest lies in the particular account of the vicar's right to some of the tithe of hay, which usually belongs to the rector. Terriers of 1638 and 1639 are preserved in the same collection:

> 1638. 26. October. Imprimis the vicarage house consisting of six field of houseing, all under one roofe, with a curtilage and garden thereunto belonging, situate nere the church, in the southeast side thereof.

> Item one meadow ground contayning by estimation two acres, unto the foresaid house and garden next adioning.

> Item the churchyard contayning likewise by estimation two acres and two little plots of ground to the value of half a yard late in the tenure of Joane Pile widow, deceased: one lying at the northside the other at the southside of the garden belonging to the Farme and bothe now in the Vicar's owne possession.

A yard was a quarter of an acre. As late as 1860, a plan of the churchyard shews the little bay at the northwest of it as "the vicar's garden". Anyone acquainted with Batheaston will readily recognise the description of the vicarage grounds and churchyard. It is disappointing that the account of the vicarage is scanty compared to that given in some terriers, for no more is known of the dwelling of the vicar of this period, than that he was taxed for three hearths in 1664–1665.

The terrier of 1639 repeats the foregoing, with the addition:

> Item that the Chappell of Katherine is a Chappell annexed unto the church of Batheaston.

> Item that it appeareth by sentence read by Dr. Ducke the herbage of the Chappellyard of Katherine belongeth to the vicar of Batheaston but we saie that in our memories the vicar never enioyed itt.

> Item that the vicar of Batheaston hath and is to have certain tythes ariseing in Katherine.

Unlike the rectory, there is no record of rights in the common fields attached to the vicarage. Indeed, it is quite clear that by the early seventeenth century there were no such rights, for the agreement of 1620 on the stinting of grazing for sheep (p. 132) allows no common to the vicar. So by this time he was almost entirely dependent upon tithes for his support.

THE VICARS

The list of clergy who have served Batheaston can never be complete. Nothing definite is known of any minister before 1260, though it is probable that the editor was correct in identifying Aiston, where Nicholas was chaplain about 1180, with Batheaston.[9] The first two certain names survive in the cartulary of Bath Abbey. The list of authorities in Table 2 shews that the bishops' registers omitted several who are known from other evidence; besides, the register

Table 2

Vicars of Batheaston whose names are known

Date	Name	Cause for vacancy where known	Authority other than the Bishop's register
About 1180	? Nicholas	—	Cartulary of Bath Abbey
1260	Richard le Gist	—	Cartulary of Bath Abbey
About 1291	Walter de Slouhtre	—	Cartulary of Bath Abbey
1323	William de Kayner	—	—
Before 1329	Nicholas	—	—
1329	Thomas de Thornton	Exchange with N.	
1343	John de Houton	—	Calendar of Patent Rolls
1349 Jan. 10	Ralph Boye	—	—
1349 Jan. 18	John Savery	—	—
Before 1379	Thomas Pokelchurch	—	Button M.S. 318
Before 1396	Thomas Wynscote	—	Calendar of Patent Rolls
1396	Lawrence Witley	Exchange with T. W.	Calendar of Patent Rolls
Before 1399	William Redhode	—	Bishop Stafford of Exeter
1399	Richard Covyntre	Exchange with W. R.	Bishop Stafford of Exeter
1401	William Cornewayll	Exchange with R. C.	Bishop Stafford of Exeter
1402	Thomas Byryg	—	—
Before 1433	William Byryton	—	—
1433	John Knocston	Resignation of W. B.	—
1434	Richard Rose	Resignation of J. K.	—
1455	Lewis ap Price	Resignation of R. R.	—
1464	Edmund Hill	Exchange with L. P.	—
1471	John Lorde	Resignation of E. H.	—
1503	John Parker, B.LL.	Death of J. L.	—
1537	William Taylor	—	Prior Holloway's Register, Harleian M.S. 3970
Before 1554	John Holder alias Auston	—	—
1569	Thomas Brytton	Death of J. H.	—
1614–1653	George Lee, B.A.	Death of T. B.	—
1654 (only)	Henry Hall, D.D.	Death of G. L.	Poor Book
1662	James Mitchel	—	—
1663	John Davy	—	—
1682	Joseph Dresser, B.A.	—	—
1707	John Hellier, B.A.	Death of J. D.	—
1717	Mark Hall, B.C.L.	Death of J. H.	—
1766	John Higson, M.A.	Death of M. H.	—
1787	Peter Davy Foulkes, M.A.	Death of J. H.	—
1797	Thomas Herbert Noyes, M.A.	Death of P. D. F.	—
1812	John Josias Conybeare, M.A.	Death of T. H. N.	—
1829	Spencer Madan, M.A.	Death of J. J. C.	—
1851	Thomas Percival Rogers, M.A.	Death of S. M.	—
1888	Arthur Meadows Downes, M.A.	Death of T. P. R.	—
1928	Edward Charles Rich, M.A.	Resignation of A. M. D.	—
1931	Conrad Douglas Richard Oakley Bankes, M.A.	Resignation of E. C. R.	—
1935	Philip Brandon Mercier, M.A.	Resignation of C. D. R. O. B.	—
1949	Reginald Arthur Evans, B.A.	Resignation of P. B. M.	—

is altogether lacking from 1363 to 1401. We do not know the "intruders" who served during the Commonwealth. The mere recital of names is not very edifying, and scarcely a hint is preserved to tell what manner of men the pre-Reformation vicars were. From the seventeenth century onwards recognisable characters begin to emerge, and the chronicler must attempt to paint them. The little that is known of early vicars is here briefly presented.

Richard le Gist only appears once after his institution, when in the following year he was witness to a deed between Lady Matilda and the Prior of Bath.[10]

Walter de Slouhtre may have been a local man. His name (Old English, Slahtreo—Sloe tree) is an early form of what later became known as Slaughter Lane, the ancient trackway which forms part of the western boundary of Batheaston, and his family may have taken its name from it.

Bishop Ralph's register records in 1329 a commission "to institute Sir Nicholas of Batheneston to the church of Netilcoumbe (Nettlecombe) vacant by reason of exchange". The "Sir" was a courtesy title accorded to the clergy. The name of Thomas de Thornton appears as rector of Nettlecombe the previous year. Of John de Houton nothing but his name and royal patronage is known.

Our next record belongs to the period of the Black Death and the terrible winter of 1348–1349. The bare account of institutions in the diocese of Bath and Wells tells a vivid tale. Excluding exchanges, in October 1348 there were two, in November nine, December thirty-one, January forty-three, and thereafter a gradual fall to reach the usual level about May. The situation must have been desperate, acolytes, men "in first tonsure" and "poor priests" being hurried into benefices. On 12 January, Bishop Ralph issued a mandate addressed to all rectors, vicars and priests that they should make known to the laity that on account of the spread of the plague — *contagium pestilentiae moderni temporis undique se dilatans* — they need not hesitate if they are overtaken with the sickness and cannot make confession to a priest, to confess to one another, and even to a woman.

In this corner of Somerset, Bathampton, Bathford, Weston and Twerton all lost their vicars. On 10 January Ralph Boye was instituted to Batheaston, and probably the pestilence had carried off the vicar, perhaps John de Houton. Immediately it struck again, killing, presumably, the new vicar so rapidly that John Savery was instituted a mere eight days later. Of him nothing is known, and the next incumbent we can name was Thomas Pokelchurch, who, as vicar of Batheaston, witnessed a deed in 1379.[11] He was probably the same Thomas who paid a shilling in the taxation of 1377. By this time surnames were general, many of them preserving the place of origin of the family. Thomas had not travelled far from the ancestral Pucklechurch.

The exchanging of benefices became a common practice in the fourteenth century, and by 1391 was such a scandal that Archbishop Courtenay fulminated against the "brokers" who arranged them, denouncing the "Choppechirches" as accursed consorts of Gehazi and Simon Magus.[12] Doubtless they secured some benefit for themselves, but the mutual advantage which persuaded the incumbents to the undertaking is far from obvious. It is recorded in the Patent Rolls that in 1396 Thomas Wynscote, vicar of Batheaston was presented to the church of Werkley (Warkleigh) in the diocese of Exeter on exchange with Laurence Witley. For knowledge of the next three vicars we depend on the register of Bishop Edmund Stafford of Exeter, which records that William Redhode of Batheneston exchanged with Richard Covyntre of Hockeworthy. Little more than a year later Coventry exchanged with William Cornewayll, vicar of Egloshayll; whose successor at Batheaston was instituted just within the year, Cornwall returning to Exeter diocese! In each of these exchanges a considerable journey was involved —Nettlecombe is near Watchet, nearly sixty miles away, Hockworthy in Devon about the same distance, while Egloshayl, near Wadebridge, lies well within the Cornish peninsula. It is difficult indeed to form a mental picture of the how and why of the transaction, from the necessary preliminaries to the slow, painful journey, encumbered by however modest a collection of worldly goods; yet it happened.

The next five vicars all resigned; William Byryton's name appears only on his resignation, which shews that the register was faulty before 1433. To us these men are only names, except Rose, of whom we know that in his early years at Batheaston he inclined to negligence. For in 1437 Bishop Stafford confirmed a decree which settled a dispute between him and his parishioners about the services to be held in the chapel of S. Catherine. The vicar must at his own expense provide a chaplain to celebrate masses on Sundays, Mondays and Wednesdays, and on festivals and solemn days, according to ancient custom. If he failed to do so, he was to pay £10 to works of piety. The threatened forfeit was a fierce one, more than a year's income. Presumably Rose complied, and perhaps established good relations with his people, for he continued vicar a further eighteen years. Lewis Ap Rice exchanged with Edmund Hill the living of Staunton Fitzherbert in the diocese of Salisbury, in 1469.

John Parker was the first vicar whom we know to have been a university man, Bachelor of both Laws. Neither University claims him among its alumni, and nothing more is known of him except that he was still vicar, and residing in the parish, when the Valor Ecclesiasticus of 1535 was compiled. So it is probable that William Taylor followed him directly in 1537; and of Taylor no more can be said.

The register of Prior Holloway[13] notes that one Henry Brunker in 1538 obtained the next presentation to the vicarage of Batheaston; the monastery was dissolved, however, the next year, so it is probable that he never enjoyed his right.

The next vicar whose name we have, John Holder, does not appear in the bishop's register; it is blank between the years 1547 and 1554, so he may have been instituted during that time. We do not know whether the religious upheavals of the Reformation affected Batheaston, or whether any vicar was expelled during the reign of Queen Mary, when clergy who had availed themselves of permission to marry were deprived of their livings.

Thomas Brytton was vicar for forty-five years until his death. His surviving signature, firm and confident, was written only six weeks before the institution of his successor, so his death was evidently unexpected. Probably of a well-known Bath family, he was resident in 1575, when, according to the bishop's return[14] some incumbents were absentees. Agnes Hickes, widow, of Chew, in her will of 1584[15] asserted that "Mr. Britten, vicar of Batheaston, owes me four pounds". Whatever the truth there, his last years suggest a dereliction, both of the vicar and of his son Thomas, who went from King Edward's School on a scholarship to Balliol College in 1598 aged eighteen, and graduated in 1603.[16] The remaining evidence comes from the Visitation Act Books.[17]

1606. Batheaston. Thomas Britten presented for preaching but two sermons since Easter.

1609. Batheaston. J. W. is begotten of a child, and nameth Thomas Brittaine jnr. to be the father thereof.

Thomas Brittane jnr presented that he preacheth without licence and hath byn often tymes forbidden by former churchwardens. That he is a common drunkard.

Katherin. Presented that Thomas Brittanie jnr

did lately serve the cure there under his father the parson of Batheaston whether licensed they knowe not and allsoe he did preached and expound the scriptures whether licensed they know not.

They went not in perambulation the last yeare nor in manie yeares before. That they had no communion. . . . Easter past except upon the Sunday last before the visitation and the parishioners had no warning to prepare themselves and the partie that ministered the same was a stranger sent thither by their vicar, which stranger did also preache theare that daie whether licensed they know not. They know not his name, but believe the said vicar can tell whoo he is.

1612. Batheaston. Presented Thomas Brittain jnr that he doth for all they know stand excommunicated.

It looks bad, but we only hear one side of the story.

George Lee B.A. was vicar for thirty-nine years, dying in 1653, aged 85. The brass replica of his tombstone, the latter now buried beneath the floor of the chancel, gives his age as 35, obviously an error, and his true age is known from a declaration as a witness. He may have been the George Lee who graduated at Cambridge in 1586.

From the touching inscription on his tombstone it may well be inferred that he was a good man, and loved by his people:

Here lyeth ye Body / of George Lee late / Vicar of this Parish / who departed this / life ye 25 day of July / Ao Dm 1653 Aetatis q / suae 85 Ecce verus / Israelita in quo Non / fuit Dolus / Vita mea / Mors Christi est.

The worst that the historian can find to say of "An Israelite in whom was no guile" is that he was negligent in the keeping of the register, which is blank for ten years until a solitary entry in his own hand the year before his death. The tremulous signatures of his latter years, at last barely legible, are very different from the bold hand of his prime, and rather pathetic.

With the death of George Lee we enter upon a period of obscurity which lasts for nine years. It was the time of the Commonwealth and the Puritan ascendancy, when, under Cromwell, some liberty of religion was allowed—but not to episcopacy. Page 79 of the register of the Bishop of Bath and Wells is blank, save for the bald statement: "During the time of the Wars viz: from 1645 to 1660 there were no Institutions". Further, hundreds of men were driven from their parishes, cruelly, even to starve, unable to earn a living. Perhaps the old man died just in time to escape ejection; perhaps a gleam of compassion enabled him to finish his days in his vicarage. We may be glad that it was so, and take leave of him with an affectionate regard.

A mystery follows: the accounts of the overseers of the poor for 1654 bear the signature "Henry Hall vicar", and the same year "Dr. Henery Hall" paid to the rate for the highways; in 1665 in the same position in the list William Bletchley, a local man, paid the same sum, "for the glibe", the implication being that the benefice was vacant. For the next three years a Mr. Nelme paid, and then no comparable entry appears. Dr. Henry Hall was never instituted, and he was evidently in the parish only a year or so. Who was he? It is impossible to be certain, but he was probably that Henry Hall, son of a cleric of Wells, who graduated from Oxford in 1634, was created Doctor of Divinity by Trinity College, Dublin, dean of Cork 1643, vicar of Harwell, Berkshire, 1654, and bishop of Killala from 1661 until his death in 1663. Unfortunately, no other example of his signature can be found, so the identification remains a surmise. Nothing is known of Mr. Nelme; perhaps he was the George of that name who entered Lincoln (Henry Hall's) College in 1650.

The known records of "intruders" and ejectments during these unhappy times, including the Commonwealth Papers at Lambeth Palace Library, do not help to fill the gap.

From the Restoration onwards the list of vicars is complete. The great dearth of ordained clergy to fill the vacant livings in 1661 and after is exemplified in the history of James Michell, described as "literate", who was instituted to the cure of souls at S. James, Bath, and ordained deacon and priest, all on 9 November 1661! His signature (Pl. 6) does not appear in the parish records of Batheaston, but is taken from his subscription of faith made that day. The entry of his institution to the vicarage of Batheaston in 1662 describes him as of Corsham. He was probably the James Michel who was instituted, also in 1662, to Draycot Cerne in the diocese of Salisbury.

His successor at Batheaston, John Davy, described as a clerk, not a graduate, was vicar for nearly twenty

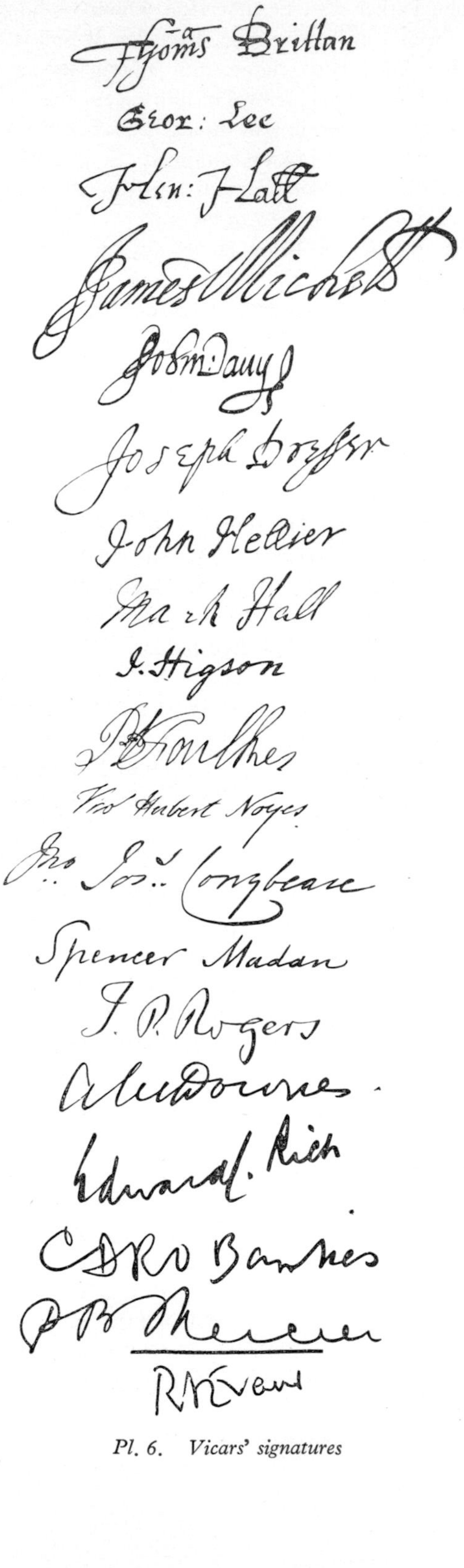

Pl. 6.   Vicars' signatures

years, and also left no hint of his disposition, nor detectable impress on the parish. His signature appears but rarely in the records, nor did he trouble himself about the keeping of the register.

The next nine vicars died in office, their incumbency totalling 206 years, and seven of them were buried here. It would be interesting to know to what extent long tenure is evidence of content. Joseph Dresser was admitted a sizar to S. Catherine's College, Cambridge, in 1671, and graduated B.A. in 1675. Besides being vicar of Batheaston, he was rector of Walcot from 1688 to his death in 1707, a doubling of parts not uncommon. The evidence, from the downright of his "A true and perfect register of all ye baptisms, Weddings, and Burials in the parish of Bath-Easton commencing April the 10th by me 1683 Joseph Dresser, Vicar" onwards, shews that he was a conscientious vicar, and he, his wife, and two of their children were buried here, so he was evidently resident. He made his last entry in the register, a burial, on Christmas Day, 1706. A wedding on 6 January was entered in another hand, and the next records: Feb. 8. Dresser, Joseph, vicar of this Parish buried. He had buried his *"charissima uxor"* in 1701, and was unique in keeping the register in Latin.

John Hellier (notes about this, and succeeding incumbents, are taken from *Alumni Oxonienses*), son of Andrew Hellier, of Salisbury, entered Oriel College in 1695, and graduated B.A. in 1698. He was vicar for barely ten years, and died, leaving a widow, at the age of thirty-seven. He is honoured as the Founder of Batheaston School. In his will he expressed the wish that his body be buried "near the outside of the Chancel Wall of the Church of Batheaston on the West side of the Church Door"; and so it was. He must have loved the place. His monument is still on the chancel wall, the inscription fast flaking away, and much of it lost, but fortunately it is preserved in the churchwarden's accounts for 1793, which include also a copy of the will:

Near this place lies interr'd the Body of John Hellier late Vicar of this parish who departed this Life the first day

of February Anno } Domini 1716
                  } [Aetatis 37]

He left by will the interest of one Hundred and twenty pounds for ever for teaching poor children of this parish to read write and cast accounts and for instructing them in the knowledge and practice of the Christian Religion as profess'd and taught in the Church of England.

The Righteous shall be had in everlasting Remembrance. Ps. 112–6.

In truth his age was never inscribed on the stone, the foundation was explicitly for boys, and there is no mention of the teaching of religion in Hellier's will! (p. 116).

Mark Hall's incumbency lacked a few months of fifty years, the record for Batheaston. His father, John Hall, was a cleric, of Smeaton, Yorkshire. Mark entered University College in 1709, aged 18, and graduated from Christ Church in 1713. He became Bachelor of Common Law in 1726. In addition to holding the living of Batheaston, he was rector of Walcot 1721–6, and rector of Ditteridge from 1726.

He was early bereaved by the death of his wife, Sarah Jenny, in 1723, leaving him with two young children, John, born 1719, and Susanna, 1721. John entered Christ Church in 1738, and was probably the John Hall, curate, who signed the Poor Book in 1774. Nothing more is known of John or of his sister.

The catalogue of Mark Hall's books is interesting as an example of the library an educated man of the eighteenth century, a country parson, might possess. It consisted of eighty-four works, more than half religious, a few volumes of the classics—Sophocles, Plato, Cicero, Virgil, Horace, Ovid, a volume of Euclid, a work with the intriguing title *Derham's Astro-theology*, a few periodicals, including *The Gentleman's Magazine*, which noticed his death. English literature is represented by a folio Evelyn's *Sylva* and the poems of Cowley! Some of the books were sold after his death for a few pence or shillings. The fate of *Sylva* is not recorded.

For the last two years of his life he was evidently unable to work. One Edward Sheppard signed a quarterly receipt for £7 10s for taking duty at Batheaston, S. Catherine and Ditteridge, and shortly before he died E. Yescombe received £3 4s for eight Sundays at Ditteridge. He was buried by his young wife, beneath the east end of the nave, where the passing feet of generations of Batheastonians have worn away much of the inscription. Let the entry in the parish register be his epitaph:

1766. Oct. 9. Buried Rev. Mr. Mark Hall Vicar

of this Parish for 50 years aged 75 A Gentleman well beloved by his parishioners and acquaintances. A copy of his will is in the parish archives (Appendix 5).

John Higson was an unhappy man. He filled many sheets of paper, and several books, with accounts of tithes due to him, often years in arrears, and at least once threatened, if he did not take it, legal action against three farmers. A letter of his, dated May 1783, is preserved at Christ Church. After remarking on his "very bad state of health", he continued:

"The Art and Roguery of Farmers are well known. And they that are in Composition, as it stood in my Predecessor's time, are almost all in Arrears, some up to three, and some up to seven years. And I cannot get any Attorney that will bring an Action against any of them. By these Means, and the Dearness of Provisions, I am run into Debt—My Health is Bad, my Spirits are low. I want an Assistant and am not able to pay One—'Tis well known that I sacrificed a very good Income in Oxford, and hitherto have had Nothing done for me. Perhaps the Bishop of London, or some other worthy Persons might take Compassion on me; if my Case was made known to Them. Pray order my name to be taken out of the College Books."

Pl. 9 (p. 38) refers to a later tithe of 1779, and gives some idea of the petty traffic which engaged so much of his attention. It is not that his troubles were exceptional—the evidence proves otherwise—but that he seems to have been excessively absorbed in his claims and grievances against his parishioners. Rotten hay and sour milk seem too often to have come his way. Perhaps, though, his preoccupation was not really unusual, only the extent of the poor man's scribblings that has come down to us. He was certainly very unhappy. What a life for a minister of religion, constantly dunning his flock for the means of existence!

He came from Moberley, Cheshire, entered Wadham College in 1740, aged 19, and took the degrees of B.A. 1743, M.A. 1747. The parish register records thus:

The Rev. John Higson A.M. late Vice Principal in St. Edmund Hall, Oxford, and twenty years Vicar of this Parish died 15th Feb. 1787 aged 66 years, and was buried on 24th Feb.

He was evidently working to the end, or nearly; for the last wedding of his incumbency was performed by him the previous 26 November.

Batheaston has not been without its absentee vicar. Peter Davy Foulkes, son of a medical man of Topsham, came of a landed Devonshire family. He graduated B.A. from Christ Church in 1771, at the age of twenty, and proceeded M.A. in 1774. *Alumni Oxonienses* states that he was of Medland, Devon, and that is all; it does not mention Batheaston. Indeed, without the record of his institution, and one signature in the churchwarden's accounts, there would be no evidence that he ever visited the place. During his incumbency, the parish was served by Edward Davies, who added to his signature the appellation Minister.

The parish register records laconically:

1797. 15 August Foulkes Peter David (sic) A.M. Vicar of this parish died in Devonshire and was buried there.

Thomas Herbert Noyes, son of a gentleman of Berkhampstead, entered Christ Church aged seventeen in 1775, was student, and took the B.A. in 1779, M.A. 1782. His incumbency of Batheaston from 1797 is the only appointment recorded of him. In contrast to his predecessor, he signed the accounts regularly, and almost always officiated at weddings. Two sons were baptised at Batheaston; one, also Thomas Herbert, after Oxford, became a barrister of Lincoln's Inn. The marriage of his son in 1878 to a daughter of T. P. Rogers, then vicar of Batheaston, excites curiosity. In the parish register is entered:

1812. August 16 The Reverend Thomas Herbert Noyes Vicar of this Parish died August 8th and was buried August 16th at Horsepath, near Oxford.

John Josias Conybeare, the only vicar to gain an entry in the *Dictionary of National Biography*, was a son of the parsonage, his father rector of Billingsgate, his grandfather Bishop of Bristol. King's Scholar at Westminster 1793, Captain of the School 1796, he was elected head to Christ Church in 1797. He won the Chancellor's Prize for Latin Verse in 1800, was B.A. 1801 and M.A. 1804. Among his many academic distinctions, he was Professor of Anglo-Saxon 1808–1812, of Poetry 1812–1821, and Bampton Lecturer in 1824, shortly before his death. He was Prebendary of York, too, from 1803.

W. S. Mitchell recorded of him[18] "I have been told he was of dark complexion, with black hair, and any stranger meeting him would have been struck by his peculiar jerky manner. He was considered to be one of the most learned men of his day".

Sacred to the beloved and revered memory of
John Josias Conybeare M.A.
Prebendary of York, and for 11 years
the faithful minister of this parish

Thus was inscribed his memorial tablet, and there is evidence that he was indeed a zealous vicar. A major benefit of his incumbency was the erection of a school building—in the churchyard, a choice which later proved an embarrassment (p. 118). This enterprise he pioneered, and to it he largely contributed. Less happy was his mutilation of the front of the vicarage, partly to provide for himself a laboratory.

His talents and versatility were remarkable. His scientific studies enabled him to publish papers on chemistry, and original observations on the geology of a number of sites, especially in the Somerset coalfield, Devon and Cornwall. By far his most memorable achievement, however, was his contribution to early Anglo-Saxon scholarship. His work is preserved in his *Illustrations of Anglo-Saxon Poetry*, which includes, besides an exposition of metre, long sections of texts, with his own translations into Latin and English, and which can still be studied with interest and profit. It was his intention that the proceeds from this *magnum opus* should be used for the building of Batheaston School, but the preparation of it took so long that he gave to the school from his own funds, and left the work incomplete at his untimely death, to be published by his brother, W. D. Conybeare.

He was seized with sudden illness on his forty-fifth birthday, and perished the next day, leaving a widow. A charming tribute to his merits is the dedication of the *History and Antiquities of Bath Abbey Church*, by John Britton F.S.A. 1824:

To the Esteemed Memory of the late
Reverend John Josias Conybeare M.A.
Who combined in his own person
the profound and modest Scholar
the liberal and enlightened Critic,
the erudite Mineralogist, the acute Antiquary,
the amiable and charitable Parish Vicar,
the sincere Friend and affectionate Relative;
This volume is Inscribed,
With sentiments of real personal regard
and sorrow for his loss,
By the Author.

Spencer Madan, favoured of Fortune, was the third of four Spencers, all clerics. His grandfather was Bishop of Bristol, afterwards of Peterborough, and his father canon of Lichfield, where he was born in 1791. King's Scholar at Westminster 1806, he was elected to Trinity College, Cambridge in 1810, following his father and grandfather, but instead entered Christ Church, Oxford, taking a first class in mathematics and second in classics in 1813, and proceeding M.A. in 1816. Being tutor to the younger sons of Charles Lennox, Duke of Richmond, he was present at the Duchess' famous ball, 15 June 1815, three days before the battle of Waterloo.[19] Several of his letters to his family at this time are extant; one of them suggests a young man serious and thoughtful, if somewhat intoxicated by the glamour of his situation:

"The Duke dined on April 6th. You may conceive the pleasure it gave me to find myself at the same table with such a man. . . . He was in the highest spirits, full of fun and drollery, and made himself the life and soul of the party. The Duke appears to unite those two extremes of character which Shakespeare gave to Henry the fifth, the hero and the trifler. You may conceive him at one moment commanding the Allied armies in Spain, and at another sprawling on his back or on all fours upon the carpet, playing with a child. His judgement is so intuitive that instant decision follows perception, and consequently, as nothing dwells for a moment on his mind, he is enabled to get through an infinity of business without ever being embarrassed by it or otherwise than perfectly at his ease."

There follows a full and very interesting account of events, before, during, and after the battle when the wretched casualties were returning to Brussels.

He was curate of Netherseale, Derbyshire, 1816–1824, Prebendary of Lichfield from 1817, vicar of Batheaston from 1823, and of Twerton also from 1825 until his death in 1851. Perhaps his social standing accounted for his appointment in 1830 as chaplain to the King. He married in 1825 Louisa Elizabeth, sister of Sir William Nigel Gresley. Of their four sons, two took orders; another two served in the Crimea, one being killed at Sebastopol.

A man of private means, he employed one, sometimes two curates at Batheaston, but there is ample evidence that he did a good deal of work himself.

During his incumbency the school was enlarged by the addition of a second storey largely at his expense, and the north aisle of the church was built.

His obituary notice in *The Gentleman's Magazine* tells that he never failed to keep his months of residence at Lichfield, and that, though he was not musically inclined, he always attended the services. Evidently his circulatory system failed gradually during several years; the end came suddenly in the close at Lichfield, and in the close he was buried. His memorial in Batheaston church records that:

> "until incapacitated by sickness, he sedulously attended to the duties of his office ever administering to the wants of the poor; whilst, by his truly Christian demeanour, he engaged the esteem and affection of his richer brethren, and to whose zeal and liberality the enlargement of this church, and of the school house on two occasions, is mainly attributable."

Undoubtedly a sincere appreciation of his merits.

His successor, Thomas Percival Rogers, son of a clergyman of Wentnor, Shropshire, entered Christ Church in 1840, aged 19, and was student 1843–1852, B.A. 1844, M.A. 1847, tutor 1850. Batheaston was his only cure, and here he laboured for the last thirty-seven years of his life, earning a great debt of his people's gratitude, though there were those who dissented at the time. Visible memorials of his incumbency are the chancel, rebuilt largely at his cost as recipient of the rectorial tithe charge, the south aisle, the nave roof and the parish school. It is mainly owing to him that features of the old church were preserved.

That he was a faithful shepherd is abundantly evident. His letter urging the enlargement of the parish church (Appendix 9) is a moving example of his zeal. An accomplished artist, his etching of the church before the building of the south aisle survives to give pleasure to-day (Pl. 7). His second wife was a daughter of C. E. Broome, the eminent naturalist (p. 97). He died suddenly, and his people gave a carved screen for the tower arch, now banished to the north aisle, and the stained glass in the window to the south of the arch, inscribing on a mural tablet that the gifts were "a memorial of the regard and affection in which he was held by all who knew him".

Arthur Medows Downes, yet another clergyman's son, of Palgrave, Suffolk, went up to Christ Church,

aged 18, in 1877, and was B.A. 1880, M.A. 1884. He came to Batheaston after a curacy at S. Luke, Old Street, London, and served for forty years. Not only a conscientious vicar, he was a keen musician as well, and himself trained the choir to a high standard. He supported, too, the lectures arranged for the village folk (p. 72), and contributed on diverse subjects. Old Batheastonians speak of him with affection, invariably as "Dapper" Downes. With his incumbency living memory is reached.

ASSISTANT CURATES

The practice of employing a curate began, it seems, in Batheaston in the late eighteenth century, and from then on, though not every vicar could afford the luxury, a line of "curates, long dust, will come and go" not 'on lissom, clerical, printless toe', but across the pages of the parish records. Two at least of them made their mark—Edward Davies who did the work for the absentee Foulkes, and William Hutchins who in 1830 was presented with "very sincere thanks for his attention to the Parish whilst under his care".

VALUE OF THE CHURCH

A bald statement of the vicar's income over seven centuries has little meaning without reference to the cost of living, a consideration which cannot be entered into here; besides, in later times there is often doubt about whether the figure relates to gross or nett income. So only a few notes are put on record, culled from standard sources and the archives of Christ Church.

1292. Batheaston Church valued at 15 marks (Bathampton 10½, Bathford 13. A mark was 13s 4d. These figures are taken from the Taxation of Pope Nicholas.)

1377. 16 marks. (The vicar's "twentieth" was 1s, i.e. taxation.)

1428. 15 marks. (For "tenth" from Feudal Aids.)

1445. 16 marks. (Beneficed clergy paid 1d. in the mark in taxation. Batheaston's assessment included a pension paid to the sacristan of Bath Abbey. Bathampton was worth 10½ marks, Bathford 6½. (S.R.S., 49, p. 34.)

1468. 12½ marks. (Benefices not taxed which are now to be taxed, Batheaston and South Stoke.)

1535. £29 6s 4½d. (Valor Ecclesiasticus. The rectory was valued at £17 13s 10d.)

Pl. 7.   *Batheaston Church 1858. Before the building of the south aisle*
          (etching by Rev. T. P. Rogers)

1783. £116 10s 9½d. (Under the provisions of Queen Anne's Bounty, Batheaston ranked as a "discharged vicarage", i.e. one excused the payment of first fruits, and a tenth of the annual income.)

1800. £163.

1835. £298.

1893. £260. (This included fees, £12 and Easter Offering, £16.)

Through the centuries, the church of Batheaston has been neither rich nor poor. To-day it is among the better remunerated of the diocese, but the income of the clergy is no longer a matter primarily of local concern.

TITHE

Until recent times the parochial clergy were practically dependent for their support on the produce of their glebe and on tithes, a tax on the produce of the land dating from antiquity. In parishes served by a vicar the usual custom was for the rector, in this case generally a layman or a religious house, to take the "great tithes", of corn, hay and wool; while the remainder, the "small tithes" fell to the vicar. For the man working the land the system meant that he was legally required to hand over a tenth of all his produce—that often he did no such thing, at least from the eighteenth century, will shortly be seen. Certain lands were always tithe-free, because they were anciently occupied by a religious house. Here they were the manor farm of S. Catherine, and most of Charmy Down Farm (in 1825, 227 and 399 acres respectively), and, for some historical reason long forgotten, 1½ acres to the north of Ramscombe Lane, called "the tithe-free land".

The common custom about the division of tithes was subject to variation in many parishes, including Batheaston. The agreement of 1262 (p. 22) entitled the vicar to the tithe of wool, and of the hay of all the meadows beside the Avon; the first he was never to lose, the second in course of time he had to share with the rector. Pl. 8 reveals diagrammatically how complicated a pattern had developed in Avonland by the eighteenth century. A terrier of the vicarage of 1623 lists fourteen other pieces of land, two only an eighth of an acre, in which by that time the vicar had some or all of the tithe hay, defined, for example, "between the two greeps where a walnut tree stands",

or "part of the ground called Stokes his close (Map 2, B68) viz. all the middle thereof from the arable in the west side to the row of trees on the east side". These instances are quoted to shew how complex was the practice that had grown up. As to why the vicar had a stake in this piece of land and not in that, no clue remains. Most of these fourteen lands whose tithe hay went to the vicar lay on either side of the road through Northend, and the enumerator can be followed travelling in his mind's eye up the valley. The parish officers listing those liable for rates worked the opposite way.

In the *Valor Ecclesiasticus* of 1535 the tithe of wool and lambs was valued at the considerable sum of £8 16s 4d. It is the more strange that the vicar's tithe of wool scarcely appears in the copious records which remain, for it was obviously an asset of special value in this district of sheep-farming and cloth-making. Yet the only mention of wool comes from the year 1781, when a lamb fleece was counted as 1½ lb. worth 8d a lb., a ram and ewe fleece 4 lb. and 3 lb.

What success attended efforts to collect the rector's tithe it is not possible to say; no record of complaint survives. For the vicar, the gathering of the means of subsistence was one long struggle, endlessly consuming time and goodwill alike. In the eighteenth and early nineteenth centuries successive vicars made many books and covered countless sheets of paper with reckonings of their claim to tithes, often years outstanding; in fact, the conclusion suggests itself that sometimes the exercise was a poor compensation for the failure of the reality. Before the end of the seventeenth century some tithes were being taken at an agreed valuation, but it was another hundred years before the composition system entirely displaced payment in kind (Pl. 9). The records left by John Higson are the richest source of information. In 1776, for instance, he took his tithe of hay in the Avonland between 20 June and 31 July, accepting some cocks, rejecting others as "rubbish". Another time he complained that his tithe milk was "sour in the churn". One of his anxieties, too, was computing his agistment, that is, his right to a tenth of grazing, in this case for his horse.

His predecessor, though, was having trouble in collecting the money due to him by composition. In 1757 the Hon. B. Bathurst owed six years' tithe for

TITHE OF AVONLAND 1724. (Shown Diagrammatically)

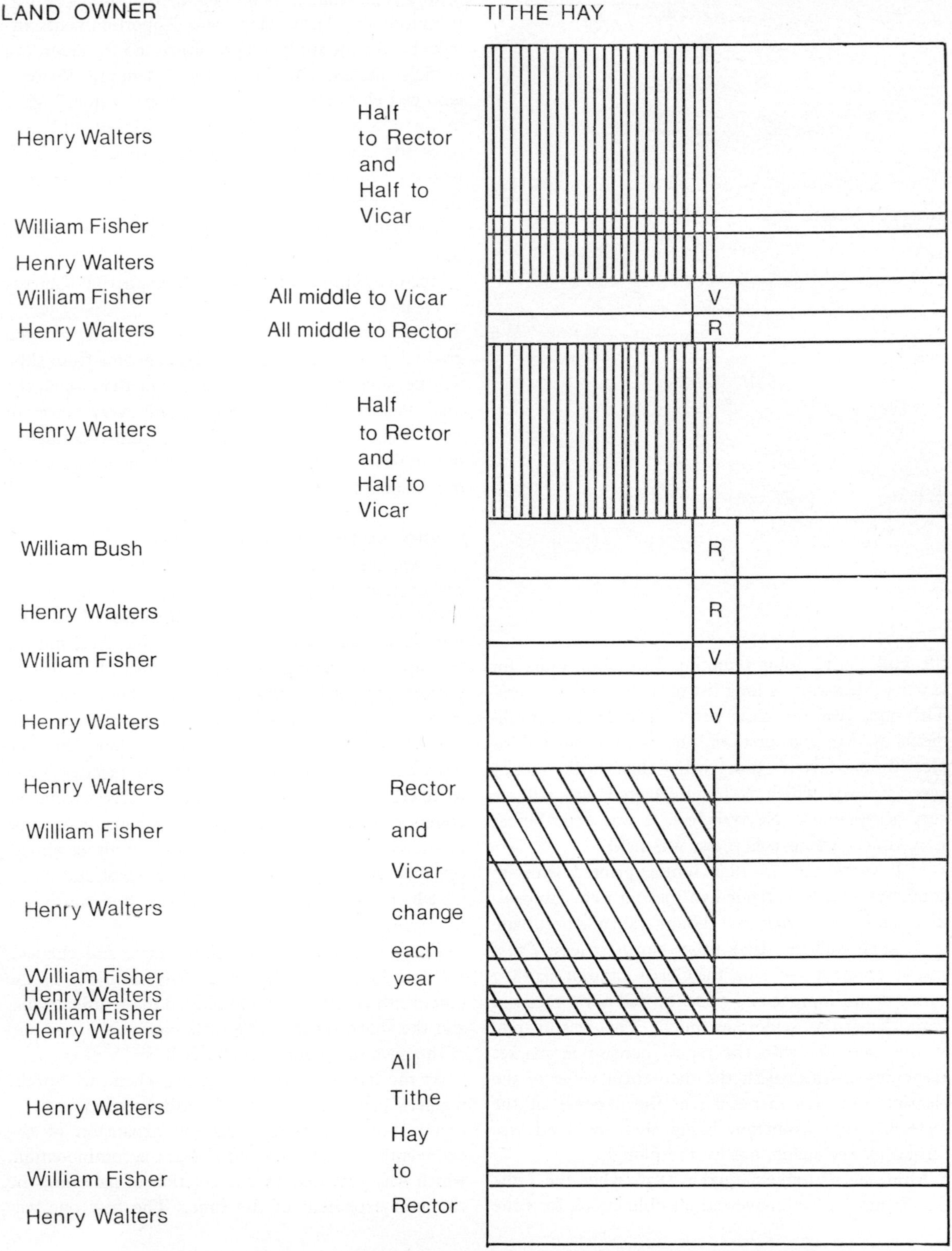

LAND OWNER   TITHE HAY

LAND OWNER	TITHE HAY	
Henry Walters	Half to Rector and Half to Vicar	
William Fisher		
Henry Walters		
William Fisher	All middle to Vicar	V
Henry Walters	All middle to Rector	R
Henry Walters	Half to Rector and Half to Vicar	
William Bush		R
Henry Walters		R
William Fisher		V
Henry Walters		V
Henry Walters	Rector	
William Fisher	and	
	Vicar	
Henry Walters	change	
	each	
William Fisher	year	
Henry Walters		
William Fisher		
Henry Walters		
Henry Walters	All Tithe Hay to Rector	
William Fisher		
Henry Walters		

Pl. 8. Tithe of Avonland 1724

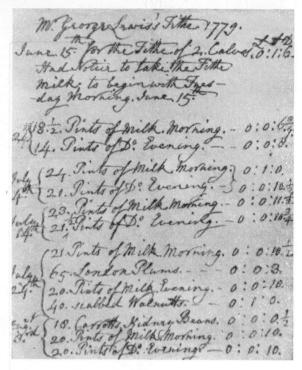

Pl. 9.   George Lewis' Tithe 1779

into a rent charge. This led to the survey which produced the Tithe Maps and Apportionments invaluable for the study of agriculture and the recording of field names. In Batheaston, Melmoth Walters, who was churchwarden and unofficial "squire", gave in £270 0s 3d, how calculated we are not told, as a basis for commutation. A larger amount, he said, would be quashed by the yeomen and the numerous small freeholders.

The sums agreed with the Tithe Commissioners were:

Rector: Batheaston £210 2s S. Catherine £46 10s
Vicar: „   £301   „   £50

The Tithe Act of 1935–1936 provided for the gradual extinction of the charge. Income from tithe will be altogether abolished not later than 1996, the final victory of the dissenters, in every sense of the term, who fought so long and obstinately the obligation to contribute to the maintenance of the Established Church.

S. JOHN BAPTIST, BATHEASTON.   THE BUILDING

There are no remains above ground of a church earlier than the fifteenth century building whose tower so splendidly dominates Northend (Pl. 10). Its four stages reach a height of ninety-four feet, and the bell openings have good stone louvres. The elegant pierced parapet is a pleasing feature. On its east face in a canopied niche an unidentified, much-decayed figure stands, or rather, curiously stoops (Pl. 11). To what benefactor or benefactors Batheaston owes its tower no one knows. Whether it derives from the coffers of Bath Abbey, or from the generosity of some unknown donor, the wealth which built it almost certainly resulted from the trade in wool and cloth, to which we owe so many of the fine towers of Somerset.

The tower dwarfed the simple nave and chancel, 108 feet long by 22 feet wide (the additions of the nineteenth century have not altered these dimensions) and the south porch. The little cote at the east end of the nave roof held a sanctus bell.

By the later seventeenth century when the churchwardens' accounts begin this building needed frequent repair, but it sufficed until the expansion of the eighteenth century demanded extra accommodation, which was provided by the erection of galleries, the common expedient of the time. The first one was

the Hill Farm, John Gunning Esq. four years for Hartley Mead, and a long list of debtors lesser sums. The next year the vicar wrote "Mr. Hall's compliments to Mr. Bathurst and he desires he will be pleas'd to favour him with this little money (£6 15s 11d) which is much wanted and will be very acceptable". Nevertheless, it was 1766 before £20, tithe for fourteen years, was paid.

J. J. Conybeare in 1823 sent a printed letter to announce that he intended to make a new composition. In it he asserted that though a detailed estimate in 1799 shewed the small tithes worth at least £325, and an eminent surveyor, for Christ Church, in 1817 gave a figure approaching £600, he had never received more than £170, seldom as much. This was in spite of the fact that with the rapid increase in market gardening in the parish the theoretical value of the vicarial tithe was increasing at the expense of the rectorial; the distinction being that the land was turned by the spade, not by the plough.

A rational system emerged in 1836, when the Tithe Commutation Act converted all obligations for tithe

Pl. 10. S. John Baptist, Batheaston
(*from a photograph by Mrs. E. L. Green-Armytage*)

built at the west end under the tower in 1727 "for the use of the Singers"; in 1792, when the village was growing fast, this was enlarged, and a new gallery, with three rows of seats, built on the north side. The faculty adds: "the church being so small as not nearly, nay hardly half spacious enough for the Inhabitants".

In 1834 a first meeting was held to consider enlarging the church, "the cost to be met by subscription and sale of pews, at not less than £5 average, according to position, the remaining pews to be let". Subscriptions brought in £650, the sale of seats £295, and the north aisle was built by Thomas Lewis, a local man. "The plans were drawn by Mr. Pinch, and much admired", and the work done "to great satisfaction, without an appeal outside the parish". The architect was the younger Pinch, designer of the Bath Literary and Scientific Institute, now the Reference Library. At the same time the ditch and walling outside the tower were constructed. The provision of an organ sited in the west gallery, and costing £87, completed the improvements. A stove, sconces, candlesticks and chandelier had been bought by subscription in 1830 for lighting and warming the church and £4 voted from the rates for fuel and candles for the year.

Soon more work was urgently needed, the rebuilding of the chancel, shortly followed by the building of the south aisle and the re-roofing of the nave. The vicar, T. P. Rogers, wrote in a letter to Christ Church that the chancel arch was only kept up by iron bars which bracketed it to the walls, the bases having been cut away, and could not have held up more than three or four years, adding "We shall have much difficulty in supporting the chancel arch during the building". This implies that the present arch is original. Rising in an uninterrupted curve from a low base, its form recalls the lower jaw of some toothless whale.

The rebuilding of the chancel was done in 1860, the vicar, as lessee of the rectory, contributing £350, while £375 was raised by subscription. Quite free of any excess of neo-Gothic exuberance, it was not built without the resistance of at least one strong evangelical, Melmoth Walters, who as the most influential parishioner vainly tried to insist that there should be no encaustic tiles, no stained glass, the ceiling wholly white, and "nothing offensive to the Protestant eye". To the vicar's scrupulous care for memorials and records of the past we owe the representation in brass of the inscriptions on the tombstones now buried beneath the floor, which is on the south wall of the chancel.

The next need was further enlargement of the church. A letter from the vicar to his parishioners,

Pl. 11.   Figure on church tower
(from a photograph by Mrs. E. L. Green-Armytage)

dated Advent 1865 (Appendix 9) set out in moving terms the inadequacies of the church to the needs of the growing population. A curious suggestion of a second north aisle was rejected, and it was decided to build a south aisle, to reseat the church, and if enough funds could be raised, to restore the nave roof. A London architect named Preedy was appointed. Of the nave roof he reported that the bosses at the intersections were richly carved and the wall plates richly moulded, the timbers being unusually large; portions of the kingposts were decayed. (These beauties were entirely hidden by the panelled plaster ceiling, only the corbels being visible). Preedy much admired this roof, and recommended its restoration; if funds were not enough to supply oak—ominous of things to come!—deal was to be stained to harmonise. He reported the next year that owing to the injudicious sinking of a vault four feet below the tower its west side was fractured from base to summit, and urged the removal of the coffins and filling of the tower base with concrete, as the only means of making it safe.

The excellent response to an appeal for funds enabled work to begin. The old south wall and the porch were taken down and carefully rebuilt to form a south aisle; this is the more remarkable because as the result of alterations and additions any harmony that the wall might originally have possessed was long disturbed, and the temptation to replace it must have been great; and though the stained glass of the east window of the aisle does not please the modern eye we may well thank Mr. Preedy and the Rev. Rogers for their restraint and respect for the past. Following the excellent example set in the rebuilding of the chancel, the delightful gargoyles, too, were re-used, with the addition of drainpipes their posture quaintly unconventional.

When it came to work on the roof, the restorers were grieved to find that the timbers throughout were so decayed that it was impossible to make any use of them; so a new roof of red deal was constructed, preserving in its main features the character of the old, and using the old corbels. The gallery at the west end of the nave was removed, and the pews of pitch pine, which do not please modern taste, installed. According to the *Bath Herald*, 8 November 1860, the discarded pews were "surpassingly tall and supremely ugly". The "three-decker" pulpit

was superseded. Finally, the firm of Skinner, of Bristol, installed a new system for "warming" the church for £55.

The church was reopened on 20 February 1868, a year to the day after the decision to build was taken, and the vicar wrote in a note book which records the entire enterprise:

"We had a most successful re-opening. . . . The day was lovely in the extreme: crowded congregations: services all fully choral. . . . The Pic-nic luncheon went off to perfection: something over 200 partaking thereof: going in by relays, but all in good humour. The total Collections amounted to £120 4s 3d. So our long trial over we have entered anew into our Sanctuary. . .

δόξα ἐν ὑψίστοις Θεῷ

Four months later, of the total cost of £1896 19s 6½d the deficit was a mere £1 18s 1½d. Batheaston had cause to be proud, and a century later may be thankful for the good taste of the restorers; but it is a pity about the "three decker". Of the little to deplore in the church, perhaps the fussy if horribly competent reredos of 1878 comes first.

The ancient font is lost, unless it is the late Norman font of S. Catherine, where baptisms would scarcely be expected at such an early date in a building of non-parochial status. Of the two fonts now in Batheaston church, the earlier, an octagonal bowl on a slender stem, probably dates from a big restoration of 1715. The other, given by Mrs. Rogers and ladies of the parish in 1869, has a bowl and shaft of Caen stone, with detached columns of red Irish marble at the angles. A newspaper spoke enthusiastically of "a new font, of beautiful design and very excellent workmanship. . . . The whole of the subjects are treated with great feeling, and shew real artistic skill in the grouping and execution". The whirligig of time failed not to bring in his revenges, for the Parochial Church Council in 1923 agreed "to recommend to the Vestry that a faculty be applied for in order that the modern Font in the Church may be disposed of". The resolution was later withdrawn. The discarded font, long forlorn in the churchyard, was restored to the church; we may not know whether the proposal rested on a revolution in taste, simple antiquarianism, or the desire for an addition to church funds. The older one is that used. The organ, by Sweetland, was built in 1875.

Pl. 12. Graffito on window in north aisle

THE CHURCH SERVICES

The earliest record of the vicar's obligations in his office is the agreement of 1262 (p. 22). Nothing further is known until long after the Reformation; the churchwardens' accounts, from 1667, witness to the common custom of the celebration of Holy Communion only three times a year, at Easter, Whitsuntide and Christmas, the bare minimum allowed. There is no other record of the customary services until 1775, when the vestry agreed to pay annually to the vicar at Easter "Ten Pounds in consideration of his officiating at Service and Sermon every third Sunday there being at present only

service two Sundays out of three". The practice continued at least to the end of the century.

About 1819 the vicar, J. J. Conybeare, replied to a general enquiry by the bishop that the accustomed services were "Double service and sermon two Sundays out of three—on the third single service and sermon". In 1826 the vestry resolved "to pay £20 out of the church rate for a clergyman to perform a second service at Batheaston alternate mornings and evenings when the vicar is at S. Catherine, the bishop having ordered a Duty to be performed every Sunday". A few years later, in 1833, the vicar was to have at least £20 for a resident curate, "to provide a second sermon, except on those mornings when the Sacrament of the Lord's Supper shall be administered". By the standard of to-day, the vicar led a life of ample leisure.

"Parish Notes" of 1899 contain, written by "J. W.", an account of Batheaston at prayer about 1840 so vivid and delightful that it merits quotation:
"The pews were very high, so that the occupants could scarcely see out, and when seated you only saw rows and rows of heads and bonnets; when it was time to stand up I was perched on a hassock, the instability of which often caused me to fall with a crash among the umbrellas in the corner of the pew, much to the discomfort and disturbance of my neighbours. The pulpit was that known as a three-decker: at the bottom sat Mr. Bell, the clerk, in the stiffest of white chokers, that rendered the turning of the head an absolute impossibility; above him in the reading desk was the curate, Mr. Nussey; and above him, in black Geneva gown, the vicar, Mr. Spencer Madan.

The men sat on one side of the aisle, the women on the other; the organ was in the gallery, which occupied the west end. When the organ played, the congregation turned round and faced it. The majority of the men wore smock frocks, and the women, in wet weather, pattens, which they formerly took off in the porch, under the stone benches, but some truant boys had on one occasion mixed the pattens, while the old ladies were at their devotions. There was a door into the chancel, and all the very grand ladies and gentlemen used to come into the church that way instead of by the big door, as it was considered more genteel. The lighting was not brilliant, standards with two branches holding candles were planted at intervals about the church, the candles were never snuffed, and as the service advanced, a cauliflower excrescence formed, materially interfering with the light. Those in front of the pulpit were, from motives of economy, never lit until just before the sermon. Sometimes the clerk had to wrestle with a damp and refractory wick, which spluttered and obstinately refused to light; the interest the congregation took in these little combats was intense. The majority of the old ladies brought lanterns with them; these were taken into the pews and blown out, so that there was a generally pervading odour of tallow. At the end of the service the lanterns were relit, and it was a strange sight: all these lanterns bobbing and flitting about the road, as though a flight of fireflies had suddenly taken wing."

After the re-opening of the church in 1868, the sexes were no longer segregated. The Holy Communion was celebrated every Sunday. T. P. Rogers had arrived as vicar in 1851 and with him, evidently, the first stirrings of the Oxford movement in Batheaston, for in 1860 Melmoth Walters in a letter to Christ Church asserted that "many families have left the parish owing to the defective teaching in the pulpit". It was not until 1876, however, the year in which "Church Rambler" wrote that the surpliced choir was very well trained, and sang very well, that the storm broke, set off by discord over the election of churchwardens. The evangelical faction issued a huge poster accusing "an Extreme Party who encourage and will uphold the Senseless and Ritualistic Practices which have lately crept into the services of our Parish Church". One parishioner asserted at the Easter Vestry that the vicar had made him a dissenter, another complained that the hubbub was disgraceful, and the two columns devoted by the press to the affair included the gleeful announcement that cries of "No popery!" were heard during the election. The vicar's supporters scored a clear victory, and Dr. Harper was chosen as churchwarden. The unhappy controversy, which must have deeply hurt the sincere and earnest vicar, was not yet over, for next appeared a manifesto in these terms:

"In consequence of the unhappy differences that have arisen between many of the Congregation of our Parish Church and the Vicar, relative to the introduction of certain objectionable practices and innovations in the Services of the Church, much painful feeling has been created between the supporters and opponents of the Vicar in these practices, and as I have taken a leading . . . part in the endeavour to restore the simplicity of our Worship, and to oppose the introduction of Ritualism in any degree or form . . .".

After the excitement generated by this preamble, it is disappointing to learn that it was circulated with a petition to represent to the vicar the desire of the parishioners that the cassocks worn by the choir should be discontinued!

The episode is related in some detail as a reminder how keen were the passions aroused in our not-so-distant ancestors by matters touching the conduct of public worship. For the historian, silence now descends on the unhappy scene, and it is good to recall that on the death of the vicar his people subscribed generously to a memorial (p. 34). From that time any controversy that has arisen between vicar and people has been handled with more circumspection.

THE BELLS

The church bells have been and are so much a part of village life that no apology is offered for examining them in some detail. In Batheaston a long story of bells and bell-ringing culminates in the completion of the peal of eight in 1967, and the bells illustrate the art of the founder during six centuries.

The treasure is mediaeval, a fine and important specimen, one of a small group of early London bells, cast probably by William Revel about 1350.[20] It carries, in beautiful Lombardic characters, the inscription: VIRGINIS EGREGIE VOCOR CAMPANA MARIE (I am called the bell of the illustrious Virgin Mary). The history of this bell is unknown; at least half a century older than the tower, it may once have hung in an earlier tower on the site, or, perhaps more likely, been brought from elsewhere when the church was held by Bath Abbey. It has good tone, and was the fourth bell of the ring of six until, in the 1967 restoration, it was thought wise to withdraw it from the peal and hang it in honoured semi-retirement as clock bell and five-minute bell. There it is safe for posterity to admire; rung full circle no one can say how soon or late it would have cracked and been ruined.

The peal of eight is described thus:

Treble: I speak for Truth   Sursum Corda
        John Taylor Loughborough 1967
                     4 cwt 2 qrs 11 lb

Second: I speak for Charity   Cantate Domino
        John Taylor Loughborough 1967
                     5 cwt 10 lb

Third: John Rudhall fecit 1824   6 cwt 1 qr 24 lb

Fourth: Anno Domini 1634 A.T. I.G. W. I.L.
        (Anthony Townsend, John Gay,
        Churchwardens, John Lott. [of War-
        minster], Founder).   6 cwt 1 qr 15 lb

Fifth: Same as fourth.   8 cwt 1 qr 5 lb

Sixth: To God be the Glory
        John Taylor Loughborough 1967
                     9 cwt 2 qrs 2 lb

Seventh: John Rudhall fecit 1824 Geo Melsom
        Ambe Emerson Churchwardens
                     10 cwt 2 qrs 16 lb

Tenor: Same as seventh. 13 cwt 2 qrs 18 lb in F.

Besides what the bells themselves tell us, the only source of knowledge about bells and ringing until recent times is the churchwardens' accounts, and the evidence they contain allows the construction of a history which, while its general outline could undoubtedly be repeated many times from villages up and down the country, may be of special interest to local people. In 1667 there were five bells, treble and second the present fourth and fifth, the mediaeval bell—then the third—and a fourth and tenor about which all that is known is their subsequent history. The bells remained five until the Rudhall restoration of 1824, when a new treble was added, to make the peal of six so well-remembered.

It is usual for churchwardens' accounts to record frequent expenditure on the upkeep of the bells and payments to the ringers, and Batheaston is no exception; small items, paid usually to the blacksmith, the wheelwright or the carpenter, appear on nearly every page. The bell wheels were a constant source of trouble, requiring to be mended or replaced almost yearly. The modern bellhanger does his work and little further expenditure, save for ropes, is to be expected for half a century or so. Though English church bells are often splendid creations, past work about them must have been by to-day's standards very crude. The thought of the village blacksmith ministering to the bells horrifies a modern ringer;

indeed, he sees a probable connection between the resolution of the Vestry in 1726, when "it was unanimously agreed on by all yt were present yt ye fourth bell wch is crack'd, shd be new cast or mended wth all convenient speed" and the black-smith's bill of 19s 4d for "repairing Bells" the previous year. There is great cause for thankfulness that so many ancient bells have survived unharmed, as the three at Batheaston.

These entries are typical of many:

1668. The ringers of Gunpoude day   2s 6d
       A rope for the third bell   3s 0d
1676. Nayles at two tymes for ye bells   1s 6d
       Mending ye bolt of ye 3rd bell   1s 6d
       Spoaks & board for ye wheel of ye 3rd
       bell   1s 6d
1691. Mending ye tenour wheele, third
       wheele, & board and nailes and
       trussing of ye treble & ye 4th
       bedding all ye rest and other things   8s 0d

It is not known to what extent peals of bells were rung to call the people to the regular services in earlier centuries. At the time our records begin the ringers were paid for ringing on 5th November, and on 29th May to celebrate the restoration of Charles II. The latter custom persisted until 1866, testimony to the value set upon tradition in a rural parish! By the end of the seventeenth century payment was a shilling a man, about what a labourer would earn for a day's work; so the perquisite was a useful one, and doubtless much sought after. Ringing was lawfully required when the sovereign passed through a parish; situated on the road from the capital to Bath, Bath-easton had not infrequent occasion to pay to demonstrate its loyalty. Royal events were of course likewise celebrated:

1677. Ringing when the queene came   1s 0d
1685. The Ringers when the king was pro-
       claimed   5s 0d
       Ringing the Corronation Day   6s 0d
1686. The Ringers at the cuming of ye King
       and Qu to Bath   4s 6d
1714. Ringers at King George's Procl   6s 0d
       Ringers at ye King's Arrivall   10s 0d
       Ringers at the Coronation   10s 0d

The sequence of crowned heads was duly celebrated and the ringers rewarded, until they earned a whole guinea on the Coronation Day of Victoria. Many other occasions of national rejoicing or lament were celebrated by ringing:

1692. Ringing when ye French were beaten   2s od
1697. Ringing for the peace   3s od

The failure of the attempts of James Stuart (the "Old Pretender") and his son ("Bonnie Prince Charlie") to regain the throne had their echoes in Batheaston:

1715. On Routing the Rebells   5s od
1745. The Ringers on ye account of ye Rebels 5s od

One occasion of ringing for an event of local importance may be mentioned. At the celebrations attending the laying of the foundation stone of the School in 1858 the *Bath Chronicle* relates that "during the ceremony the bells of the parish church poured forth a joyous peal, which tended greatly to enliven the proceedings".

Some of the major work done on the bells should be put on record:

1709. Hanging the bells   £9 5s od
1726. New casting the Fourth Bell and
     all other Expense concerning
     the same   £18 0s od

This is the outcome of the resolution already mentioned. The recast bell was never satisfactory, and before the end of the century was regularly presented as "cracked" at the visitation. The parish put up with it until the next restoration:

1824. Mr Rudhall's Bill   £103

The Rudhalls were a famous family of Gloucester bell-founders. This bill was for the casting of the new treble (the present third) and the recasting of the present seventh and tenor. An amusing reminiscence on this episode was contributed by an old parishioner to the parish magazine in 1899:

"My father, he wor a ringer for 60 years. Them bells was rung fust time for his weddin. Why, there used to be only fower bells and a cracken one, and my father, he used to rottle this 'un during the service becos he wanted to make the Parish get a new 'un. Ans so they did. Well, Mr Conybeare wor Vicar at that time, and he wouldn't hev nothing to do with 'em, and I hev heerd say, as how he said he didn't care if he never heered 'em rung. Nor he didn't. He wor away for three months from home and they wrote and told him that the bells wor all paid for and finished but he never heerd 'em, for he died while he wor away. And it wor while he was a-lyin dead that my

father wor married. And Mrs Conybeare she said that if my father wouldn't have the bells rung at his wedding, she would give them their wedding dinner, so they only just rose the bells, and rang 'em out of Church, and let 'em fall again, so that as I told you, they was rung fust of all at my father's wedding. Well, my father wor a ringer for 60 years, and when he died in Mr Rogers' time the Church was being built again, so they could nor ring a peal for him here, but only toll one bell, and then they went up to Kattern's and rung a muffled peal for him there."

1881. The bells were re-hung in a new frame at a cost of £325, including some repairs to the tower, and the installation of a chiming apparatus. Asking Christ Church to give some help towards the raising of the money, the vicar wrote that they had not ventured to ring the bells for more than a year. The floor of the ringing chamber might have fallen into the church, and the workmen asserted that the timbers were put in when the tower was built. "No wonder the ends were mere powder." Dates scratched on the jambs of the window shew that to this time the bells were rung from the stage above the present ringing chamber.

1929. The bells were hung on ball bearings, and more repairs to the tower were made.

1962. The bells were narrowly saved from destruction by a fire which charred the frame. The bellfounders advised a thorough restoration as the "go" of the bells was far from good, but the parish did not feel inclined to face the cost, and the bells were merely re-hung.

They were always difficult to ring, mainly because they were hung so high in the tower, resulting in "tower shake", as ringers say, and awkward handling. By 1966, it was obvious that soon the choice would lie between a full restoration and unringable bells; an appeal to the parish was made, the response was magnificent, and the job was done. The bells were tuned, hung in an iron frame ten feet lower in the tower, and a new bell cast to replace the mediaeval one, all at a cost of £4,500. The gift of two trebles augmented the ring to a good peal of eight. On 4 June 1967, the Bishop of Bath and Wells, Dr. E. B. Henderson, dedicated the new bells, and charged the churchwardens with the care of the peal.

We know nothing of the degree of skill attained by

the ringers in previous centuries, nor do we know when the art of "method" ringing, as opposed to set, or "call" changes was introduced. In 1897 John Taylor became Tower Master, and set about the exacting task of training a competent band. At the same time Mrs. Pagden, of Batheaston House, gave an excellent set of handbells. Years of faithful practice were rewarded on 4 June 1907, when the first full peal on the bells was scored, 5040 changes of Grandsire Doubles, in 3 hours 3 minutes. It is fitting that the names of the successful band should be remembered, and interesting to note their occupations:

Treble: Jesse Hallett. Gardener.

Second: Thomas Davies. He rose at 4 o'clock, walked four miles to Box Quarry, worked as a blacksmith until 6 o'clock, and walked home. Past seventy years of age.

Third: Arthur Cordery. Head gardener at Hill House.

Fourth: John Taylor (Conductor). Head gardener at Batheaston House.

Fifth: Oliver Derham. Coachman at Hill House.

Tenor: Thomas Taylor. Son of John Taylor. He left the village to learn farming, and was killed in action in 1918.

Jesse Hallett alone of the band lived to ring on the day of the dedication of the new bells sixty years later to the very day.

S. CATHERINE'S CHURCH

The church of S. Catherine is a plain little building in a lovely setting, probably late Norman in origin, from the evidence of the north capital of the tower arch, but having no external feature earlier than the fifteenth century. It was built or rebuilt by Prior Cantlow of Bath Abbey in 1490, as the contemporary stained glass of the east window tells. The four lights shew the Virgin, Crucifixion, S. John and S. Peter.

Pl. 13. S. Catherine's Church

Much of the glass is original, but the figures were restored during work on the church in 1846. The pretty little wooden pulpit probably comes from Prior Cantlow's time. The font is considered to be late Norman (Pl. 14). In the chancel is a monument with canopy and two kneeling figures, Captain William Blanchard (died 1631), and his wife.

The tower was rebuilt in 1704. The six bells are hung "dead", but they chime the quarters with a pleasantly rustic sound. Until 1927 the old four were hung for ringing, and were rung once a year, on the afternoon of Christmas Day, when the Batheaston ringers walked up the valley for the purpose, and found strenuous work in handling them.

The treble has no founder's mark and no inscription except the date 1616. The other three bells are pre-Reformation. The second and third came from the famous Wokingham Foundry, and were cast by

Pl. 15.   Roger Landen's stamp

Roger Landen or his successor, probably about the mid-fifteenth century. The second is inscribed: Sancta Maria Ora Pro Nobis and the third: Sancte Necollae Ora Pro Nobis. Both carry the stamp of a lion's face invariably used by Landen in addition to his own mark.[21] The tenor is by Thomas Gefferies of Bristol, who died about 1545, and it is inscribed: Sancta johannes baptista ora pro nobis, with a stamp which has the letters t.g. The identity of t.g., a number of whose bells are to be found in the neighbourhood of Bristol, was unknown until a lucky discovery of recent years.[22]

In 1927 the 1616 bell was recast, and a new treble and second added to make the present chime of six. The organ was given in 1927 by the Hon. Richard Strutt.

BAILBROOK CHAPEL

The vicar, T. P. Rogers was anxious about the hamlet of Bailbrook, which, he wrote in 1855, had 45 houses and 300 souls and a good mixed school, but needed a clergyman and chapel. In the hope that a perpetual curacy might be formed he wrote to Christ Church that the inhabitants

"having no Chapel among them nor any of the better classes resident, and living what they consider a long distance from their Parish Churches, they are for the most part an unsatisfactory and disorderly set. On Sunday afternoons they congregate together in the lanes or fields to gamble or create disturbances to the great annoyance of the few better disposed. I have been among them myself to try to stop this, and at one time my churchwarden (Mr. Walters) regularly went up there every Sunday afternoon. The only result was to force them to change their quarters to the adjoining parish".

Pl. 14.   Font, S. Catherine's Church
(drawing by Peter Coard)

Nothing was done until some time in the 1880's when George Vezey, a licensed Lay Reader regularly conducted evening service. In 1891 an appeal was made for funds to erect an iron mission chapel. The cost was to be £200 with furniture. The bishop of the diocese dedicated the building on 4 July 1892.

It says much for the enduring qualities of corrugated iron that the chapel, though decidedly dilapidated, still stands and is in use.

THE VICARAGE HOUSE

The vicar of Batheaston has dwelt "to the south east of the church" at least since the seventeenth century (p. 27), and probably long before that the site was set apart for his house and garden. At the archdeacon's visitation in 1615 it was reported that the vicarage was in decay and needed repair. The house noted in the terrier of 1638 was of one storey, otherwise it would have been described as "chambered over", or a similar expression; it was evidently a modest building.

The present vicarage, a house of two storeys, of coursed rubble and stone-tiled mansard roof, originally pleasant if undistinguished, has lost any charm which the west elevation, facing the street, may once have possessed. It was obliterated by the grimly utilitarian addition, including a room for a laboratory, clapped on to it by J. J. Conybeare, vicar from 1812 to 1824. There is no record of the erection of the house, but indirect evidence points with probability to Mark Hall (vicar 1716 to 1766) as the builder. A valuation of the living of 1800[23] stated that the late incumbent spent £500 on it and his predecessor at least £200 more. (This was probably the extensions to the north, now separated as Vicarage Cottage.) The implication is that neither was responsible for the original building. The previous vicar, Mark Hall, in his will (Appendix 5) directed that six labouring men that had been employed about his house should carry his coffin. The likeliest occupation for the six labouring men was the building of the house, suggesting a date not long before 1766. The style of the east elevation, which is little altered, is in agreement.

THE CHURCH HALL

A serious defect in parish life was made good in 1952 with the building of a church hall. A fund for the purpose had been opened a good many years before, but had little success until a special "drive" brought the necessary subscriptions, and a much-needed meeting place was provided.

BATHEASTON CHURCHWARDENS' ACCOUNTS AND VESTRY MINUTES

The surviving churchwardens' accounts are in three books, beginning in 1667, 1762 and 1833, with no intervals in the record. All are in good condition, legible, and on the whole shew a fair standard of literacy and conscientious care. From the uniformity of the writing it is obvious that each set of accounts was written up for the Easter Vestry. There were no separate Vestry minutes before the nineteenth century, one book being used for all purposes.

The names of those paying the church rate, and the amount paid, are always recorded, so that we have a regular list of householders, except the indigent, and some indication of their relative prosperity. Similar lists are preserved in the accounts of the overseers of the poor (p. 98). Unfortunately, addresses in the modern sense were unnecessary in a small community, and the invariable formula was "B. late A". So it is rarely possible to assign holdings to the familiar names. It is a curiosity of history, with an ironic twist, that only during the Commonwealth was there statutory authority for the levying of a church rate. Nevertheless, an Act of 1868 abolished the "compulsory" church rate! Those liable to pay "to church and poor" were originally the owners or occupiers of property worth twenty shillings or more a year. At Batheaston the parishioners paid up well, and the amounts in default, when recorded, are usually quite trivial, until 1869, when naturally many non-churchmen refused to pay, and still more the following year.

For almost a century from 1667 a single rate brought in about £10 and this on the whole covered the outgoings, which ranged from about £5–£20. From time to time it was necessary to levy a much heavier rate; in 1715, for example, £800 was raised "for repairing and beautifying the church". In 1824, three double rates for recasting three damaged bells realised £153 16s 6d. The rate was usually calculated at a theoretical penny in the pound. In the nineteenth century the scale is always recorded, usually six farthings. In 1870, this amounted to £57, but only

£31 was collected, because of the recent deliverance from "compulsion". In 1872, the Vestry decided that the deficiency in the accounts should be cleared by offertories, collections to be taken at the morning and evening services. By these means, £190 was raised in 1874, but the amount given declined in the years following. From this time, deficiencies were usually made up by gifts, continuing the practice, begun in the eighteenth century, of raising funds by subscription for special purposes.

The dismal era of the Jumble Sale opened in 1913, when £17 5s 7d was secured by this means, to supplement collections which amounted to less than £100 a year. Fifty years later the picture is changed. Christian Stewardship was introduced in 1962 and about £1400 a year is raised under that scheme; to which is added £400-£500 of collections in church, all the latter being sent outside the parish.

The records so fortunately preserved for us, deeply interesting in themselves, and, with those of the overseers of the poor, vividly illuminating the day-to-day concerns of a village community, do not in essence differ from those of other rural parishes. Quaintnesses abound, and though on the whole the churchwardens were respectably literate for their period, some occupants of the office depended on hearsay, not precise diction, for their orthography; meaning, of course, not the lack of conventional spelling, which was in any case not standardised, but oddities such as:

> 1687. Rate for Repairing the Church and Other Neserarys there unto Blonings.

> 1702. ospetell muney   15s 4d
> bear when the parish mett   4s 0d
> voisitation & tow Mr. Dresar [Dresser]   15s 6d
> A boibell   £3 4s 6d
> glaesing the winders   6s 2d

The passing of the accounts at the Easter Vestry was signed by from two to twelve parishioners, until in 1819 appears: "Signed on behalf of the vestry J. Conybeare", and thereafter the vicar always signed as chairman.

No indications of feuds or quarrelling ruffle the calm serenity of the Vestry. In 1765, it was noted that the Vestry "adjourned to the Lamb Inn". Apart from that a single touch of levity enlivens the pages. Between 1703 and 1710 William Russell, parish clerk and a talented artist, embellished the records with his accomplished doodles. Across the

foot of one page swims a sprightly fish, entirely composed of squiggles; on another is a fine bird, of peacock shape, but lacking the tail. Another jeu d'esprit is a male face of worldly aspect, framed in squiggles, and looking from between a pair of angel's wings. A lean, long-nosed face, so typical of the period, appears three times, and must surely be a caricature. The same artist left a splendid dragon in the Poor Book (Pl. 16).

Pl. 16. *Dragon in Poor Book*

The primary duty of the churchwardens being the repair and upkeep of the church, care of the churchyard, and the provision for divine worship, we find much of the accounts taken up with items for this purpose. Apart from major works, the impression is of endless patching and tinkering. Windows constantly needed glazing and doors mending. Most years the plumber was at work, often sending a bill for several pounds, a large part of the income. Loads

Pl. 17. *More idle moments of a parish clerk*

of lime and freestone often came in. Scarcely a year passed without payment to the carpenter for mending or replacing bell wheels.

The big restoration of 1715, already mentioned, was a heavy expense spread over three years. The bills are too many to be quoted in full, but some items are of special interest:

For Alder Poles, Ropes, Hurdles etc, being Expences in Scaffolding	£2 13s 2d
63 Bush of Brown hair	£1 11s 6d
for white Hair	18s 9d
W. Rawlins for halling 2 Load Deals Lafts Sand from Bristol	£1 10s 0d
To Mrs Cottle for Nails	6s 11½d
Beer for Plumers and Painters	14s 6d
for Pitch	6s 5d
Mr Price Bill for Deal Bords	£31 2s 0d
W Web mason for 320 Foot paving stone Carriage and work	£6 3s 6d
Holiday ye Plumers Bill	£28 5s 0d
W Strange for 88 Sacks Lime	£4 8s 0d
Cannings Glasiers Bill	£3 19s 6d
Tho Amesbury 2 Bills for Irework	£3 3s 0d
Shephard a Bill for joints & Nails for ye pew doors	£1 8s 0d
Stone and Work at ye Font	13s 0d
Henry Lewis Bills for Timber about Roof, Belfree & Sills & for Oak Bord for ye Seats and for Work	£40 18s 6d
Hellier ye Painter for work	£5 10s 0d

Of items of expenditure on furnishings of the church this selection is typical:

1670.	A planke for a seate	1s 8d
1677.	Cleaning ye flaggon and boule	6d
1682.	A cloth for ye Communion table and making	9s 6d
1683.	A prayer book, a book of Cannons and 2 paper books	12s 0d
1685.	2 bulls to kneell on	2s 4d
1691.	Mending the Church seats	6d
1718.	A pewter bason	3s 0d
1721.	Plate for ye Communion Table & a Brass pin to Hang Mr Halls Hat on	1s 6d
	Mending the top of the Font	3s 0d
	Carrying the top of the Font to Bath & back	1s 0d
1732.	A Lintern for ye Gallery	4s 0d

1755.	4 doz Butts for the Seats & Matts for the Communion Steps	£2 14s 0d
1758.	three Brushes and a Mop for the Church	7s 10d
1761.	Ordered at the vestry that the churchwardens are to get the church whitewashed with all speed	
1764.	Eight Bras Screwes against the Gallorey	2s 6d
1774.	4 new pews	£13 17s. 9¾d
1782.	A Chalice for the Sacrament	£2 2s 0d
1790.	for Childs Furms	£2 12s 0d
1796.	2 yds Plush at 8/6d per yd for pulpit cushion & shalloops for the Same	£1 1s 0d
	3 yds fring 13/6d Bobs 9/0d for same Making of the same	3s 0d
1806.	2 Women for Washing the Church	5s 0d
	3 Boys for Carring Water	1s 0d
1830.	Painting the King's Arms	£3 3s 0d
1832.	Matting for chancel	£1 4s 5d
1841.	Paid for replacing brass articles broken and stolen in an act of sacrilege	£15 14s 3d
1844.	Clearing stools of moth	6s 0d
1881.	Weekly cleaning of church for year	£6 13s 0d
1910.	Drapery for Church for King's Funeral	£1 7s 0d

Some of the larger works on the church are noted in the account of the building, and on the bells in the account of them.

OTHER EXPENDITURE

Bread and wine

Bread and wine supplied for the Communion was, of course, a regular item throughout the accounts. It is well known that inordinate sums were often spent on sacramental wine, and the explanation offered lies in the words of the Prayer Book: "If any of the Bread and Wine remain unconsecrated, the Curate shall have it to his own use". Even so, far more wine than could possibly be needed was commonly supplied, and obviously there was often abuse of the provision. At Batheaston, if some allowance is made for the perquisite of the clergy, expenditure on wine, though the amount varied, was not regularly excessive:

1686.	Bread and wine at Christmas	4s 6d
	Bread and wine at Easter	9s 0d
	Ye Sacrament on Palm Sunday	5s 2d

(Wine cost about two shillings and threepence a quart.)

1757.	Wine at Whitsunday, Christmas and Easter	16s 6d
1849.	12 qts imperial of wine	£3 0s 0d

By this time, the Communion was being celebrated monthly, on "Sacrament Sunday", so assuming that the quaint custom of supplying the vicar's table persisted, the amount was not greatly excessive. Before the end of the century, the amount of wine bought was only enough for its proper purpose.

The surplice

The surplice was an important piece of parish property, and appears regularly:

1683.	Washing the surplus	1s 0d
1686.	Washing ye Sarplis	2s 0d

Through the eighteenth century the surplice was usually washed four times a year, at a total cost of ten shillings. For many years, Peter Cannings was the launderer.

1733.	10 ells & ½ yd of holland	£2 12s 0d
	an ounce of fine thread	1s 0d
	washing and mending the old surplice	3s 0d
	making the new surplice and washing the same	14s 6d

The churchyard

The churchyard scarcely appears in the accounts before 1752, when it is recorded:

	Wm Fisher Grubbing making and planting Church Yard Hedge 16½ Lugg	£2 0s 0d
	16 Hundred of Plants	8s 0d
	making the low Hedge	8s 0d

The next year the hedge was weeded twice, at nine-pence each time, and thorns were bought to mend it. From this time, there are regular items for care of the churchyard, such as:

1763.	5 days cleaning Churchyard at 9d the day	3s 9d
	Cleaning Churchyd Dich	1s 0d

The next year, "cuting ye nettles Chyd" cost 2s 3d and the item appears annually for some years. There are payments for weeding the paths, and, nearly every year in the 1790's, for clearing snow. Concern about the state of the churchyard is a recurrent theme through the nineteenth century. A long line leads to the vigorous and effective volunteers of to-day.

In 1831 a bankwall was to be built under the hedge towards the street on the east side of the churchyard. This is familiar to anyone who knows the village. There are entries concerning fives playing:

1767.	Diging up of fives Place	1s 0d

This was done more than once.

1802.	Replacing the stones to prevent Fives playing against the Church	2s 0d

The game of fives was known in England at least from the fourteenth century. Fives playing may have taken the place of the juvenile diversion noted in 1696:

	hewing ye quoines of ye Church porch to keepe ye boyes of ye leads	6d

The force of this procedure is not obvious.

Other expenditure

The first entry in the year's accounts is nearly always for the visitation, when the wardens were sworn in. A typical one:

1685.	At visitation for our dinner and other expenses	18s 4d

Until about the end of the eighteenth century the vicar's dinner at the visitation cost an unvarying half-crown. An exceptional entry occurs in 1718:

	Spent at ye Lamb when the Rural Dean visited	16s 6d

A regular visitor to the parish was the apparitor, a minor official whose duty it was to carry round such things as proclamations, and forms of prayer for special occasions—all of which had to be paid for—and collect the copy of the register required annually, as well as messages. He figures in the Batheaston accounts as parriter, apearrator, ye par, and even once as bariter.

1677.	Ye parriter for warning to vizettation	1d
1696.	the pareter for a prayer book and a proclemation for a fast to June ye 26th	1s 6d

(This was in time of war with France.)

1697.	A proclamation Against Swearing and prophaning the Saboth	1s 0d

After the early eighteenth century the apparitor no longer receives personal mention, but special prayers and proclamations continue thick and fast, some of them very interesting:

1746. Instructions Consarning ye Cattle   1s 6d

This entry is repeated three times, appears the next year, and in 1751 as "Orders relating to the Horned Cattle". Outbreaks of disease among cattle, known as "murrain" or "distemper" probably included foot and mouth disease.

Wet summers, with bad harvests and hard winters, at the end of the eighteenth century, were a cause of privation and suffering:

1795. Letter from Sessions to put against the
          Church door about Bread   6d
          Prayer for fast day the 9th March   1s 6d
1800. Proclamation for frugality   6d
          King's proclamation upon Acct of
          Bread   1s 6d
1810. Prayer for a Bundant Harvest   1s 6d

Special prayers were to be paid for on occasions of national rejoicing, such as:

1797. Thanksgiving prayer for the Victory
          gained by Duncan over the dutch
          Fleet   1s 6d
1798. Thanksgiving prayer for Nelson's
          victory   1s 6d
1805. Form of Prayer for a fast on Nelson's
          Victory   1s 6d

The last two occasions were the battles of the Nile and of Trafalgar, with the death of Nelson.

Among events concerning Royalty may be noticed several special prayers, fasts and thanksgivings for the recovery of King George the Third from attacks of mental illness, and in 1802 for his escape from assassination.

Briefs

The church brief was much used in the seventeenth and eighteenth centuries as a means of collecting money for good causes. The brief, with Royal sanction, was sent to every parish, where it was to be read out in church, and a collection made as the people left. It seems that the system was much abused, especially in the eighteenth century, and a great deal of the money never reached its intended destination; congregations became more and more resistant, and the church brief gradually died out.

At Batheaston, it was evidently the practice usually, not to make a collection in church, but to give a shilling from church funds. The first page of the extant accounts contains entries for nine briefs, each one shilling, no mean sum when the year's income averaged ten pounds. There is a quaint entry for 1670:

Laid out for a Jugg of beare when I had
          acquittance for the money for the briefs   2d

On a few occasions a special collection was made, and the accounts are interesting:

Monye collected in the parish of Batheaston this yeare 1670 in November by virtue of his Matis Briefe for ye redemption of English Captives taken by the Turkes.

This brief realised thirteen shillings, given by 34 persons, mostly in sums of a few pence. Jeremy Richmond and Henry Blanchard each gave a shilling, and John Fisher half a crown. In 1680, 14s 9½d was collected "for redeeming captives in Argeea" (Algier) and other briefs for a similar cause were given special attention during the next few years. The usual description is "taken by the Turks". In 1750, six briefs brought in only 1s 7d, and soon the church brief ceased to circulate.

Hospital money

In the early accounts a regular levy of fourteen shillings and ninepence appears four times a year under the heading either of "hospital money" or "maimed souldiers". Elizabethan legislation required parishes to contribute to the relief of sick or maimed soldiers and sailors, who received a pension. A local man might benefit. At the Wells Quarter Sessions in 1670 John Horseman of Batheaston was admitted to a yearly pension of forty shillings in the place of Thomas Sellock of Dunkerton, deceased. "A poor man who faithfully served King Charles the First in the late unhappy wars."

Passengers and Travellers

Finally, payments to persons traversing the parish with a magistrate's "pass" were a heavy drain on the funds, and must have borne especially hard on a parish through which passed an important route such as the road from London to Bath and Bristol. In 1667, there were twenty-four entries, single persons, twos and threes, and once sixteen together. The usual sum was a penny a head. Seamen likewise were relieved; they were especially numerous in 1670, probably having left their ships at Bristol, or returning thither, and they each had twopence.

A few items taken almost at random evoke a vivid picture of this itinerant company. "A great loss" seems almost a technical term.

1668. A souldier that lost his Arme	3d
1670. A greate bellied woman	4d
A sea captaine his wife and his boy	6d
A distressed woman of Meere and her family	3d
1677. A man for a greate loss	3s 0d
1683. 28 men women & children which had great loss at sea	1s 6d
A man that was taken by the turk	6d
1691. Given away this yeare to travellers, maimed souldiers and poore distressed Irish	£5 3s 6d

Even including the regular levy for hospital money, this was a large sum for a country parish to give, and it was exceptional.

In the early eighteenth century, travellers disappear from the churchwarden's accounts. The reason is not less distress, but that these itinerants were regularly relieved by the overseers of the poor (p. 112). For the ratepayer, the change was immaterial, for what the churchwardens did not require of him, the overseers, their underlings, did.

Dissent

Early references to nonconformity are scanty. In the unhappy days for puritan ministers after the ejections of 1662, let us hope that Batheaston received kindly the dispossessed vicar of Wotton under Edge (which parish gave him £13 a year as he was in want), and the late rector of Combe Hay, who are both recorded as preaching here in 1669.[24] Calamy, visiting Bath in 1692 wrote of the latter: "There I conversed with good old Mr. Creez, who lived then in that city, a worthy man, though of a melancholy disposition".

An entry in the parish register tells that in 1732 Elias Harford (baptised 1663) was buried "at ye Quakers pound", the little enclosure to the south of the London Road, just in Bathford parish. This is the only reference to quakerism. The tenets of the sect which in 1794 petitioned the bishop to license a

house in the possession of Eleanor Gale "to be a place of meeting for Protestant Dissenters" are unknown. There were six signatories, including Thomas Lewis, Gent. and Francis Sainsbury, both prominent inhabitants.

The next mention of nonconformity was in 1797, when a certificate was granted for a house for "an independent denomination". This was a new enterprise, for the six petitioners included none of the above. They were probably Wesleyans, for "Church Rambler", 1876, passed "the curious old building used by the Wesleyans as a meetinghouse since 1797, to be rebuilt ere it falls down". Unfortunately, Wesleyans have not in the past been careful of their archives, and the point has not been proved. There is the almost inevitable tradition that John Wesley preached at a farmhouse in the village; very probably true, for he passed through many times on his journeys to Bath and Bristol. One example: "27 March 1786. The snow which fell in the night lay so deep, it was with much difficulty we reached Chippenham. Taking fresh horses there, we pushed on to Bath".

The new church was duly built, and an active membership continues.

Two other certificates for dissenters' meetings, both in private houses, were issued, in 1844 and 1846, but of them nothing more can be said.

The Congregational Church in Batheaston was formed by the Rev. Robert Rew and twenty-five persons who on 13 March 1868 resolved:

"That for the glory of God and for mutual edification and strength, we do form ourselves into a church and join ourselves to the Congregational Body of Christians."

Their decision arose from the custom of a group of people who for some years had met regularly for worship in the old Poor House (p. 100). Their venture prospered, and their church, of Banner Down stone with a slate roof, was opened on 25 April 1871. About 1910 the Church became owner of the Poor House, usually known as the Mission Hall. Good relations with other Free Churches in the district have been a notable feature, and though the body has had its ups and downs, it retains its influence in the village, and celebrated its centenary in 1968.

A wooden hut put up for the use of the Roman Catholice of the neighbourhood in 1948 was replaced in 1967 by a permanent building, a bold essay in modernity, but brutally unregarding of its surroundings. Square in plan, with its hyperbolic paraboloid roof of slightly uneasy copper foil resting on two corners, the interior is arranged crosswise, with the sanctuary in the peak. The church is mainly of untreated concrete blocks, but rectangles of coloured fibreglass form the peak. The effect is not displeasing from within the building, but from the London (Bath) Road, especially in sunshine, the experiment, dominating the houses below, is blatantly aggressive. The low corner, at the entrance to Northend, is more tender of the traditional scene. The architect was Martin Fisher, and the cost about £40,000.

There is in Batheaston a hopeful response to the oecumenical movement.

Chapter 6

Parish and People

Every parish must have a history,
every parish has a register,
every person has a parish.

BISHOP STUBBS

I T IS necessary now to review as far as may be the rural community and its everyday life and institutions; from which was fashioned, slowly and in the main haphazard, the picture that we know today. We must look at the developing society, its organisation, numbers, customs, discipline, and the evolution of those aspects of existence necessary to the ordered life of a modern community. In doing so, it must not be forgotten that all this came about through a natural process of makeshift and compromise, and that our ancestors would be at a loss to understand our mania for planning and uniformity.

As the manorial system fell apart, during the sixteenth century especially, the parish became the unit of community as well as of religious life, and for three centuries was for local purposes practically autonomous; managing its affairs without interference, provided that it found such taxes as were levied by the central government. Chief among the parish officers were the churchwardens, chosen from among the more prominent inhabitants. Local custom varied; in some parishes a rotation was observed according to the property a man occupied. There is a solitary reference in our records: In 1777 John Hooper was chosen churchwarden "for the Cold Bath Farm" (Map 1, 18). The origin of the office is obscure, but it dates back at least to the fourteenth century. The term is misleading to the modern ear, for the churchwardens were accountable not only for the church, its upkeep other than the chancel which was the responsibility of the rector, and its services, under the incumbent, but also for all matters concerning community life. A list of churchwardens is in Appendix 10.

The overseers of the poor were in being from the later sixteenth century, always subordinate to the churchwardens. The surveyors of the highways (waywardens) originated in the Highway Act of 1555.

Usually, but not always, these offices were in Batheaston served before that of churchwarden. The hayward, in origin an official of the manor, was concerned with the management of the common fields, the upkeep of the pound, and the securing of stray animals. Though the hayward is rarely mentioned in the records, the deed of 1719 (p. 133) makes it clear that his was an active office.

The constable, legally subordinate to the justices, was responsible for law and order, had powers of arrest, and in many places, but not in Batheaston, kept separate accounts. His office, too, dated from distant antiquity. The office of tithingman is also ancient, originating in a system of mutual responsibility for good behaviour in a tithing—once perhaps, very long ago, a unit of ten families. His relation to the constable in general is obscure—in some places he was regarded as an assistant, others had one officer, but not both. Batheaston had two tithingmen, one for Easton and Amorel, the other for Easton and Catherine. The vicar recorded, in connection with the decision to assess taxes between Bathford and Batheaston on a parochial basis, not as tithings, which had included part of both parishes, (p. 5) that separate tithingmen were annually chosen at the court leet for the liberty of Hampton and Claverton for Easton and Amorel, and at the hundred court for Easton and Catherine. It is not at all clear how the duties were apportioned between the constable and the tithingmen. They are mentioned from time to time, usually in the overseers' accounts, rarely by name, and mostly in connection with taking up miscreants and keeping them in custody. About the middle of last century there are lists of names, from which a number of constables were to be chosen by the justices; a more organised system was coming into existence. The lists appear each year until 1872, after which there is no further mention of the constable, at least in the old sense; but of course by this time a fully professional police force was in being. The last mention of a tithingman was in 1834, when one of them was paid half a crown for arresting a wrongdoer.

When a man's turn to serve a parish office came he had little option, though many, doubtless, were less than willing to undertake duties which might well bring them into conflict with their neighbours. In 1722, Walter Parry was fined £2 10s 0d for refusing the office of surveyor. On the other hand, it could be advantageous to a newcomer, as the service gave a settlement (p. 107). All the offices were unpaid, except that the constable and tithingmen might get a gratuity on an item-of-service basis, and from the late eighteenth century an assistant overseer was appointed with a small salary, probably to do most of the work.

The parish meeting, so curiously known from at least the seventeenth century as the Vestry, met by law in Easter week or within a month after Easter, to choose the churchwardens and overseers for the next year. The surveyors of the highways were chosen by the justices from a list supplied by the Vestry.

The parish clerk was a paid official, permanent in his post, and sharing with the churchwardens, the constable and the tithingmen the prestige of being sworn in his office. The name of Anthonie Anlie, the earliest clerk of Batheaston so remembered, is only known because at a visitation in 1609 it was presented that he was not sworn. In church it was the duty of the clerk to lead the responses, and in Batheaston, which retained its "three-decker" pulpit until the restoration of 1868, he had the glory of occupying the bottom deck. He was also usually responsible for the keeping of the parish register, a duty not always taken with proper seriousness, to the chagrin of the historian and the genealogist. The clerk, for obvious reasons, might act as schoolmaster; William Russell certainly did, and a very good hand he wrote. A list of parish clerks whose names are known is in Appendix 11.

The nineteenth century saw the end of independent parishes. The new Poor Law of 1834 replaced the Overseers of the Poor by the Guardians of the local Union. Highway Boards took over the upkeep of roads. The process of devolution was almost completed by the formation of County Councils in 1889.

An Act of 1894, however, required parishes of more than 300 souls to set up Parish Councils, and Batheaston's met for the first time on 12 December of that year. This step marked the final division into ecclesiastical and civil parishes. At present fifteen members, the Council cares for footpaths and playing fields; responsibility for lighting was transferred to the County Council in 1968. It sends five representatives to the Committee of Batheaston Freeholders (p. 142), and administers Smith's and Weaver's Charities (pp. 148, 150). Perhaps its most valuable function is in making representations as necessary to the Rural District Council and the County.

POPULATION

Expert studies lead to inferences that the population of England may have been about one and a half million in 1086, when the Domesday survey was made; that it rose fast in the thirteenth and early fourteenth centuries, to reach nearly four million, and was drastically reduced by the plague of 1348–1349, the Black Death, in which perhaps a third of the nation died. Recovery was slow, and the population of 1500 is estimated at only two and a half to three million. By 1600 it is thought to have reached four and a half million, and by 1700 five and a quarter. The first census, that of 1801, recorded nine million, that of 1901 thirty-six million.

Few and fortunate are the parishes whose population can be counted with any approach to accuracy before 1801. For most, the evidence enables only estimates which may be far from the truth, and this is especially so in dealing with small communities, such as Batheaston, and even more S. Catherine, in which statistical significance is difficult or impossible to obtain. For this study every known source in which records might survive has been investigated. Disappointments are many, either because valuable lists are no longer extant, or because lists that do survive can be shewn to be wholly inaccurate as evidence. As an example of the first, the Poll Tax of 1377,[1] much used in population studies, exists for Bath and for Wells, but not for Bathforum Hundred; of the second, the Muster Roll of 1569,[2] another valued source, which should list all able-bodied men between sixteen and sixty, contains not one name of the twenty-two who are mentioned in a Court Roll of 1565!

Such records as there are mostly apply to a section of the community only, such as ratepayers, or provide evidence of the number of households. Neither can be translated into an accurate population count. For the latter source, it is suggested that a multiplier of 4.5 gives the best approximation, and it has been used here; of course, it takes no account of changes in birth and death rates and social habits. Again, the number of children not brought to baptism in the parish church is an obvious possible source of error. So in what follows it must be kept in mind that suggested figures are at best approximations; nevertheless, it is feasible to discern trends which illuminate the evolution of Batheaston.

The earliest evidence comes from 1086, when Domesday Book enumerates forty-eight workers in what is now Batheaston and S. Catherine. Assuming that these were heads of households, they may represent a population of about 216, a prosperous community.

The next information is in the Exchequer Lay Subsidy of 1325–1326[3] which taxed all worth £1 a year or more, that is, most heads of families except the very poor; but it is well known that many escaped paying, so the lists may only be used to indicate a minimum (Appendix 3). We must take account of two lists, (E)Stone with twenty names, and Aumarle Chaumflour with twenty-five, but the latter part of this entry is torn off. Aumarle (p. 20) was the original of Amorel and must be counted as part of Batheaston, though Shockerwick, which can never have been populous, and was never a parish, was included. It is safe to say, therefore, that at least forty-five paid the tax, representing 202 persons; but how many did not pay can never be known, and the total population must have been greater. It is worth noting that of twenty-four who paid a fine at the Manor Court of S. Catherine in 1310, twelve (or their presumed heirs), paid the Lay Subsidy, while the other twelve are not represented. Though the Subsidy lists are of limited value in estimating population, they do furnish interesting material for assessing the relative importance of neighbouring places.

For more than two centuries following, no source is known to exist which enables any conjecture on the local population. How many died in the terrible Black Death, in which Somerset suffered severely, we do not know; probably the vicar, for whom successive replacements were instituted during the worst month, and if he, doubtless many of his people too.

The next evidence comes from the Ecclesiastical Census of 1563,[4] which enumerates households, and is believed to be accurate. The entry reads:

Batheaston, being A parishe church hathe L householdes.

Katheren, A chaple annexed therunto hathe VIII housholdes

From this we may suggest a population of 225 for Batheaston, and 36 for S. Catherine; little greater than five centuries before, but that accords with evidence for the country generally.

From 1620 onwards there are lists of those who paid the poor rate nearly every year. In 1620, also, all those having a stake in the common fields of Batheaston subscribed to an agreement about grazing rights (p. 132). Forty-nine names appear in one or both lists, so we may count so many heads of families, plus an unknown number excused payment of the rate because of their own poverty. (Only five women, and no men, received parish relief). The same year eleven men of S. Catherine paid the poor rate, making in all sixty families of some substance, slightly more than the total of all households in 1563. Evidently the population had increased. Twenty years later it had probably grown further, for forty-four paid the poor rate for Batheaston and thirteen for S. Catherine; that is, of course, assuming no great change in prosperity. The number of ratepayers remained fairly constant through the later seventeenth century, suggesting little change in total population.

Next to be considered is the evidence of the parish register. Unfortunately, the first book—records were ordered to be kept in 1538—is lost. The earliest surviving one begins in 1634, but the baptisms for two years, and the burials for four, in the first quarter of the century are preserved in the copies required to be sent to the bishop each year.[5] Fragmentary as this record is, the numbers are consistent with those from 1634, implying that there was no great change during those years. J. C. Cox suggested that for the seventeenth century three times the number of baptisms in a decade gives a fair approximation to the total population; for want of a better, this multiplier is used for the eighteenth century also in Table 3. Totals of burials are there shewn for the sake of their bearing on population trends; from about 1710

E

Table 3.   Population estimated on baptisms

Years	Baptisms	Burials	Estimated population
1634–1642	91 (9 years)	60	303
1671–1680	105	94	315
1681–1690	88	95	264
1692–1700	91 (9 years)	84	303
1701–1710	136	78	408
1711–1720	136	140	408
1721–1730	163	121	489
1731–1740	201	—	603
1741–1750	206	—	618
1751–1760	193	—	579
1761–1770	211	—	633
1771–1780	254	—	762
1781–1790	305	—	915
1791–1800	408	—	1224

onwards, however, burials from elsewhere, especially Bath, are entered in increasing numbers, so that quite a traffic of corpses grew up, unaccountably, for while some of the bodies were doubtless of persons who had a right to burial in Batheaston churchyard, many of the names are unfamiliar, and rural interment seems to have been a fashion. Many of the inscriptions in the church commemorate non-residents. For the present purpose "foreigners" are omitted in counting burials to 1730, after which there are so many, and the figures so improbably small without them, that the evidence is quite unreliable.

For the nine years 1634 to 1642, the register seems to have been properly kept. It then ceases abruptly until a solitary entry in 1653 in the hand of the very aged vicar. Desultory entries were made thereafter, as well as lists of baptisms of several families, obviously written as a belated record. The failure of the register is in keeping with the chaotic state of the Church during the dismal years of the Commonwealth, and was general at that time. The register seems to have been kept conscientiously from 1671, except that the year 1691 was not entered.

The large excess of baptisms over burials in 1634–1642 points to a population increasing quite fast, and it is unfortunate that we cannot tell what was the check which seems to have kept numbers fairly constant for the rest of the century; the likeliest is epidemics. The fall in the birthrate 1681–1690 is

not significant statistically, numbers being so small, but it may mean that young people were leaving the village. The great increase in baptisms in the decade 1701–1710 does indicate a growing population; a period, too, when burials were fewer than average. The next decade shews an almost exact balance between births and deaths; an epidemic in 1711 went some way to account for the steep rise in the death rate. The population increased through the eighteenth century, more rapidly in the second half, as in the country generally. Many new houses were built in the village at this time.

These estimates based on the register make no allowance for children not baptised in the parish church. There is, however, evidence that the figures are not much too low, for Collinson's *History of Somersetshire*, published in 1791, says that the population of Batheaston was "nearly a thousand", and our calculation for the previous decade arrives at 915, a very fair approximation.

A nearly true count is reached with the first census, that of 1801 (there is evidence that some people avoided inclusion) and thereafter the nation was numbered every ten years, 1941 only excepted (Table 4). A calculation based on baptisms, decade by decade to 1870, falls short of the true population by from one to four hundred, not surprising when dissent was well established, and some children were not baptised at all. The only exception, that for

Table 4.   Population 1801–1961 from census figures

	Batheaston	S. Catherine
1801	1072	79
1811	1298	112
1821	1330	127
1831	1783	154
1841	2191	159
1851	1795	135
1861	1698	84
1871	1645	160
1881	1637	136
1891	1725	112
1901	1648	109
1911	1585	129
1921	1560	86
1931	1513	97
1951	2694	112
1961	3307	90

1791–1800, when the calculated figure exceeds the true one for 1801, reflects an unusually large number of marriages in that decade.

A note to the report on the 1841 census remarks that 103 persons in a private Lunatic Asylum are included (Bailbrook House, p. 91), and 265 labourers on the Great Western Railway and their families. Stoppage of the silk factory (p. 145) had led to the departure of 164 persons. It is interesting, and perhaps surprising to the modern mind, concerned with the problem of excessive population, that numbers in Batheaston shrank fairly steadily until 1931; the great expansion is, of course, a phenomenon of recent years.

Less is known of the population of S. Catherine than of Batheaston. Bishop's transcripts for five years survive, the earliest 1598, the last 1630.[6] They record fifteen baptisms, eleven burials and five marriages, an average of three, two and one a year; this implies a larger community than the eight households of the Ecclesiastical Census of 1563. Between 1620 and 1662, there were thirteen or fourteen ratepayers; after that, the rate was made separately from Batheaston, and the record of it is lost. The earliest extant register of S. Catherine begins in 1752.

The census returns shew fluctuating numbers since 1801. The report on that of 1871 notes that the population had increased with the reopening of

the paper mill (p. 145); evidently many of the paper makers had migrated during the 1850's. The paper mill closed finally some time before the Monkswood Reservoir was built (p. 146), which probably accounts for the second exodus. S. Catherine has suffered a falling population, too, in the twentieth century; according to an old resident nineteen cottages have disappeared within his lifetime.

In Fig. 8 is seen the age distribution of the community in 1851 and 1951. The high proportion below the age of fifteen in 1851 is notable, especially

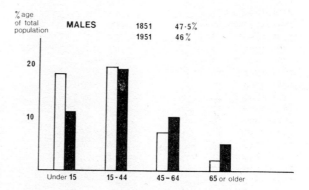

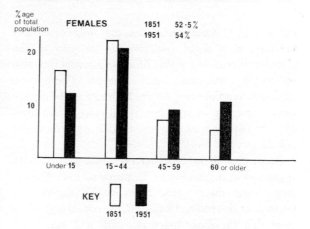

Fig. 8.   Age distribution of population (Batheaston)
1851 and 1951

as the population at that time was tending to fall. It illustrates the well-known fact that fewer children reached maturity. It shews, too, the much improved prospect of seeing old age at the present time.

ILLEGITIMACY

Illegitimacy, even if not baldly stated, can always be deduced from the entry of baptism. Table 5 gives the figures so obtained to 1870. Allowing for

Table 5.   Illegitimacy

Years	Illegitimate Births	Percentage of Baptisms
1639–1642	3	3·3
1671–1680	0	0·0
1681–1690	3	3·4
1692–1700	4	4·4
1701–1710	1	0·7
1711–1720	2	1·5
1721–1730	4	2·5
1731–1740	6	3·0
1741–1750	8	4·0
1751–1760	3	1·5
1761–1770	8	4·0
1771–1780	10	3·9
1781–1790	10	3·3
1791–1800	14	3·4
1801–1810	17	4·8
1811–1820	9	2·4
1821–1830	11	2·4
1831–1840	33	5·6
1841–1850	21	3·8
1851–1860	13	2·9
1861–1870	13	2·8

the effect of small numbers, the only consistent variation is a slight rise towards the end of the eighteenth century; at this time the national rate rose so sharply as to cause much concern. There is no difficulty in accounting for the high rate in the decade 1831–1840, for of nineteen illegitimate births from 1837 to 1840 at least six were to girls working in the silk factory (p. 145).

From 1840 to 1860 between 6% and 7% of births registered in England were illegitimate. Even if there were some discrepancy between the number of bastards registered and baptised, the conclusion seems clear that the illegitimacy rate was well below the average for the country.

MORTALITY AND EPIDEMICS

The parish register of a small community shews many chance fluctuations in the number of burials. It is possible, however, to pick out a few occasions when it is almost certain that an epidemic was killing. In 1636, for example, when the average of

burials was 6.6, seven persons were buried between 30 September and 26 October, not a time of year when mortality is likely to be heavy. There is strong evidence of an epidemic in 1711, when twenty-eight people were buried, nine of them, including Dr. Panton (p. 79), between 17 July and 30 September; the annual average for five years before and after was only 12.8. Smallpox was always about, and from time to time broke out in virulent form, and this is the most likely cause. The Poor Books, however, provide plenty of evidence that poor families might be nursed through the disease without a death, four of them in 1735 alone, a year in which deaths were not excessive. Also, where the overseers recorded a death from smallpox, often no other member of the family succumbed. The Black family, however, lost three children from smallpox in 1769, and probably it accounted for many of the deaths among children, for whom 1770 was an especially bad year. In general, and fairly consistently, from a third to a half of the burials were children.

Cholera reached England in 1831, and we know that it visited Batheaston (p. 105), but the deaths for that year were not excessive. There was probably a worse outbreak in 1735, when the parish buried eight persons, including four children, in two months.

Little can be deduced about the incidence of tuberculosis. It probably accounted for the early deaths of three of Dr. Panton's daughters. The death of several members of a family within months or a year or two is occasionally suggestive.

How many Batheaston women lost their lives in childbirth cannot be determined either, but to judge from the evidence of Freshford register, in which the cause of death is sometimes entered, the sad outcome was a common one, though the midwives employed by our overseers seem to have escaped calamity (p. 105). In the register three instances occur of the baptism of a child just before or just after the burial of the mother, and there were probably others. These were clear cases; but stillbirth, or no birth, would more usually accompany the catastrophe, and of that there can be no evidence.

PEOPLE

The list of surnames which persist for long periods in a community offers many features of interest. In

Fig. 9 are shewn the long-lasting names of Batheaston. Of course, families were likely to be in the village for some time before and after their name appears in any record—at most a generation from the seventeenth century onwards, much longer in earlier times, for which records are scanty and far apart in time. Also, lineal descent can rarely be guaranteed; there is frequent evidence of families migrating to and from neighbouring parishes, and of course names tend to be common in localities wider than parishes. Nevertheless, the list shews the small number of names which persist for several centuries, and that few of the "old Batheaston families" can claim residence for more than two or three hundred years, some much less.

Two at least of the early names (Appendix 1), de Hertlegh (Hartley) and de Ocford (Oakford) were certainly of local origin, and names such as atte Broke, atte Mulle, atte Townsend, Uphill, Woodward (first seen as "le Wodeward") may well have been so. Surnames were not universal before about 1300. Of these early Batheaston names, only the Biggs (Bygge), Beamans (mostly of S. Catherine), Somervells (Somerhylle), Stibbs (Stybbe), and Woodwards survived the Middle Ages, and none has lasted to the present day. The metamorphosis of Balman, through Baman into Beaman can be followed in an undoubted sequence related to property. Stibbs constantly appear in early documents, and there seems to have been nearly always a John of the name in the

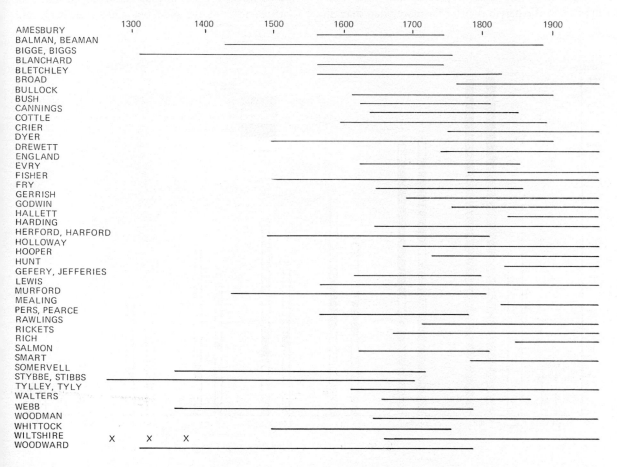

Fig. 9.   Persistence of families

parish. The family is commemorated in Stibb's Piece, but now usually called Stubbs, and Stibb's Hill (Map 2, B26, C48).

No family can be shewn to have lasted for 500 years, though several achieved more than 400. As continuity of the Wiltshires cannot be presumed, the Fishers have the longest record, and their name appears in the parish register far more often than any

is plenty of evidence, at least in later centuries, of migration, sometimes between distant places, more often parishes close at hand. The records of examinations relating to settlement (p. 107) and of removals (p. 107) establish this. From 1754 the parishes of the contracting parties were required to be entered in the register of marriages. From that date to 1812, 17% of the men belonged elsewhere, and

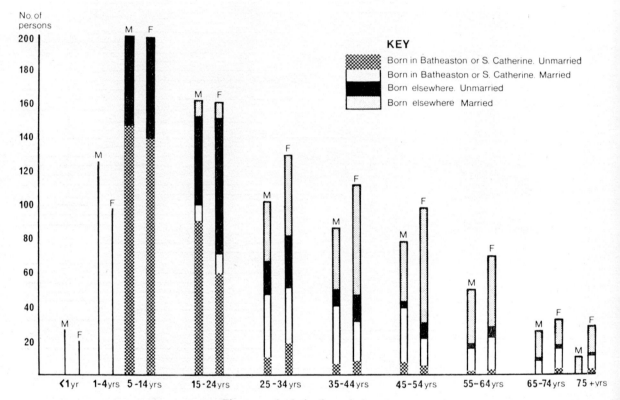

KEY

▨ Born in Batheaston or S. Catherine. Unmarried
▫ Born in Batheaston or S. Catherine. Married
■ Born elsewhere. Unmarried
☐ Born elsewhere. Married

Fig. 10.   Analysis of population 1851

other. One line became gentry (p. 75), and there were always humble folk bearing the name, but relationships are obscure. Another family exceptionally strong in numbers was Lewis. The Dyers, too, maintained a long history; the census of 1851 has sixteen young males, almost all locally born, but the name died out in the village soon after 1900.

So much for the families that stayed. Many more names appear in the records for a decade, a generation, a century, and disappear; occasionally to reappear. Some families, of course, died out; but there

6% of their brides. The latter figure is surprising in view of the probability that weddings ordinarily took place in the woman's parish; the total of immigrant women must have been larger, probably much larger.

Exact figures, again surprising ones, are obtained from the 1851 census, the earliest to record place of birth. An analysis is seen in Fig. 10, which shews that well over half of the adult population was born elsewhere. (The proportion is even more startling for S. Catherine, thirty-nine of fifty-five aged twenty-five or over. These figures are included in the total). If agricultural labourers are considered separately, a hundred and thirty-two were local, sixty-two born within ten miles, and twenty-six came from farther away, i.e. 40% were not natives. Only six of the twenty-one farmers were local men. The finding, too, that in each age-group the women exhibit the greater mobility is quite unexpected. In this matter of migration, though, the occupants of the large houses, both resident owners and their domestic staff, had an effect in obscuring the picture of a mainly rural community. (The inhabitants of Bailbrook House Mental Asylum are excluded.)

So the myth of the stable, almost-closed community is false, at least for Batheaston. Moreover, with the flourishing city of Bath so near, it is certain that considerable movement thither took place; it has already been pointed out how the handy refuge and the convenient anonymity it offered must have beckoned fugitive bondmen in feudal times. In recent years rapid growth has been due almost entirely to immigration, and at the present time only a small fraction of the population consists of native Batheastonians.

Though most of the inhabitants were employed on the land, the community was until recent times almost self-sufficient. In 1778 the vicar listed the parishioners from whom he claimed tithe, 102 of them, presumably most of the more substantial, including:

Gentry	10
Farmers	21
Shopkeepers	6
Cloth trade, carpenters	5 each
Bakers, maltsters	4 ,,
Master gardeners, blacksmiths, masons, shoemakers, tailors	3 ,,
Tilers, butchers	2 ,,
Thatcher, innkeeper, miller	1 ,,

Between them they could supply most of the necessities of village life, and of course there were others not liable for tithe. The rather disproportionate number of gentry reflects the heyday of Bath and the period of villa-building.

Analysis of the 1851 census reveals a community continuing well provided with practitioners of the basic trades. There were still twenty-one farmers. The list is not otherwise comparable with the one

above, because of course it includes employees, whose predecessors of 1778 would not all pay tithe. Gardeners (masters and men) numbered thirty-two, agricultural labourers 199 in Batheaston, twenty-one in S. Catherine. The scope of occupation had widened and there were now four coal merchants, five hairdressers (one a "frizzler", crossed out and altered). A French polisher, too, was in business. Cloth-making had ceased, but at S. Catherine there were three leather-dressers, and five paper-makers (p. 145). There was still a thatcher, a Jones, whose family for generations followed the trade.

Women's occupations, other than domestic (nineteen were "churwomen") were limited to dress-making (thirty-five), laundering (fifty-one), and fifteen females claimed to be school-mistresses—probably tiny "dame" schools flourished. The conclusion must be that some of the dress-making, laundering and teaching was on a very small scale.

INNS

Second only to the church, the inn stood at the centre of village life. There the churchwardens and Vestry refreshed themselves after disposing of parish business, there the justices met when occasion required—an enquiry, perhaps, into the credentials of "intruders" (p. 107) or the binding of a parish apprentice (p. 109); there the coroner would hold an inquest, there sick and injured strangers were nursed at the expense of the parish (p. 112); and there, of course, the villager, when he could afford it, enjoyed company and his thirst.

The ancient inn of Batheaston was the Lamb (Map 1, 9). In 1684 Richard Cock paid the poor rate—a shilling it was—"for ye Lamb". Described in his will as a carpenter, Cock was a man of some wealth, and his will was proved in the Prerogative Court of Canterbury.

Not long before 1740 the innkeeper was Samuel Fuller, founder of the Bath coachbuilding business. In 1751 he was fined 10s "for suffering tipling in his house on Sunday 3rd November"; if his premises were not otherwise well-conducted there is no mention of it, and he certainly retained his official patronage.

"Last week died Mr S. Fuller, who kept the Lamb at Bath-Easton. His death was occasioned by a Fall, which 'tis supposed fractured his Scull, he living but a few hours after".[7] According to another account, he fell from his horse at his own door.

His son William succeeded to the business, and his rebuilt inn was a pleasing feature of the village Street for nearly two hundred years. The portion on the left was dated $W^F_{1771}R$, that on the right $W^F_{1779}R$ (Pl. 18).

Pl. 18.   Lamb Inn

About the mid-nineteenth century the Lamb acquired a Flag, and continued to be so known. Its

Pl. 19. Lamb Inn sign
(*from Wheatcroft:* "Picturesque village rambles")

recent history was one of decay; on a confined site, there was no harbourage for the motor car. Trade declined, and in 1962 the licence was surrendered. The premises stood forlorn awaiting a buyer who never came, and the old inn was pulled down in 1968.

It is not possible to trace the history of other inns in the village; a change of sign was a commonplace, and the New Inn mentioned in 1728 may have become the Bell in 1744 or the Crown in 1755. Neither survives. The White Hart appears in parish records from the early nineteenth century. The present George and Dragon and White Lion were built about 1830; the former was remarkable in continuing home brewing until the 1960's.

Sandy Bank, the solitary inn of S. Catherine, beloved, but unable to provide convenience to the modern standard, closed in 1966.

LAW AND ORDER

Some examples of wrong-doing and punishment in the feudal period have been given (p. 15). The power of the Church to exact obedience and punish sin was still to be respected in the seventeenth century, when local records become plentiful. A few examples from the archdeacon's visitations illustrate this:

1615. Maria Jeffery is presented that she hath stood excommunicated this 2 monthes or theire about for not paying her chargis in the Archdecons court shee having a base child and hath don her penance for the same And accuseth Richard Blake to be the father of her child wch is gon out off their parish.

John Humfrie is presented that he did keepe tipling and drinking in his house being an alehouse at the time of divine servic on Sunday the 25 of June last past, his house was full of strangers comeing thither to be merry yt being the morrowe after their revell daye (p. 66).

Anthonie Lacie and John Gay doe often tymes frequent alehouses and doe use to be drounke.

1620. William Dobers and Elizabeth Anlie are presented for living in bedd and board as man and wife and yett they are not married wherefore there hath bin for the space of these 7 moneth and for all this there is a comon fame and reporte amonst the honest parishioners of Batheaston.

1633. Anthonie Harvord is presented for a

negligent frequenter of his parish church he hath byn presented for not receiving the holie communion at Easter last but hath receaved noe punishment for that offence to theire knowledge.

William Lewis a taylor is presented for a common swearer, a verie poore bodie.

By the eighteenth century the civil law was dealing with Sabbath breaking and dunkenness. The following episodes are recorded in the overseers' accounts because half of a fine inflicted by the magistrates was given to the poor:

1752. (Five men named) fined 3s 4d for playing Fives on Sunday 8 June. (Four men named) sat in the Stocks three hours for the same offence not being able to pay the penalty.

As for swearing, an Act of 1745 prescribed graduated penalties, 5s an oath for gentlemen, 2s for yeomen, and 1s for labourers, and for a time entries such as these are frequent:

1749. John Kirton Shoemaker forfeited £1 for being Convicted before the Justices for Swearing ten Oaths.

1753. William Fisher Gentleman 30 profane Oaths £7 10s.

Oaths were usually counted in round numbers—presumably an approximation!—but the best score was made by F. Fisher, Labourer, who in 1770 paid £3 4s for sixty-four!

Failure of Sunday observance was punished to the middle of last century. In 1808 appears the startling entry of a payment to the tithingman for "attending the Town Hall to receive a fine paid by Children for gambling on the Sabboth day". In 1820 four persons were placed in the stocks for the same offence, and thirteen boys summoned and fined. As late as 1852 four boys were fined for gambling on a Sunday.

The stocks were an important piece of parish property, and items for their repair are frequent in the accounts. A new pair was made and the old iron and three locks repaired in 1777. An engraving of the old church of 1783, in the Hunt Collection of Bath City Library, shews them at the top of what is now School Lane. The surviving stocks were made by John Cottle in 1833, and cost £2 8s 0d, including the stool. An old inhabitant recalls his mother telling how the last occupants were a couple who "were very drunk". About 1920 they were placed in the churchyard and there remained forlorn, falling into decay

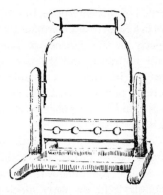

Pl. 20. The stocks
(from Wheatcroft: "Picturesque village rambles")

until 1969, when they were removed and treated for preservation as an unusual relic of village life.

It seems that for a short time only Batheaston possessed a lock-up, called indifferently the "round" and the "blind" house, of which several survive in the neighbourhood. The Vestry in 1815 decided "to Fix on an eligible Spot on Which to erect a Lock-up House"; where it stood is forgotten. It frequently needed repair, probably because of violent treatment within and without, and in 1830 the Vestry agreed to remove it and fit up a strong room in the Poor House instead. A window there retains iron bars.

The punishment of minor offenders by whipping was for so long a favourite deterrent that it is curious that more than two centuries of parish records yield a single instance:

1821. Paid the Tything Man for Flogging 3 Men
        by order of the Magistrates   15s.
      Paid the Police Officers for keeping them in
        custody 3 nights   £2 5s.

At this time misbehaviour was causing a good deal of trouble. Several women were being supported while their husbands were in jail. Unemployment was probably largely to blame. A message was received from Bathford Vestry in 1821 asking co-operation to ensure the closing of the public houses "by the hour of ten every night through the year without exception of any day or days whatsoever". Four persons were to patrol the village in pairs each night, and be paid 1s 6d, to be raised by a "voluntary" rate of twopence in the pound. The public houses were to be visited at 10 o'clock looking for suspicious characters. Nothing more is recorded of this enterprise, but in 1832 it was decided to form a Society of Guardians for the protection of property in the parishes of Batheaston, S. Catherine and Bathford, and the next year a subscription was to be raised to establish a watch. Nothing more is noted of that, either, and before long the responsibility for police work was to pass from the parishes.

Of major crime in Batheaston little is recorded. Several prisoners were carried off to the Bridewell at Shepton Mallet for unknown offences in the eighteenth century. In the early nineteenth was a case of manslaughter, several assaults, the assault and robbery of Mr. Pobjoy in 1842; one Cummings was transported for fifteen years in 1842 for an act of sacrilege in robbing the church. The keepers of several "disorderly houses" were punished by fines. Perhaps the commonest offence was desertion of a wife and family, an endemic disease. The chasing and arrest of absconding fathers of bastards was a matter of much moment to the overseers, who foresaw another body to be kept from starvation, and is noted elsewhere (p. 111).

CUSTOMS

Perambulation of the parish boundaries at Rogationtide is a venerable custom, the procession accompanied by the minister, who, according to Elizabethan injunction, was to admonish the people at convenient halting places. The people of S. Catherine in 1609 reported at the visitation that there had been no perambulation "the last yeare nor in manie yeares before". The occasion was naturally an opportunity for jollification, and the mentions of it in the records, usually at quite long intervals, are items of expenditure. Peter Cannings of the Bell wrote in 1685: "Beere from my house at procession", and an entry for cimnel (simnel) and cakes in 1691 probably related to the custom. In 1712 appears:

Beer and Diet for the Processioners   £3 7s 0d
24 dozen of Niggs on the Procession day   12s 0d

Niggs were balls of tough wood used in the game of Not. Each side, armed with bats, tried to strike the niggs into their opponents' goal.

From 1755, when £4 10s was spent "going in procession about the Parish", the custom seems to have lapsed until it was revived in 1823 by Melmoth

Walters who, with characteristic earnestness, summoned representatives of contiguous parishes to debate boundaries which in many places were half forgotten. A strenuous walk occupying two days, refreshment was evidently provided, for the "perambleation bill" came to £3 3s 6d. The revived custom was repeated several times, the last in 1837.

It is difficult to account for the name Procession Way, which attaches to a field adjoining the Fosse Way (Map 2, B41). Possibly from this point the procession customarily made its way back across the fields, omitting the remainder of the journey southward to the river as not being debatable.

The feast day of the patron saint, in Batheaston S. John Baptist, 24 June, was the occasion for a grand "revel". There is reference to it in the visitation of 1615, when John Humfrie was presented for allowing tippling during the time of divine service on Sunday, 25 June "the morrowe after their revell daye".

The time came when the revels were thought to occasion too much disorderly conduct and profligacy, and the magistrates determined to put an end to them. An announcement appeared in the *Bath Chronicle*, 23 May 1776:

BATHFORUM DIVISION

Whereas the Custom of keeping Revels in the several parishes within the division aforesaid, hath occasioned idleness, drunkenness, riots, gaming, and all manner of vice, immorality, and profaneness, amongst the lowest class of people, to the evil example of others, and the great disturbance, damage, and terror of the well disposed, as well as tending greatly to the increase of the poor: therefore we, Justices of the Peace, do hereby strictly enjoin and command that all such Revels be from henceforth suppressed, and all fencers, bearwards, common players of interludes, minstrels, jugglers, persons using any subtil craft to deceive or impose on His Majestie's subjects, or playing or betting at any unlawful games or plays, all petty chapmen and pedlars not being duly licensed or otherwise authorised by law, and other idle and disorderly persons, who shall presume to appear at any such Revels, will answer the same at their perils. All Victuallers or Alehousekeepers are not to sell any ale or other liquors at those times, or have their licences suppressed.

The sequel, *Bath Chronicle*, 20 June 1776:

Parish of Bath-Easton, Bathforum Division, and County of Somerset.

Whereas we, the Minister, Churchwardens and Overseers of the parish aforesaid, having received an injunction from His Majestie's Justices of the Peace acting in and for the division aforesaid, for the suppression of the Revel annually held in our parish, We do therefore give notice, that the said revel will in future be discontinued, and that all idle and disorderly persons appearing there will be prosecuted according to law.

An unamiable rustic custom which continued well into the present century was the baiting of adulterous couples. Life-sized dummies representing the man and woman, cloth-covered and with painted faces, were stuck on poles and carried round the village on three successive nights, amid an uproar contrived by beating on pots and pans. At intervals the procession halted for the singing of ribald doggerel made up for the occasion, not omitting, of course, the dwelling of the victims. On the third night tradition required the burning of the effigies at the customary site, the orchard where Lower Northend now stands.

The parish magazine for July 1914 contains the following, written by the vicar:

"We deeply regret the unseemly demonstrations and processions that took place on June 22 and the following two days. We cannot imagine that such things do any good, but they do definite harm to the large number of young people who take part in them. We should be glad to think there won't be any more."

The date chosen for the orgy, with its climax on the Patronal Festival, doubtless recollected the old revel, enshrined in folk memory. In spite of the vicar's rebuke, and the attentions of the police, it was nearly twenty years before the custom was acted for the last time.

SPEECH

In past ages the countryman, if he wrote at all, spelt as he spoke. So the speech he used can be recovered fairly well from the evidence he left in writing. Especially he tried to reproduce his long vowels. Examples here quoted are from parish documents.

Sarvis	Maake
Parson (person)	Laafull
Sarge	Caase
Thare	Raate
Roider	Harse
Woife	Carsway (causeway)
Boibel	Wooerke

SOCIETIES AND CLUBS

The nineteenth century saw much beneficent activity directed to insurance and mutual help, but knowledge of most of the institutions is fragmentary.

Batheaston Society

Batheaston Society offers five guineas for the return of Seven Fat Wether sheep from a field near Batheaston Bridge, if stolen. If strayed, half a guinea from John Broad, butcher (*Bath Journal*, 31 December 1798).

An advertisement noticed by chance. Nothing has been discovered of this society, its rules, or how long it endured.

Batheaston Female Friendly Society

Instituted 29 September 1802. Enrolled, under an Act of 1829, 17 October 1831. The rules, which are undated, probably date from this time.

The Society was for relief in sickness, old age and infirmity; the encouragement of moral and virtuous conduct, general benevolence and frugality. There were patronesses, one of them to be the vicar's wife, honorary members and 101 general members, the age of admission fifteen to thirty. The Annual General Meeting was on Whit Monday, after (compulsory) Church, and followed by (compulsory) Tea Drinking.

The subscription was 3d per week, the allowances 5s a week if in bed up to thirteen weeks: 3s a week up to a year, 2s 6d "for such further period as she shall continue ill". For a confinement 16s was allowed. The Society paid £5 10s for the funeral of a member, each member to attend and afterwards pay 1s; for a husband's funeral, £2 2s. Drinking in public houses spelt expulsion. The rules end:

"The Ladies who conduct this Institution cannot conclude these Rules without earnestly exhorting the Members of this Society to the most strict observance of the Sabbath Day, in their religious duties, both public and private; particularly their attendance on divine service, without which, it is feared, that their labour will prove in vain and that they will have cause to repent the neglect of those means of spiritual improvement, which can alone ensure their eternal happiness."

On the wall of the north aisle of the church is a tablet, surely an early example of the misuse of inverted commas:

TO THE MEMORY OF
MRS WALTERS
"PATRONESS" OF THE
"FEMALE FRIENDLY SOCIETY"
IN THIS PARISH
ESTABLISHED BY HER BENEVOLENCE
AND DURING THIRTY FOUR YEARS
FOSTERED BY HER CARE
THIS TABLET IS INSCRIBED
BY THE MOURNING AND GRATEFUL
"MEMBERS" AS A TOKEN OF
THEIR RESPECT AND AFFECTION
A.D. 1836.

How long the Female Friendly Society outlived Mrs. Walters no one knows.

Society for the relief of Lying-in Women

Existing knowledge of this society is comprised in the list of rules (Pl. 21). Without date, unfortunately, it must lie between 1824 and 1851, the period of Spencer Madan's incumbency. The exclusion of women in their first confinement is puzzling; so are the nature and purpose of flannel barrows and grits. The vogue of castor oil lasted a century at least.

Batheaston Provident Society

Founded in 1830, this cannot have been the earliest attempt at providing help in hard times, for in 1802 the overseers recorded a payment of 2s 6d, being Francis Hodge's Club Money. Besides, in 1821 an institution called the Old Club lent £400 towards the cost of the Poor House (p. 100).

"The object of this Society is to induce Mechanics and Labourers residing in the Parish to make weekly deposits of such sums of money, however small, which they may be able to lay by during the Summer, and which shall be expended for them by the Directors of the Society, Rev. Madan, President, Capt. Carroll, Treasurer, M. Walters,

Secretary, in the first week in December in every year, either in the purchase of coals or of such articles of clothing or bedding as the Depositors may require for themselves or their families, or in the Payment of their Rent at their own option. And in order to induce persons to make deposits, a small addition will be made to each deposit in proportion to the amount thereof".

This Society was later associated with a Penny Club for Sunday and Infants' Schools, which paid out in vouchers for shoes or boys' clothing. The Society gave out, too, loans of cotton blankets and coverlids for winter.

In January 1847, a time of dearth, a meeting of the Society called for a subscription to buy coal, establish a soup kitchen and prepare porridge for sale at cost. Gentlemen and others having gardens were asked to supply vegetables. Rice was bought in bulk. The appeal brought in £17 10s from twenty-one people.

Annual accounts of this Society were kept until 1865, when they ceased abruptly and without comment. Whether it was dissolved then, or if not when, it is impossible to say. The accounts of a Provident Fund are printed with the Church accounts for 1911.

Independent Medical Club

A worn and torn printed sheet, undated, is the only relic of this institution that has come to light. It included the parishes of Batheaston, Bathford, S. Catherine and Swainswick. Its object was "to enable the Second Class of Poor to insure to themselves Medical and Surgical Attendance and Medicines, during Sickness, independent of Parochial Aid. Servants receiving up to seven guineas annual wages, and others not earning more than a guinea a week were eligible for membership. Annual subscriptions were from 4s 6d to 11s 6d according to the size of family. Members were to furnish their own bottles, leeches and bandages, and attend on the Medical Gentleman when able; otherwise be visited at their own houses. Habitual drunkards and persons notoriously addicted to profligate habits, or who were known to be idle and disorderly, or had been convicted of felony, were not to be admitted. Sick persons could only join on procuring two healthy ones to enter at the same time.

It may be noticed that the provident societies whose traces have been followed here were under the

SOCIETY

FOR THE RELIEF OF

LYING-IN WOMEN,

IN THE

PARISHES OF BATHEASTON AND ST. CATHARINE.

THE design of the INSTITUTION is to furnish those Women who shall be eligible according to the following Rules, with Medical attendance during their confinement, the use of a Bag for five weeks, and some Articles of nutriment, and Medicine as specified in the Rules.

RULES.

I.—THAT each Member shall pay an Annual Subscription of Five Shillings, which shall entitle them to one Ticket.

II.—That each Member shall be entitled to any additional number of Tickets upon paying Five Shillings for each additional Ticket.

III.—That every Woman to receive the benefit of this Charity must have resided Twelve Months at least in one of the above mentioned places. She must have been in the habit of attending some place of Public Worship, and of sending her Children who are above Six years of age to some convenient Day-School, and all her Children who are of a proper age to the Sunday-School.

IV.—No Woman is eligible who is the Wife of a Man-Servant in place.

V.—No Woman is eligible in her first confinement.

VI.—Every Woman who is desirous of receiving the benefit of this Charity must make application for a Ticket from the Treasurer, Mrs. MADAN, Six Months before it will be required, have her name registered, and deposit her Ticket in the hands of the Treasurer, paying Two Pence Weekly, or Eight Pence at the end of every Four Weeks, when the Ticket will be returned to her signed by the Treasurer.

The Bags will contain:—1 Coverlid; 1 pair Sheets; 1 Bolster Case; 2 Shifts; 2 Night Caps; 2 Bedgowns; 1 large Wrapping Gown; 1 Square Flannel; 2 Flannel Barrows; 2 Caps; 2 Shirts; 2 Bedgowns; 2 Pinafores; 12 Towels; 1lb. Soap; 1½lb. Rushlights; 1½lb. Sugar; 1 Paper of Grits; and a small bottle of Castor Oil.

As considerable expense attends the furnishing the Bags, it is suggested that a small donation from the Subscribers occasionally, will be acceptable.

Mrs. MADAN, *Treasurer.*
Mr. CONWAY EDWARDS, *Surgeon.*

C. HUNT, PRINTER, BATH.

Pl. 21. Society for the Relief of Lying-in Women

patronage and benevolent control of Church and Gentry; no wonder, for they were found among the parish archives in the custody of the vicar. Friendly Societies were founded in large numbers from the eighteenth century onwards, by no means always under patronage. They were encouraged by the Government, which saw in them the hope of relief from the burden of supporting the poor, and enacted sundry laws which bestowed privileges upon them; hence the term "enrolled". Many of them failed through offering unrealistic scales of benefit, others through mismanagement and squandering of funds, especially on Club Nights. A feature common to them was the annual feast day, usually at Whitsuntide, which included a church parade and the famous "walk".

Margaret Fuller[8] has made a close study of the subject, and catalogued the many societies whose rules or other records are known. There is no entry for Batheaston, but the "Old Club" of 1821 implies the existence of a "New Club", and there may have been others. Whether these were the ones of which Mrs. Wheatcroft wrote in 1899 there is no knowing, for they left no record.

"Whitsuntide has just passed, which reminds one of the abolition of the walking of the village Club. This was the time of their great Saturnalia. There were two in Batheaston; one had its head-quarters at the 'Lamb and Flag', the other at the 'White Hart'.

"Each had its flag; not a common banner; its silk was covered with various devices, and it must have been of considerable weight; but it was con-sidered a great honour to bear it, and the lucky person who obtained this envied post had to pay five shillings for the privilege. Each clubman wore a large rosette pinned to his coat or smock, and a bunch of flowers (the larger the better), the favourite one being the stock or gilly-flower. Between nine and ten o'clock the band arrived, and the Club started in procession to visit the houses of the chief inhabitants. The flag was waved before the door, and the Club received donations, either of money or refreshments (principally the latter), so that when it was time to march to Church many of the members were, to say the least, of cheerful countenance. The flags were hoisted into the gallery, and drooped over the front. The Vicar

then preached an appropriate sermon, and took the chair at the dinner which followed. He left early with the Doctor, as they knew the ale was strong, and inducive of argument; and the wives knew it too, and were on the look-out to get their men home before the fun became quarrelsome, and the legs unsteady. On Club night each member had to attend and pay his contribution; if not, he was fined. Of course, it was necessary to drink some-thing 'for the good of the house'. The great institution was the 'Box', it was the centre round which the Club revolved. It has three keys, one kept by the landlord, the other two by officers called stewards. The Box could only be opened by these three persons being present together. The Club books were kept in the Box, if a man was ill, he went to the Box, and if at the end of the finan-cial year anything was left in the Box, it was divided amongst the members. Later in the Whitsun-week the lady at the great house entertained the women and children at tea on the lawn. The band played on the terrace, where the quality had their tea, the others were regaled at tables on the lawn. The entertainment was not deliciously cheerful, but they enjoyed it".

Mrs. Wheatcroft's informant, whoever he was, evidently spoke of a time before 1868, for the last gallery in the church was removed then. Which was the "great house" is not clear.

Most of these small local societies were eventually absorbed or superseded by the large affiliated "orders" which made rapid advance during the later nineteenth century. Their successors in Batheaston were the Ancient Order of Foresters, and the Loyal Order of

Pl. 22. Loyal Order of Ancient Shepherds, c. 1900

Ancient Shepherds. Miss Blathwayt remarked in her diary the Foresters' Church Parade, 22 July 1894, headed by the Batheaston Avon Vale Band. Again, in 1904, she described them marching past Eagle House, wearing green sashes, on their Whit Monday walk. Old Batheastonians of course well remember these occasions, and one at least, a march of the Shepherds, probably about 1900, is visually preserved (Pl. 22).

With the advent of national insurance the local branches declined and were dissolved. A branch of the Ancient Order of Buffaloes, which came later, and was flourishing in the 1920's, had the same fate, and thus perished a colourful and generally beneficient feature of village life.

The Nursing Association

"A Permanent Nurse is urgently needed." Thus reported a committee of ladies in March 1898, adding that a London Nursing Association which trains Village Nurses will supply one, with "various necessary appliances" for £30 per annum. Mr. Charles Harper, of the Manor House, would be the medical adviser. So Batheaston has had the valued services of a resident nurse for seventy years; in 1931 the Association built for her a bungalow, which it still administers. Unfortunately, early records are lost. In 1911 the nurse, whose salary was then £46 16s od, paid 1,747 visits, as recorded in the Church Year Book.

In 1930 the Nursing Associations of Bathford, Bathampton and Batheaston were amalgamated, and the next year Swainswick was added, and an additional junior nurse appointed to help in the large district so formed. With the coming of the National Health Service in 1948 the State took over the main responsibility, the system of subscriptions, supplemented by small payments for service, which had

Pl. 23. Ancient Order of Buffaloes, c. 1924

enabled the Associations to pay their way, was abolished and a free service instituted.

Societies for social and educational purposes had their day. A Reading Room was in existence before 1859, when it was used for the Provident Society's distribution. It probably catered for the gentry.

An undated prospectus announced the formation of Batheaston and S. Catherine's Working Men's Association. The vicar was to be chairman, ex officio, the annual subscription was 4s, with an additional shilling for the Lending Library. There was to be no smoking on the premises.

This venture probably accounts for the fading inscription on a house in Vale View: Working Men's Institute 1878. Sometime later, needing larger premises, it was proposed to buy and equip at a cost of £800 part of the late Rawlinson and Padgen's Brewery, close at hand. The ground floor was to be a Drill Hall for the 14th Avondale Rifle Volunteers. Above were rooms for Bagatelle or Billiards, Reading; and Smoking, respectable at last.

Nothing further is known of the fortunes of the Institute until 1906, when the opening of the Rifle Club on the premises is described in the Blathwayt diaries. Lord Roberts was to come, but had to be in the Lords that day. His deputy in the course of his duty addressed the Church Lads' Brigade, paraded for the purpose. The Club was enthusiastically supported; Miss Blathwayt recorded with pride in 1908 winning a silver spoon. During the sterner years ahead it declined, of course. There was a later revival, but it finally perished of inanition. The Church Lads' Brigade was disbanded in 1911 in favour of the Boy Scouts. The premises are still the headquarters of the Billiard Club.

PUBLIC SERVICES
Sanitation
In a place so hilly as Batheaston, and so well provided with springs, some device for dealing with running water must have been long in use. The entry for 1669, quoted from the accounts of the surveyors of the highways (p. 126) is the earliest written reference. A fry was a drain consisting of brushwood laid in a trench and covered over. There are a few references to drainage in the eighteenth century:

1775. 6 load broad stones for covering the fry	12s 0d
1787. Pd Bakehouse opening the Fry as Leads to the Vicarage House	6d
1800. The shore at the Bridge and from Penthouse.	

This is the first use of the word sewer. Here it probably meant a ditch lined and covered with stones, known locally as a ruckle, draining off water, and contributions of sewage from those conveniently placed. There is a record of extending it, by joint enterprise of the parish and the Turnpike Commissioners, in 1818.

The squalor, and the stench from refuse and excreta, which seemed a natural and inevitable accompaniment of human life, are hard to imagine, but persisted in diminishing degree through the nineteenth century, as will be seen. A note of 1848 lists nuisances to be abated in various parts of the village under three headings: heaps, privies and cesspools. For the fastidious to be inoffensive to themselves and others was difficult enough; human nature being what it is. . . .

Evidently a dispute arose about responsibility for the developing sewage system, for the Vestry Order Book contains in 1870 the following remarkable statement: "A letter having been received from the Secretary of State, stating that the Vestry were the proper Sewer Authority and were competent to act in the matter of the Sewerage in Fry's Lane. . . . Stephen Rawlings undertook to lay a 9″ socket glazed pipe, without mortar, 'at proper depth', with a ruckle drain on each side of the whole length, at 2s 3d per yard, finding the materials." The special problem there was spring water.

Under the provisions of the Public Health Act of 1875, Batheaston Parochial Sanitary Committee was appointed in 1876, Major-General Whistler Chairman, Captain Struan Robertson Secretary. The latter gentleman "with kind consideration brought to the first meeting a Minute Book 3s 9d, Account Book 1s 0d, Inkstand 1s 6d, Blotting Book, Pens etc 1s 5d, which the Committee, thanking him for his kind forethought, decided to purchase". This Minute Book, preserved by a happy chance, served until 1904, and the notes which follow, taken from it, give an idea of conditions when the Committee began work.

A sewer draining three houses on the Batch caused offensive effluvia in passing through cottage premises below. The drain was to be reconstructed with 9″ socket pipes (the universal remedy). There was "a foul and dilapidated slop drain to a foul open privy with cesspool underneath the floor at two cottages at North End". Drains and privies from a large number of houses in Northend discharged through an open ditch into the brook. A cause of offence in Banner Down Road was a horse kept in a back kitchen!

In 1883 the brook at Stambridge obstructed, and, foul with sewage, was cleared from the river to the school at a cost of £10. A recurrent trouble—and no wonder!—it was blocked again and again. In 1903, an angry letter complained that the accumulation of sewage there had not been cleaned out for five years, and reminded of complaints at the Coronation festivities in the previous year. "It is of no use to view the Brook occasionally. You must LIVE near it to feel its fragrance". The Minute Book ends with a proposal to run a sewer up the valley, past the school, and up School Lane to Northend. This was done.

About 1908 the old stone sewer which ran along the north side of the Street, and had served for close on a hundred years, was replaced by a socketed pipe laid across the gardens in line with the river, and discharging into a main which at that time carried sewage to a plant at Newton S. Loe, now to the sewage works at Saltford.

Collection of house refuse began in 1884, in a very small way, for it took place in July, October and March! The cost varied, but was usually about £20 a year. In 1903 the Rural District Council, now taking over functions previously discharged locally, accepted a tender of £25 for scavenging. Responsibility for sanitation has long been extra-parochial, and does not concern the Parish Council.

TRANSPORT

The history of organised transport for Batheastonians dates back little more than a century. From 1860 Mark Coles, of Stambridge Buildings, appears in the Bath Directory as an omnibus Proprietor. Before the end of the century there was a regular omnibus service, and the fare from the Lamb and Flag to Bath was 2d. Powered by two horses, and known facetiously as "the matchbox", the omnibus journeyed from the Crown at Bathford twice a day.

Electric trams came to Batheaston in 1912, and old residents remember the excitement when the first one clanged along the Street. They ran until 1938, when they were replaced by motor buses.[9] To-day incessant traffic thunders through, and the suffering public longs for the promised by-pass.

POSTAL SERVICE

A rudimentary postal service was available to private persons from the sixteenth century, but letters were usually only carried between large towns, and that irregularly. Local communications were taken by any trustworthy person who happened to be making the journey. Or perhaps some individual was recognised as the village messenger. Batheaston's "horse rider" of the last decade of the seventeenth century may have been such an one. He often received poor relief and frequently appeared in the overseers' records:

1691. a Cote and a par of Hos for the Hos Roider.
1692. a shirt, shoes and Apron for the Horsrider.
1696. Isaack Smith ye Hors Rider.

This is the only mention of his name. He had no successor.

In the early years of the nineteenth century village post offices were being set up. The practice varied, but usually the recipients had to collect their letters. There was a post office in Batheaston not later than 1823, when the occupant paid a highway rate. The first issue of the Bath Directory, published in 1858, lists William Garraway of the Post Office as "letter carrier". His premises were the house called Acbar House.

In 1870 in response to:

"Appeal to provide a Velocipede, at cost not exceeding £8, for Charles Nathaniel Ruddock, Rural Postman for Batheaston and Bathford in recognition of his good services and anticipation of increase in duties with reduction of postal rates"

a machine was bought for £1 10s and repaired for £4! Local records contain no further references to postal services.

Water

In accordance with the Bath Waterworks Act of 1846 a reservoir was constructed in Chilcombe Bottom (Map 1) and a supply of piped water provided to such of Batheaston as was conveniently placed.

Bath Corporation became a landowner, and in 1856 had property valued for rating purposes at £522. A small reservoir was made at Monkswood (Map 1) in 1870, and in 1894 the much larger one which still supplies a large part of the City's water. Batheaston profited from the needs of its rich neighbour; in 1883 the water from three wells at Bailbrook was found unfit for use, and a pipe was laid from the Corporation main, which was nearly 1,000 yards away. To-day, only a few of the more remote homes depend on spring water.

Gas

The church and the entrance to the churchyard were lit by gas in 1868, but street lighting did not come until 1881. Discussions on the desirability of installing gas lighting took place at the annual Vestry meeting in 1856, 1865 and 1875. On the last occasion the press reported that "proceedings were of a very disorderly nature". The proposal was carried by fifty-eight votes to nineteen, but it was another six years before any good came of it, while the church's lamp still shone in solitary and appropriate splendour.

A public subscription relieved the burden on the rates, and twenty-five lamps were installed. They were to be lit at dusk until 11 o'clock, 12 on Saturdays, 10.30 on Sundays; but not at all on moonlight nights. (They were in fact lit on 122 of 182 nights from November to May). In 1888 the Vestry voted £40 to pay for a year's lighting, and the "lighting season" was decreed to be 5 September to 12 May.

John Shell, for many years the lamplighter, is well remembered by old residents, who tell how into advanced age it was his habit to run between one lamp and the next. About 1900 he earned 8s a week at this task.

Electricity

Electricity came to Batheaston about 1925.

Pl. 24. Coronation of Edward VII, 1902. Commemorative tree planting
(The lamplighter can be seen holding hat on left of picture)

Chapter 7

Notable Houses,
Families and Persons

I think we might have a volume on the Historic Houses of Batheaston.

MRS. L. WHEATCROFT

S. CATHERINE'S COURT

The group formed by the Court, Church and tithe barn is pleasing from any aspect, and is nobly set in S. Catherine's valley. The stone-tiled Court retains internally relics of the grange which belonged to Bath Abbey, and which may date from the time of Prior Cantlow in the late fifteenth century. The oldest feature visible externally is the fine north front (Pl. 26). The masonry of the eastern half is uncoursed and appears to be late mediaeval. The porch, of ashlar, an addition of 1610, and the western half of the front may come from the same time, with new windows inserted in the eastern half to correspond.

The house was much altered and enlarged in succeeding centuries, the last additions, the library, and the orangery, being of the present century. A terraced garden with a magnificent yew hedge believed to have been planted by William Blanchard in 1610 enhances the picturesque scene.

The history of the Court's owners is outlined in the account of the manor of Easton and Catherine (p. 13).

NORTHEND HOUSE, MIDDLESEX HOUSE AND FISHERS

Northend House (now Eagle Cottages) a fine building (Pl. 27) is difficult to date. The stonework would be consistent with 1642 (p. 76), but if this is John Fisher's mansion the vertical oval windows in the gables must be insertions, for they are characteristic of the late seventeenth century and early eighteenth. The same applies to the sundial. The house was much altered internally about 1710–1715, and the western annexe was probably built at this time.

The porch of Middlesex House (Pl. 28) is dated 1670, and the house as a whole is consistent with this date. The front has three steep gables, each with a vertical oval window. The house has been much disfigured by later alterations.

For more than 200 years the prosperous Fishers (there were humble Fishers in the village) were mighty in Batheaston, equalled only by the Walters. Whether they derived from the Richard Fisher who paid the Lay Subsidy in 1499 Thomas, perhaps his son, who paid 7s 4d rent in Batheaston and S. Catherine in 1539 and the Lay Subsidy in 1545, or the John Fisher of Hampton who leased the manorial mill in 1566, cannot be determined.

The head of the family was always John.

John Fisher d. 1615
|
John Fisher d. 1626
|
John Fisher 1613–1684
|
John Fisher d. 1710
|
John Fisher d. 1749
|
John Fisher 1696–1765
|
John Fisher
|
John Fisher d. 1827, aged 53.

It is remarkable that the parish register yields such incomplete information about them.

The first John was well established before the end of the sixteenth century, holding of John Harington a copyhold which included common for 100 sheep on Holts Down. He was a freeholder

75

Pl. 25.   Tithe Barn (behind house,) Church and Court

too, and in 1598 with Thomas Blanchard contested the extent of the right of common in their freehold lands of Robert Pile and Thomas Stockes.[1] He could have been the John Fisher of Hampton mentioned above.

The second John added substantial possessions. At his death in 1625 he was the owner of nine properties, eight in Batheaston, one in Tatwick (p. 139). His Batheaston holdings amounted to about 300 acres, between a quarter and a fifth of the agricultural land of the parish. Among them was "the Seven Acres, at North End" (Map 2, B99); this is the earliest mention of Northend that has been noted. He was described as a clothier, and the wardship of his son John was sold to Francis Fisher for £20. His widow, Edith, was rated for the main holding until 1631, when her place on the list was taken by Mr. John Chapman, followed by John

Smith to 1641. The next year, 1642, the third John, now aged twenty-nine, paid a somewhat larger rate "for his means (mansion) at North End". This suggests that the young heir had built North-end House for himself. That the family held it is certain. This John also prospered, and by his will, dated 1681, disposed of sundry properties elsewhere, as well as in Batheaston. Among the overseers of his will was named "my kinsman, Mr. Edward Midell-sett of Warminster", an obvious clue to the origin of the name Middlesex House.

The next John Fisher, in 1665 "John Fisher the younger", bought "the New Mill" for £105 (p. 144). This was the manorial mill on the brook below the church, adapted for grist and fulling, and he was evidently trading as a clothier. Near by, in 1670, he built Middlesex House. The initials J.F. on one side of the entrance porch, and a blank shield on the other, suggest that he was at the time unmarried. He may have moved to Northend House after his father's death, for William Harford "of Middlesex", was churchwarden in 1698.

Both houses remained in the family through the eighteenth century. About 1719 Northend, as it was generally called, seems to have belonged jointly to the John of the period and his brother Francis, the latter also holding Church Farm (The Farm, p. 140). From 1750 "the occupiers of Northend", unnamed, were rated, until in 1768 William Fisher was in possession, presumably he who died in 1777, leaving a large progeny; a memorial of this branch of the family is on the south wall of the chancel. In 1789 his son William owned Northend House, the occupant being named Cowles.

The senior branch of the family, John following John, continued to live at Middlesex House. From the third John onwards they assumed the title "gentlemen". There seems to have been some doubt of their accepted status, though, for when in 1750 John Fisher was fined forty shillings for swearing twenty oaths he was described as "yeoman",

and fined at the rate laid down for yeomen (p. 65), but the entry adds "commonly called Mr John Fisher". The Fishers were hearty swearers, for in 1751 John "the Younger" paid for "six prophane Curses" at 5s od each, the rate for a gentleman, and two years later "30 profane Oaths" cost William £7 10s (p. 65). This was not the end of their misdemeanours, for in 1793 his son "Mr Thos Fisher being a Fine in Drunkenness" paid 5s.

By this time the family, though still wealthy, was declining, and thenceforth makes little appearonce in parish life. The last John died in 1827, probably childless. Middlesex House was then let to one Jonathan Ettell, a market gardener, but by 1836 the widow, Mrs. Jane Fisher, was in residence again, and continued until her death about 1863, her sister, Mrs. Sarah Price, the last proprietor of the mill on the brook below, living with her. Since then, Middlesex House has had a number of owners.

The later history of Northend House is obscure. At some date unknown the original house and the eighteenth century additions to it were divided into four dwellings, the present Eagle Cottages.

Pl. 26. North Front of S. Catherine's Court

Pl. 27. Northend House
(drawing by Peter Coard)

Each John Fisher in his turn served the parish offices, and their signatures may be seen on many records of Vestry and other meetings, but their influence on parish life, apart from their power as landowners, was far less than that of the Walters family; this is remembered, that is forgotten.

PINE HOUSE, PANTONS AND CLOTHIERS

Pine House (Pl. 29) is of coursed rubble. The earliest portion has two gables facing the street, two-light mullioned windows and a two-storey porch of ashlar, with the date 1672, which is consistent with the character of the building. Additions comprise an eighteenth century wing to the north, with an elegant cornice, and at right angles to it a wing which probably dates from the time when the house was used by clothiers.

The porch bears the initials $_R^P{}_M$. They belong to Richard Panton and Mary his wife. The arrangement was a common convention, used also on trade tokens (p. 145). The origin of the family is uncertain:

in the records of the seventeenth century the name is written Pontin, Ponton, Ponting, as well as Panton, and there is no knowing how many families were concerned. Between 1620 and 1641 the overseers' rate list clearly transforms Richard Ponting into Richard Panton, and he may have been the father of the builder of Pine House; the latter signed himself indifferently, while his son Charles was Ponton at his baptism, Pantan at his burial, and Panton in his epitaph.

Richard Panton was a medical man, and according to the epitaph on his monument, now in the vestry, was as successful in his treatment of the mentally afflicted as of the physically sick

Epitaphium

In funus Domini Richardi Panton,
Eximii peritissimique medici,
Qui desiit mori decimo sexto die
Septembris, anno Domini 1684.
Alter en Hypocrates jacet inferiore sub urna,
Qui modo Pantoniae gloria stirpis erat.

Aegros sanavit non solum: sed furiosos
Ingenio veteri reddidit ille viros.
Nobilis ars, fortuna, genus, patientia, virtus,
Singula sunt paucis; sed data cuncta tibi.

His son Charles was born at Batheaston, 23 April 1662, and died 30 August 1711, probably during an epidemic (p. 60). Of Lincoln College, Oxford, he was B.A. in 1682, and Extra Licentiate of the Royal College of Physicians in 1686.[2] According to this source, he succeeded to his father's practice. He appears in the church rate of 1687-1688 as Dr. Panton. If his epitaph is to be trusted, he, too, was a learned physician, and no less an amiable character: ". . .

Pl. 28. Middlesex House porch

amans erat maritus indulgensque pater bonus vicinus, vir justus, in pauperes benignus, vereque pius domi et ecclesiae venerator".

After his death his widow, Cecilia, always referred to in lists, uniquely, as Madam Panton, resided in the parish, a prosperous widow, until her death in 1744. Of their four daughters, three died young, Cecilia in 1712, aged twenty-one, Betty in 1716, aged twenty-six (her funeral slab is near the doorway to the vestry). Ann, widow of Isaac Selfe, of Melksham, in 1740, aged thirty-four, "after a long illness, fatal to her sisters".[3] Mary, the eldest, baptised in 1687, makes no further appearance.

Piecing together the evidence of parish records, particularly the order of names on rating lists, and the amount charged, it is probable that Madam Panton sold Pine House to James Walters, son of the first Henry Walters (p. 81). The *Gloucester Journal*, 23 January 1739, contains this advertisement:

> To let, house at Batheaston, with dyehouse and store, long used as a clothier's. Enquire of Mr James Walters in Batheaston.

Dyehouse Lane and Dyehouse Bridge figure in the Highway records of the period, and by elimination must be the passage which runs through the out-buildings of Pine House and the bridge over the brook at its lower end. (Map 1, 24).

James Walters married Mary Clement, daughter of Thomas Clement, gentleman. James Walters died in 1739, and in 1742 his widow married Thomas Drewett, a drugget maker of Colerne. A reference to his "Mansion House situate in Batheaston lying opposite the church"[4] proves his association with Pine House. His widow outlived him to 1770, and in 1764 paid tax for forty-three windows which still exist.

Their son Samuel was described in the Jury List of 1787 as "clothier, infirm".

The *Bath Chronicle*, 4 September 1856 reported the visit of the British Archaeological Association, when the pine tree in the garden of Mr. Rawlison, who at this time occupied Pine House, was much admired. "The respected vicar told the company that it was known to be upwards of 300 years old and that the Marquis of Lansdowne's gardener had paid it a visit to include it in a work on pines". The venerable tree (one must be sceptical about its great age in the absence of evidence), perished soon

Pl. 29.   Pine House, east front
(drawing by Peter Coard)

afterwards, for Mrs. Wheatcroft, writing in 1899, noted that Henry B. Inman, who had the house when she visited the village, planted the splendid Wellingtonia, which still thrives, from a pot thirty years before i.e. about 1869.

BATHEASTON HOUSE AND THE WALTERS

Batheaston House (1712) is faced with ashlar, and keeps its stone-tiled roof. Evidence of an older house is retained in the basement. The main front looks south to the river Avon, and still shews the features depicted so delightfully in the eighteenth century. (Pl. 30.)

Much of the material on which this account is based is taken from *The Personal Life and Family History and Pedigree of John Eldad Walters*. (Privately printed 1882.) It includes quotations from two documents, now apparently lost, said to have been found in the chancel of Batheaston church. The first, dated 1732, was signed by the elder Henry Walters; the second, 1775, by Henry his son.

The story of the Walters family in Batheaston, a story of unofficial "squiredom" for nearly 200 years, begins with Eldad (1640–1706), son of Edmond Walters, gentleman, of Piercefield, Monmouthshire, who came to Batheaston to learn the clothing trade. His name first appears as Eldad Watores, in 1665, when he was chosen as overseer, though he is not previously recorded as paying the poor rate. He prospered, and by 1684 was designated Mr., an unusual distinction at that time. Thrice married, his first wife is only known to have been named Elizabeth, and of Bristol. The second, Mary, was a daughter of Henry Blanchard, of Batheaston, a clothier, probably the one who was churchwarden in 1649. The document of 1732 described him as "an eminent clothier in his time, though he did not get much money". Eldad and Mary had at least eleven children. She died in May 1685, two young sons following her within a fortnight. He married in 1694 Rebecca, daughter of Thomas Blanchard, descendant of William Blanchard, who had bought the Hill Farm (p. 25, Map 1, 14) as well as the manor of Easton and Catherine. Thomas was in possession of the Hill Farm, and having no son, Rebecca brought the property, together with the lease of the parsonage and the advowson of Batheaston (p. 24), into the Walters family.

Eldad Walters' funeral slab may be seen in the central aisle of the church, the inscription partly illegible. In 1888 it seems, during a sequestration, the churchwardens had the coat of arms cut out and destroyed, and the space filled with cement, because it wore out the matting!

His son Henry (1667–1753), followed his father as a clothier. He succeeded to the property of his grandfather, Henry Blanchard, including a house on the site of Batheaston House. This he demolished and on the foundations built the present house. He also bought the Cold Bath Farm (Map 1, 18), where Elmhurst now stands. This Henry Walters was Justice of the Peace for Somerset and Wiltshire in 1714 and High Sheriff for Somerset in 1715. From his time to that of his great-grandson Melmoth, practically every document or transaction of any importance pertaining to Batheaston bears the signature of a Walters, almost invariably at the head if others had occasion to sign. Uniquely powerful in the community, the Walters were generally beneficent.

The second Henry (1722–1797) had neither trade nor profession. A Justice of the Peace and Lieutenant Colonel of the Somerset Militia, he kept a large establishment and a coach-and-four, and added to Batheaston House two wings. The fine barn behind Elmhurst, now a dwelling, originally belonging to

Pl. 30.   *Batheaston House, c. 1750*
(*from a painting in the possession of the Walters family*)

*Pl. 31.   Pitching Hole—stable of Batheaston House
(drawing by Peter Coard)*

Cold Bath Farm, bears his initials and the date 1750. The parish records interested him, and it may well be owing to him that so much was preserved. Some documents bear notes in his hand, and occasional observations of interest.

His son, Thomas (1757–1847) was educated at Winchester and Christ Church, Oxford. Between 1812 and 1817 he sold the Cold Bath Farm (which was then dismembered) and other property, to pay the cost of reducing the size of Batheaston House by removing the wings built by his father, and redeeming Land Tax. His finances were embarrassed, too, by buying up a long lease of Hill Farm. which had been granted "on improvident terms". He joined the Coal Company (p. 146) and lost money in that. His fortunes declined so much that it needed a legacy to his wife to add to the comfort of their last years by keeping an open one-horse carriage. His wife's devotion to the Female Benefit Club is commemorated on the wall of the north aisle (p. 68).

Melmoth (1793–1868), the last of the Batheaston Walters, was a barrister practising in Bath and a bachelor. He gave much time to village affairs, and was probably somewhat autocratic. Among other activities he revived the practice of perambulating the parish bounds and left full accounts of strenuous circuits, each occupying two days, between 1823 and 1835 (pp. 4, 66). An earnest evangelical churchman, the monograph tells us that "the Lord's Day Society especially engaged his vigorous mind and energies". He was a churchwarden for thirty-four years. Ripples of the Oxford Movement reaching Batheaston encountered his determined opposition (p. 43). He was a generous benefactor to both church and school, giving land for the rebuilding of the latter, as well as money (p. 119) and a Melmoth Walters Prize. The parish records which his grandfather had cherished interested him also, and his handwriting becomes very familiar to the student of them. Less acceptable was his gift of a deed of 1535, the second oldest belonging to the parish, to the British Museum! (p. 24).

This minute was recorded in 1866:

The Parish in Vestry assembled desire to express their deep regret at the retirement of M. Walters Esq. from the Office of Churchwarden, and to record their grateful sense of his unwearied kindness and courtesy in fulfilling the duties of the office throughout the long period during which he has held it.

After the death of Melmoth Walters the family sold the Hill Farm, Batheaston House remaining their property until 1921, when it was sold on the death of Mrs. Pagden, a tenant of many years, and a generous friend to the village.

After a time the house suffered a period of neglect and became sadly dilapidated. Thanks to the enthusiasm of its present owners it has been restored to its former beauty.

EAGLE HOUSE, THE WOODS AND THE BLATHWAYTS

The common belief that John Wood, senior, first and greatest planner of Georgian Bath, built Eagle House is easily disproved. The west wall of the early building bears the date 1724, under the initials

Pl. 32. *Eagle House (drawing by Peter Coard)*

S.C.; but Wood came to Bath in 1727. Mowbray E. Green, the architect who designed the upper storey built in 1906–1908 over a western extension of the house, was much interested in Eagle House, as containing some of Wood's earliest work in Bath, and he drew attention to its importance in his *Eighteenth Century Architecture of Bath*. He was especially impressed by the doorway, of which he wrote a detailed description.[5] The account which follows owes much to his observations.

The house is faced with rubble, suggesting an origin not later than the seventeenth century. The courses below the eaves and most of the east wall are of ashlar, perhaps dating from the insertion of the eighteenth century windows. Whether this was the work of Wood or of S.C. is uncertain. Confidently attributed to Wood are the main doorway and the embellishments of the east wall, dated 1729. The crowned head on the keystone of the doorway is supposed to represent Queen Caroline, the wife of George II. Green wrote:

> "The house appears to have been altered at three different times. The ground was originally much lower than at present, and the old doorway stood immediately under this one, but the house was probably altered in 1724, and Wood also made some improvements when he came to reside about 1729, among them this doorway and probably the shell-headed recess and the eagle surmounting the front towards the road. It was his first home in Bath, but he did not stay long, moving afterwards to 15 Queen Square".

The identity of S.C. is not known, but the only Batheastonian of the period of suitable status who bore those initials was Samuel Clement, the brother of Thomas (p. 79). He died in 1728, a date which well fits the arrival of Wood the next year, and directed that his body "be decently buried in the parish church of Batheaston under the seat or pew I usually sit in, and a marble monument (not a large one) in the window above the said seat or pew". It may still be seen.

Obscurity surrounds the later association of the Woods with Batheaston. Their name appears in no rating list, and neither of them served a parish office. We have Collinson's authority that the younger Wood lived in Northend, and that of his

Pl. 33.   Doorway of Eagle House

obituary[6] that he died at Batheaston. The name appears but once in the parish records, in 1776, when "Mr Wood's butler" was in trouble with the overseers about a bastardy.

For the next hundred years there is nothing of importance to record of Eagle House. In the year 1882, Lieut-Colonel Linley Blathwayt, whose father had been rector of Langridge, and who had retired after long service in India, bought the house, with $4\frac{1}{2}$ acres, and came to reside there with his wife, Mary his young daughter, and William, his infant son. The family were earnest diarists—one could almost say obsessive—solemnly recording the events of each day, however trivial. This curious habit produced a huge collection of volumes which contains material for a detailed reconstruction of the life and milieu of a leisured Batheaston family during sixty years, and illuminates, too, village life and customs in their humbler aspects. The diaries alone are a cause for thankfulness to the local historian, but there is much more. Linley Blathwayt, a man of acute mind and many interests, and a scrupulous recorder of his observations, was notable in several fields. An entomologist of distinction, he contributed the section on Insects, except Lepidoptera, to the *Victoria County History of Somerset*. A large proportion of his specimens were attributed to Batheaston. An enthusiastic photographer, he followed up every advance in the subject, and was experimenting with microphotography and colour photography in the early years of the century. His studies of eminent suffragettes have fortunately survived.

The first motor car in Batheaston was his, a 6 H.P. Oldsmobile, costing £150, registered F.B.46 on 18 January 1904, and many were his adventures in this machine. There are those still living who recall with relish the gangs of urchins who lay in

Pl. 35.   *The first motor car in Batheaston*

wait for his return from Bath, trusting that his engine would fail on Penthouse Hill, in the sure expectation of sixpence apiece when their united labours took him to the summit. Nevertheless, and in spite of constant mishaps, within a few months of taking up motoring he covered the thirty miles from Marlborough in two and a half hours. The pioneer machine was known to the family as Bodo, and served until 1911. Meanwhile, in 1906, a second car, made in Bedford, was obtained and named Dodo.

A Fellow of the Linnean Society, he laid out at Eagle House a garden in which he grew and propagated plants not commonly seen, as well as more usual subjects.

About 1905 he became interested in the women's suffrage movement, which from then until the events of 1914 brought a truce in the battle occupied much time for himself, his wife and daughter. Mary Blathwayt was busy in such activities as handing out leaflets, chalking slogans on pavements, organising and attending meetings; but the Blathwayt women never joined the militants. Eagle House received a long succession of visitors about the business of the Cause, as well as women released from prison after hunger strikes. Then Linley had the idea of inviting prominent suffragettes to plant each a tree in the upper part of his garden—conifers for members of the Women's Social and Political Union, hollies for lesser followers. Between April 1909 and July 1911 at least forty-seven trees were

Pl. 34.   *The Eagle*
(*from a photograph by Linley Blathwayt, 1904*)

planted, and his diary records seventeen different named conifers. It was his practice to have made for each one a plaque recording the planter, the tree and the date. Nearly all the famous names were there—Despard, Fawcett, the Pankhursts. The following entries come from Mrs. Blathwayt's diary:

22 April 1909. First tree planting. Lady C. (Constance Lytton) shewed how she was first prejudiced against militant methods till gradually step by step she found she must go to prison herself. I suppose future generations will give honour to these noble people. When the Cause becomes the fashion we shall have the stupid people in it.

23 April. Beautiful day for the planting and L. photographed the three in a group at each tree. Annie (Kenney) put in the West one, Mrs P. (Pethick) Lawrence, South, and Lady Constance the East.

7 February 1918. The Reform Bill passed yesterday ... Women cannot vote before the age of thirty. Wives of men entitled to vote can vote as well as women in their own right and university women also have the franchise. L. has a telegram from Lillian Forrester "Greetings. Votes for women". L. and I walked through the trees this afternoon and wondered how quietly this had come at last, but the war occupies all our thoughts.

Pl. 36.   First tree planting (see text)
(Left to right:
Annie Kenney, Lady Constance Lytton
and Mrs. Pethick Lawrence)

The Blathwayts were predictably concerned to promote cultural interests in the village. In 1909, for example, a course of lectures "for the village people" received this mention in Linley's diary: "My lecture on spiders. Worked up from spiders in geological times, bringing in Mr Scott White's Primitive Man and Mr Downes' coming astronomy lecture, and about the infinite, finishing by saying with the ancients 'Light, more light'." During the session the vicar lectured also on Insect Mimicry and Dr Moorhead on Bacteria. The women of the family contributed to the cause of education by giving lessons on the violin and on French to village children. Mrs. Blathwayt added to her benevolence by arranging dental care for a number of children at her own charge. The fourth member of the family, William, wrote slight verses and published them in several volumes.

Linley Blathwayt lived until 1919, Mrs. Blathwayt until 1939. Their son and daughter lived on at Eagle House, where Mary, the last survivor, died in 1962. The upkeep of the house had been neglected of late years, and work on it was an urgent need. What very nearly took place, the destruction of this fine and historical house, is scarcely credible.

"Eagle House, Batheaston, a 'listed building', once the home of the Woods, may be pulled down. At their meeting last night, the City Council agreed with a Planning Committee recommendation that they could 'see no objection' to the demolition of the building ... The committee had gone into the question of whether or not it was a practicable proposition to preserve the house, and it had been decided that it was not. They were now backing up Somerset County Council by informing them that 'this is not a piece of practical preservation'."[7]

Happily, this huge mistake was not the end, for the house found an enlightened purchaser who had no great difficulty in making a sympathetic and thorough restoration, and in consequence this important building still graces the village scene.

The greater part of the land was sold separately, and consigned to "development". It is discreditable that when it was prepared for building the machines which destroyed the suffragettes' trees—the arboretum was by this time sadly overgrown—blithely smashed the remaining plaques.

BATHEASTON VILLA

Batheaston Villa (Pl. 37), a not greatly distinguished building of the eighteenth century, is a listed house under the Town and Country Planning Act 1947, largely because of its literary associations. Its most striking feature, on the south side, that towards the Avon valley, is a large bow window, the height of the house, battlemented, the upper storey with a balcony supported on wooden Corinthian columns, and having a neat iron railing. The entrance, on the north side, has a porch with four Ionic columns.

In the garden is a pretty little rotunda, its dome supported on eight Roman Doric columns. It has associations with Lady Miller's gatherings.

LADY MILLER AND HER CULT

About the year 1772, there returned from a tour of Italy a Captain, later Sir John, Miller and his wife, bringing as a memento of their travels a marble vase found not long before near Cicero's villa. The home of the Millers was Batheaston Villa, of which Horace Walpole wrote in a letter of 1766:[8] "They have a small new-built house, with a bow window, directly opposite to which the Avon falls in a wide cascade, a church behind it in a vale, into which two mountains descend, leaving an opening into the distant country. A large village, with houses for gentry, is on one of the hills to the left. Their garden is little, but pretty, and watered with several small rivulets among the bushes. Meadows fall down to the road; and above, the garden is terminated by another view of the river, the city and the mountains. 'Tis a very diminutive principality with large pretensions". The last sentence suggests a foretaste of what was to come.

Lady Miller, aspiring to fame as a patroness of letters, and holding a not lowly opinion of her own literary merit, was for several years the presiding goddess of a cult which achieved considerable notoriety at the time, and even a tiny niche, though not as the lady intended, in the history of English literature. At Batheaston Villa the Millers provided a weekly entertainment for the poets and poetasters visiting or living in Bath, the *sine qua non* for admission to the circle being strict social acceptability and propriety. The meetings were held in the morning, and are well recollected in the contemporary

Pl. 37. Batheaston Villa, the bow window

descriptions, comments, and specimens of poesy which this account contains.

At first the contestants were to complete a set of rhymes handed out the previous week, a device recently imported from France, and called "bouts rimés". Later, a subject upon which verses were to be written was announced. Always the destination was the same—the marble vase that could have been Cicero's; thence to be conveyed into an adjoining room, and submitted to judgement. The "prize" being then bestowed upon him who might aptly be called Victor Ludorum, a cold collation, said by some irreverent to be the best part of the entertainment, was consumed, and everyone returned to Bath.

Lady Miller inspired more wit outside her circle than within it, but if notoriety was her aim, she achieved it. Everyone knew about the Batheaston

Vase. London society laughed at her pretensions, the press could be very scathing, the offerings to the vase were mostly of little worth. Nevertheless, besides the scribblers and foolish idlers of Bath this vulgar, if kind-hearted woman attracted others whose literary merit exceeded the best that she could fairly hope to capture. Garrick and Anstey (of the *New Bath Guide*) contributed, and whether or not Sheridan wrote for the vase, he mentioned her in the printed dedication of the *School for Scandal*.

Four volumes of *Poetical Amusements at a Villa near Bath* were published between 1775 and 1781. They were sold to benefit the Bath Pauper Charity, of which Sir John was president, and the first volume was sold out within ten days of publication. Lady Miller herself was the anonymous editor. Perhaps the worst that can be said of her is that she had an unrestrained appetite for flattery, and no sense of satiety. Page after page is filled with absurd adulation of Lady Miller, and the fact that she published it proves how voraciously she gobbled it.

From time to time a less reverent tone, even a touch of satire, crept into the vase, and doubtless many of her guests were secretly laughing at her foolishness and vanity, but the story that some licentious lines sullying the purity of the vase brought the meetings to an abrupt end, finally and for ever, cannot be true, for Lady Miller was editing yet a fifth volume at the time of her sudden death, and there is nothing to suggest that a final adjournment had taken place.[9]

In 1773, Walpole wrote:

"You must know, that near Bath is erected a new Parnassus, composed of three laurels, a myrtle tree, a weeping willow, and a view of the Avon, which has now been christened Helicon". To him also we owe an oft-quoted account: "They hold a Parnassus fair every Thursday, give out rhymes and themes, and all the flux of quality at Bath contend for the prizes. A Roman vase, dressed with pink ribands and myrtles, receives the poetry, which is drawn out every festival; six judges of these Olympic games retire and select the brightest compositions, which the respective successful acknowledge, kneel to Mrs Calliope, kiss her fair hand, and are crowned by it with myrtle—with I don't know what. You

may think this a fiction, or exaggeration. Be dumb, unbelievers! The collection is printed, published—yes, on my faith! there are bouts-rimés on a buttered muffin by her Grace the Duchess of Northumberland ... many by Mrs M. herself, that have no fault but wanting metre; and immortality promised to her without end or

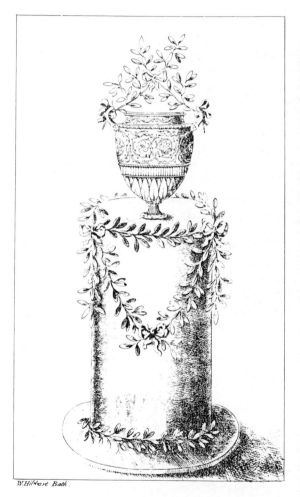

W. Hibbart Bath.

Pl. 38. *The Roman vase at Batheaston Villa* ("Poetical amusements")

measure. In short, since folly, which never ripens to madness but in this climate, ran distracted, there never was anything so entertaining, or so dull".

Johnson's opinion was predictable. Though his friends the Thrales visited the Millers, there is no record that he met them during his visit to Bath, but Boswell preserved this conversation:

"Lady Miller's collection of verses by fashionable people, which were put into the Vase at Batheaston Villa, near Bath, being mentioned, he held them very cheap: 'Bouts rimés' said he 'is a mere conceit, and an old conceit now; I wonder how many people were persuaded to write in that manner for this lady'. I named a gentleman of his acquaintence who wrote for the Vase. Johnson: 'He was a blockhead for his pains' ".

The Reverend Richard Graves, a man of letters of some merit, and rector of Claverton for fifty-five years, wrote "I counted one morning above fifty carriages drawn up in a line from Bath Easton, towards Lambridge; and was at one time present at it, with four duchesses, the duchess of Cumberland, Northumberland, Ancaster and Beaufort".[10]

Here are some specimens of the verses contributed to the pastime which attracted so much attention; first, one of the bouts rimés:

To hail thy wished return, delightful	Spring!
Behold how fair a train their chaplets	bring!
Blythe as the feather's songsters, warbling	free,
Who own thy genial power on every	tree;
Soft as thy zephyr's wings, when balmy	rains
Have scattered fragrance o'er the smiling	plains;
Oh! ne'er while these adorn the grove and	field,
Shall fair BATHEASTON to Arcadia	yield

Also in the first volume appears:

A New Ballad

Ye belles, ye beaux, ye wits and all,
From concert, cotillon, and ball,
Come, come with me, attend the call
Of Miller, at Batheaston.

The eighth—and last—verse:

But hither, prythee, hither flee,
Ye Muses nine, and Graces three,
And follow, follow, follow me
To Miller, at Batheaston!

On one occasion the subject set was Simplex Munditiis. It produced this *jeu d'esprit*:

Simplex Munditiis is the word.
Thus, Miller spoke, the poet heard,
And turn'd, and turn'd it o'er again,

Yet to no purpose rack'd his brain;
He found the Latin was too hard,
To be express'd by English bard,
As thus he sought how to translate,
And bit his nails, and scratch's his pate:
Egad! cries he, I've found it out,
The fair one sure thought me a lout,
Not to perceive the cunning elf
By Simp. Munditiis meant herself.

One more specimen, from volume three:

An Offering to the Urn
Lord N— ————t.

Why range o'er Bath in useless search, to find
Whatever charms the sense and soothes the mind?
While all that Love can wish, and Reason feast on,
Is in this Circle found, at sweet Batheaston.

Among satirical verses written at this time, not as contributions to the vase, were the following, attributed to Garrick by the Reverend Francis Kilvert, when addressing the Literary and Philosophic Association in 1858:

Miller! the urn, in ancient times, 'tis said,
Held the collected ashes of the dead;
So thine, this wonder of our modern days
Stands open day and night for lifeless lays.
Leave not unfinished, then, the well-formed plan,
Complete the work thy classic taste began,
And O! in future, ere thou dost inurn 'em,
First raise the pile funereal, and—burn 'em!

Fanny Burney described Lady Miller as "a round, plump coarse-looking dame of about forty, and while all her aim is to appear an elegant woman of fashion, all her success is to seem an ordinary woman in very common life, with fine clothes on. Her movements are bustling, her air is mock-important, and her manners inelegant". She added, though, "So much for the lady of Bath-Easton; who, however, seems extremely good-natured, and who is, I am sure, extremely civil".[11]

She died in 1781, aged 40, and it is perhaps only fair to her to quote a little of the eulogy which appeared in *The Gentleman's Magazine* with the announcement of her death. "The wealthy and the indigent will have equal cause of regret; for she did not study to enlarge and multiply the elegant entertainments of the former, with more assiduity than she sought occasion to administer to the comforts of the latter ... Few persons in the county of Somerset could be less spared, by the sons of riches or poverty, to an early tomb; nor will any be more sincerely lamented by both". Exaggerated language, no doubt, but she must have had the merit of a kind heart, and perhaps this outweighs her silliness.

According to a note written inside the front cover of volume one in the set of the Poetical Amusements belonging to Bath Reference Library the original vase was presented to the Bath Park Committee by Mr. Edwyn Dowding in 1865. What became of it is unknown, and Lady Miller is all but forgotten; not quite, though, for she has the distinction of a mention in the *Cambridge History of English Literature*, where she is identified by W. H. Hutton as "the undoubted original of Mrs Leo Hunter".

Long after Lady Miller Batheaston Villa had another brief moment of respectable notoriety, when Mrs. Tollemache, a clergyman's widow, and a keen suffragette, refused to pay income tax. The Commissioners raided Batheaston Villa, seized a pair of entrée dishes, a cruet set and a cream jug, and offered them for sale at the White Hart. The first and only bid, of £23, was made by a friend, and as the claim was only about £20 the farce shortly ended with the buyer presenting to Mrs. Tollemache her own silver. A number of prominent suffragettes carrying banners NO VOTE NO TAX attended, and afterwards held a protest meeting on a wagon outside the Lamb and Flag, when Mrs. Tollemache's daughter said that her mother had refused to pay the taxes because she had no voice in the way these taxes were spent. Taxation without representation was tyranny.[12]

OTHER NOTABLE HOUSES

The Street of Batheaston has Vienstown House (Pl. 39), an interesting building, its external features dating probably from the early years of the eighteenth century. Nothing of its history has been discovered; a likely guess is that one of the clothiers built it. A drawing of 1868 by J. T. Irvine, clerk of works to Sir George Gilbert Scott, shews it already with a little shop window (Pl. 1).

Number 2 The Batch (Pl. 40) is a house of some distinction, which fortunately can be dated. In the

Pl. 39. Vienstown House
(drawing by Peter Coard)

lefthand (southern) gable is an inscription which can just be made out—the letter M, following a letter which has disappeared, and below, the date 1727. In a short time this clue will have quite decayed.

At the extreme north of S. Catherine is the Grey House, previously S. Catherine's End Farm, a pleasing building of the *genre* of Pine and Middlesex Houses, with oval windows in the two gables, and retaining its stone tiles. The front is more or less symmetrical, but the masonry of the north-west corner of the ground floor is older, and may be co-eval with the barn, built by Thomas Sallmon (p. 18) and dated 1617. The rest of the front is probably of the very early eighteenth century.

At least four farmhouses from the seventeenth century still stand. Radford (Pl. 41) is perhaps in part of the first half of the century. The masonry is uncoursed. J. T. Irvine, who sketched it in 1865 noted that the latticed windows were removed soon afterwards. The old Church Farmhouse, now Church Cottage, is of similar style and period.

Upper Northend Farmhouse, the only one still in use as a farmhouse, probably dates from about 1630, though part of the north side of the front may be a rebuilding. It has an attic in a dormer gable, and a variation in the form of a gabled porch the height of the house.

Lower Northend Farmhouse (Pl. 42) is of three periods, of which the portion to the left, i.e. next the road, may be the earliest. The centre portion is probably before 1630, the right wing of the early eighteenth century.

Many new houses accompanied the expansion of the eighteenth century. There are at least fifty mansard roofs in Batheaston. The late eighteenth century saw Bailbrook House (previously Lodge). It has two blocks of two storeys, each façade with four large Ionic pilasters, connected by an elegant hall of one storey, with galleries and an oval lantern and externally more Ionic pilasters. It was built by John Eveleigh about 1786 for a Dr. Denham Skeet, at a cost of more than £12,000.[13] According to the same authority Eveleigh designed Camden Crescent, and was made bankrupt in the building of Grosvenor. Bailbrook House was illustrated by Collinson (1791). Its medical connections began early, for in 1812 a Dr. Barber was rated for "the Great House". The next year it was sold, with 130 acres, for £14,700. About 1819 a short episode owing to the benevolence of Lady Isabella King was described thus by Pierce Egan:[14] "a recent establishment formed for the reception of decayed ladies of respectability and high rank, under the patronage and sanction of her late Majesty". Within two years the house changed hands. About 1836 a Dr. Spry had it and established a mental hospital, mainly for private patients, but is said to have kept pauper lunatics in the basement cellars.[15] From then burials from Bailbrook House begin to appear in the parish register—there were five in eighteen days in 1840—an epidemic, evidently. Later proprietors were Dr. John Terry, who took an active part in parish life, to 1886, and Dr. Lionel Weatherley, to 1907. The house is still a Mental Hospital.

OTHER NOTABLE PERSONS

George Aust and Sarah Mayes

It is worthy of record that
GEORGE AUST
A pauper boy indebted for his early
education to HELLIER'S CHARITY
rose by the blessing of God on his
diligence and good Conduct to the
high and honourable offices of under
Secretary of State, Commissary
General of Musters, and Secretary
and Registrar of the Royal Hospital Chelsea.
He was born in the year 1740, and died
Feby 11 1825, in the 86th year of his age.
'Seest thou a man diligent in his business
He shall stand before Kings' Proverbs 22 29.
His second Wife was the Honourable
Mrs W. MURRAY, formerly SARAH MAIZE
born of humble parents in the Fosse Lane
in this Parish, Authoress of a
treatise on EDUCATION.
The outline of the romantic story may be read,
the cynosure of innocents, on a gilt-lettered board

Pl. 40. No. 2 The Batch
(drawing by J. T. Irvine)

Pl. 41.   Radford
(drawing by Peter Coard)

in the big schoolroom of Batheaston, almost certainly placed there by Melmoth Walters. The harvest of a search of possible sources enables some expansion of the account.

In the year 1738 the overseers paid 2s to Thomas Aust "for writing the account"; this is his first appearance in the records of Batheaston. The next year, 1739, on 30 June, Thomas Aust and Anne Low were married in Batheaston Church. Anne, daughter of the Rev. George Lowe, rector of Claverton, was baptised there 2 December 1709. Her father died when she was in her tenth year.

The young couple went to Corsham, where George, their eldest child, born 6 February 1741, was baptised 22 March. In 1747, Anne Aust, with George and three younger children, was removed as a pauper from Corsham to Batheaston, on the grounds that her husband, having served for five

or six years as a covenant servant to Henry Walters, had gained a settlement there, which laid on Batheaston the duty of providing for his destitute family. As to what became of Thomas Aust there is no clue; he was not buried at Corsham.

The lot of a pauper was hard, and this was Anne's. The 11s paid by the overseers for carrying her poor bits from Corsham would not sweeten her welcome. In spite of her origin in a clerical family, her examination concerning settlement is "signed" with a **X**. The parish allowed her 4s a week, reduced to 3s in 1750, paid her rent of 35s a year, and occasionally bought clothes for the children, such as "2 pair of shoes 4s 10d, cloth to make shirts 10s 6d". In 1749 the poor woman forfeited a week's allowance for daring to appear in public not wearing the pauper's badge (p. 110).

In 1752 the family caught smallpox; all recovered,

and the cost to the parish of nursing them was £2 11s 11½d. Next year, Anne's name is not on the list of those receiving weekly pay, but she earned 4s "For Ciping of James Dancy After he Came From the Ospetol". The future was perhaps not quite such a humiliation, for she seems to have made a living lodging the Dancy boys, whose father had deserted them, and making their clothes, and the overseers helped her no more. We may hope that her remarkable son did. One more fact about her is known: on 7 February 1782 Mrs. Anne Aust

age of twenty-four. It is noteworthy that the overseers did not pay the usual premium; perhaps Henry Walters did. Batheaston sent him off with £3 10s of Gift Money, probably to buy his outfit. His indenture is endorsed in the hand of the second Henry Walters (died 1795) "George Aust has since been and still is in the Secretary of State's office and is Married to a Lady of Fortune". His career of galloping success can be traced in some detail, but of the "Lady of Fortune" and his wooing of her nothing can be found out.

Pl. 42.   Lower Northend Farmhouse
(South elevation, from a measured drawing by Peter Coard)

from Batheaston, aged seventy-three, was buried at Claverton. The title, by no means general, implies that she had achieved respected status. There is pathos in the thought of her aged body, after the hard struggle, borne across the river to rest in the churchyard she knew as a child.

It is likely that Henry Walters took an interest in George Aust, not only as a bright boy, but as the son of his old servant. He probably arranged his apprenticeship in 1752 to John Jeffery, gentleman, of Bath, to learn Writing, that is, Law, until the

In the book *The Foreign Office*[16] he is mentioned several times. In 1769 he was a clerk in the Northern Department, earning £80 a year, plus an augmentation of £70 from Post Office funds. In 1790 he became one of the two Under Secretaries in the Foreign Office, where his salary would be £500 per annum, but fees and perquisites may well have increased his emolument to more than £2000. In the view of Tilley and Gaselee, though, he "does not seem to have made much mark on the office". In 1795, apparently to make room for George

Canning, he was transferred from the Foreign Office, and became Secretary and Register of the Royal Hospital, Chelsea, appointments which he held until 1816. He was paid a salary of £500 and provided with a house and a generous supply of coal. In the *History of the Royal Hospital*[17] Captain Dean writes:

"A select Committee on Finance, which visited the Royal Hospital in 1798, during an exhaustive inquiry into every aspect of the public administration, found much to criticize. George Aust, the Secretary and Register, was also drawing over £1800 per annum as Commissary-General of the Musters. He lived in Kensington, and the only occasions on which he went to Chelsea, apart from the annual muster and monthly Board meetings, were when he drove over in his coach to collect his share of the garden produce".

On 4 November 1744, Sarah Maze, daughter of John and Elianor, was baptised in Batheaston Church; her sister Jane followed three years later. The family was not of long standing locally, but John was probably that John, son of John and Sara Mays who was baptised in 1703. (The name appears in various forms—Mays, Maze, Maize, finally Mayes.) John Mayes, who died in 1750, was never on parish "pay", but for several years had a handsome share of the Gift Money, which suggests that he was of poor health and circumstances, but of good repute. Widow Mayes, too, had a generous allocation of Gift Money, but she, also, avoided accepting regular support, and so never had the humiliation of ranking as a pauper, as Anne Aust had to do at this time. She had one of the parish houses in the Fosse Lane (Pl. 45), and was still living there in 1775.

The sources for the history of her daughter Sarah are the *Dictionary of National Biography* and *Burke's Peerage*, but of the first thirty-nine years of her life they have not a word to say. In 1783 the poor child of Batheaston reappeared in splendour as the bride of the Hon. William Murray, Captain R.N. and brother of the Earl of Dunmore, a Scottish peer. Her husband, of whom she wrote with eager praise, was then forty-nine, and this was his first marriage. After three years he died.

Mrs. Murray's contribution to English letters was not her treatise on Education which, if indeed she wrote such a work—would that she did!—was

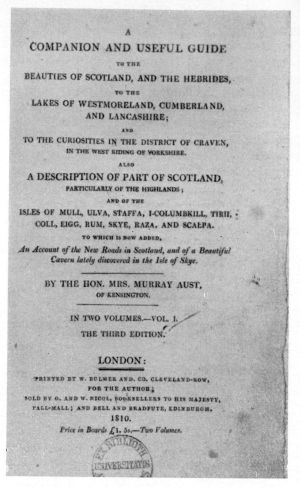

A

COMPANION AND USEFUL GUIDE

TO THE

BEAUTIES OF SCOTLAND, AND THE HEBRIDES,

TO THE

LAKES OF WESTMORELAND, CUMBERLAND, AND LANCASHIRE;

AND

TO THE CURIOSITIES IN THE DISTRICT OF CRAVEN, IN THE WEST RIDING OF YORKSHIRE.

ALSO

A DESCRIPTION OF PART OF SCOTLAND, PARTICULARLY OF THE HIGHLANDS;

AND OF THE

ISLES OF MULL, ULVA, STAFFA, I-COLUMBKILL, TIRII, COLL, EIGG, RUM, SKYE, RAZA, AND SCALPA.

TO WHICH IS NOW ADDED,

An Account of the New Roads in Scotland, and of a Beautiful Cavern lately discovered in the Isle of Skye.

BY THE HON. MRS. MURRAY AUST, OF KENSINGTON.

IN TWO VOLUMES.—VOL. I.

THE THIRD EDITION.

LONDON:

PRINTED BY W. BULMER AND. CO. CLEVELAND-ROW, FOR THE AUTHOR; SOLD BY G. AND W. NICOL, BOOKSELLERS TO HIS MAJESTY, PALL-MALL; AND BELL AND BRADFUTE, EDINBURGH. 1810. *Price in Boards £1. 5s.—Two Volumes.*

Pl. 43. Title page of "A Companion and Useful Guide"

never published, but her *Companion and Useful Guide to the Beauties of Scotland, etc.* (Pl. 43) which went to three editions between 1799 and 1810. This remarkable work related the travels of the author, this elderly widow who travelled in her own chaise many of the most inaccessible roads of Scotland, visited the finest scenery and the greatest waterfalls, for which she had insatiable enthusiasm, and many great houses, and set down her adventures and impressions in lively and entertaining prose. Her endurance was equal to her appetite for travel; necessarily, for she braved not only difficult scrambles to view sights on which her heart was set, but the disgusting hospitality of remote Highland hovels mis-called inns—though, truly, in her wisdom she

[viii]

" ce gros bon sens qui court les rues ;" I am able to relate, in my own fashion, what my eyes have seen. But you, Gentlemen, frighten me.—Should you discover faults, and faults in abundance I fear there are, be generous, as the mastiff is to the babbling lap-dog, who looks with calm dignity at the Lilliputian, passes on, and takes no notice: so that if your consciences will not permit you to give me a word of encouragement, I entreat you to be silent. On the contrary, should my child be thought in the least worthy of your approbation, I shall rejoice, and ever think myself obliged to you.

I am, Gentlemen,

with great respect,

your most obedient humble Servant,

S. MURRAY.

Kensington,
March the 30th, 1799.

Pl. 44. End of introduction to "A Companion and Useful Guide"

carried with her bedding and provisions against the intolerable worst.

Pl. 44 reproduces the end of the introduction to her first edition. Let the reader now judge for himself. The extracts are from the third edition:

Provide yourself with a strong roomy carriage, and have the springs well corded; have also a stop-pole and strong chain to the chaise. Take with you linch pins, and four shackles, which hold up the braces of the body of the carriage; a turn screw, fit for fastening the nuts belonging to the shackles; a hammer, and some straps.

For the inside of the carriage, get a light flat box, the corners must be taken off, next the doors, for the more conveniently getting in and out. This box should hang on the front of the chaise, instead of the pocket, and be as large as the whole front, and as deep as the size of the carriage will admit: the side next the travellers should fall down by hinges, at the height of their knees, to form a table on their laps, the part of the box below the hinges should be divided into holes for winebottles, to stand upright in. The part above the bottles, to hold tea, sugar, bread, and meat; a tumbler glass, knife and fork, and salt-cellar, with two or three napkins: the box to have a very good lock. I would also advise to be taken, bed-linen, and half a dozen towels at least, a blanket, thin quilt, and two pillows; these articles will set a traveller quite at ease, with respect to accommodation; the blanket and quilt will be very seldom wanted, however, when they are, it is very pleasant to have such convenience in one's power (p. 41).

With my maid by my side, and my man on the seat behind the carriage, I set off, May the 28th 1796 . . . Before I proceed, I will however inform you, that I think I have seen Scotland, and its natural beauties, more completely than any other individual. I was alone, nor did I limit myself as to time. I took great pains to see everything worth seeing: and perhaps had better opportunities, than most other travellers, of exploring almost every famous glen, mountain pass and cataract, by having a great many good and kind friends and relations by marriage, in Perthshire, and other parts of the Highlands; whose hospitality and kindness are stampt upon my heart, and will not be forgotten by my pen, when I describe the country (p. 45).

I was desirous of seeing the southern end of it [Loch Ericht], near Rannoch. Eight miles was the distance named; but I am sure it is fourteen at least. I was placed upon a shelty, which was led through the Gaur river by a Highlandman, hip deep; but he cared far less for that, than I did for the splashing of my petticoats. As soon as I left the side of the Loch, to mount the river Ericht's side, I could no longer take care of myself; therefore the good Highlandman became my friendly leader. I stuck as fast to the pummel of the saddle as I could, and thus mounted, I descended such places as were sufficient to scare a lowland female out of her wits. At the end of a mile or two we quitted the bank of the river, and every track that had been gone before us, entering on the roughest and most uneven boggy, rocky, watery, black mountain moor, that human being ever explored. It was with the utmost difficulty that the poor little beast could keep upon his legs, though born and bred on such wastes; but there is a sagacity in the shelties not easily credited. (p. 317).

As I was creeping down the crag side, the children and women came to the doors to gaze at a fearless female stranger, scrambling alone amongst the crags. Comerie hache (how do you do), and la-mah-chuie (good day to you), were nearly the only Gaelic words I could say to them; but here, as well as in all the other sequestered Highland glens, English is in some degree spoken. As I have a great passion for water falls, I wished to reach that of the Lochy, but knowing distances in Scotland to be often misrepresented, I much doubted the accomplishment of my desire. The Scotch wee bit is nearly equal to their mile, and a mile with them is almost double the distance of an English measured mile. However, I enquired at the village, and was told it was not so much as one mile; nearly which I walked, and met a man with a cart loaded with hay; the driver told me he thought it might be a mile and a wee bit; another Highlandman came in my way. 'How far is it to the fall of the Lochy?' 'I ca'nae say, but it maun be twa miles or mair'. I still advanced, not from any further idea of reaching the fall, but to take a nearer view of a house prettily situated before me. The evening was closing fast, when meeting a woman, I had the curiosity to question her about the distance to the fall. She could scarcely understand me; but by words and signs she, as I supppose at last comprehended I meant the fall of the river; for she shook her head and said, 'mony miles; it maun be pick mirk ere ye'se at the fa''. I then totally abandoned my project, and turned about" (p. 354).

It is tantalising to know nothing whatever of how this remarkable woman acquired an education and a husband the son of an earl: but all search has been in vain. She was kindly and generous, as her writing abundantly shews, most unlikely to neglect her kin, and it is strange to find her widowed mother living in a tiny parish house just seven years before she made her dazzling marriage; perhaps worldly success came suddenly. Mrs. Mayes was not buried in Batheaston.

The climax of the romantic story was reached in 1801, when George Aust Esq. married the Hon. Sarah Murray, the poor boy and girl of Batheaston united in their old age. An astonishing couple, Sarah was probably the more interesting character, and perhaps the more estimable.

There is little more to tell. Mrs. Murray Aust died in 1811 at Noel House, Kensington, George Aust in 1825. Whether they ever revisited childhood scenes that must have held unhappy memories is not known. Ann, the elder of George's sisters, from 1799 to 1817 paid rates for a quite substantial house in Batheaston. After her death the rate was charged twice to George Aust, Esq. and then the house was sold. The fate of his brother and his other sister is uncertain, but it is likely that Thomas benefited from his brother's worldly success and was that Mr. Thomas Aust of the General Post Office whose death at Brompton in 1788 is recorded in *The Gentleman's Magazine*.

William Wilberforce (1759–1833)

Though never a permanent resident, Wilberforce was wont to retire to Batheaston for periods of rest when exhausted by his parliamentary labours. In 1803 he remained for three months, and thus recorded in his diary his arrival on 3 September:

> "Delighted with the beauty of our new villa. Weather delicious. Afternoon and evening read and heard, out of doors, in a lovely arbour by the river. This is a beautiful country".

A favourite haunt was a shady spot beside a steep bank of the river. On 25 October he wrote that some impulse caused him to move his stool back from the brink; within minutes the stool broke and flung him on his back, but not in the river. He could not swim.

William Lonsdale (1794–1871)

William Lonsdale was born in Bath, commissioned at fifteen, and retiring on half-pay in 1816, came to live at his mother's house in Batheaston.[18] This was probably the house known as Lonsdale Villa. He gained an entry in the *Dictionary of National Biography* as a noted early geologist, and his name is especially associated with the distinguishing of the Devonian System. While here he established the museum of the Bath Literary and Scientific Institution, and was its honorary curator from 1823 to 1828, earning a lasting reputation for precise accuracy in everything he undertook. In 1829 he accepted an invitation to become curator and librarian of the Geological Society, and moved to London.

Christopher Edmund Broome (1812–1886)

In the year 1848 C. E. Broome came to live at Elmhurst (Map 1, 18), a house which early in the century replaced the old Cold Bath Farm (p. 82). A distinguished botanist, he is remembered for his pioneer work on Mycology. Batheaston supplied many of his specimens, and his collection of fungi went to the British Museum after his death. With the Rev. L. Blomefield, another eminent naturalist, he made a herbarium which was a valued possession of the now defunct Literary and Scientific Institution. A shy man, not much inclined to publicity, Blomefield has recorded what a delightful companion he was on the regular botanical walks which provided many specimens for the herbarium.

Broome, no less outstanding as a gardener, established at Elmhurst a collection containing many rare plants, some of which were sent home from abroad by one of his sons. After his death it was removed to form the nucleus of the Botanical Garden of which Bath is so rightly proud, and which at first very properly bore his name.

Blomefield's account and appreciation of Broome are preserved in the *Proceedings of the Bath Field Club*.[19] Batheaston Parish Vestry recorded a resolution proclaiming "their deep sense of the loss the Parish has sustained by the death of one, who as Guardian was unremitting in the discharge of his duties, and who also faithfully served the Parish for many years in various other important offices".

Of course there were humble folk, too, who made their little mark. For several generations the Cannings, usually a Peter, were handymen about the church, probably sextons as well. Some interesting story must lie behind the record of that William Murford, who on 28 December 1642 stated and signed his disbursement for the poor, adding (the entry is crossed out) "upon other employment for King and Parliament". It is a pity that the history of the "hos roider" cannot be known (p. 73).

In 1798 a child was found abandoned or lost at Canning's Grave (Map 1, 19). Perhaps she was old enough to say that her name was Grace. The surname Trouvée (soon Trouvey) was given her, and she was boarded for 2s a week. About 1812 she disappeared from the record—not buried, or married, or apprenticed by the parish, perhaps she was sent elsewhere to service; just a passing figure in village history.

Lydia Loveday earned mention. Between 1774 and 1794 she presented the parish with six bastards, only two of whom survived infancy. Nursed through smallpox, subsidised at her frequent excursions into motherhood, she received help from the overseers at other times until soon after 1800, when she took to "weekly pay" of half a crown. Lydia continued to draw her "pay" until the overseers' accounts ceased in 1836. Later in the year, however, she went to the churchyard, aged eighty-five, still at the expense of the parish.

Chapter 8

The Poor

Ere I again, or one like me, explore
These simple Annals of the VILLAGE POOR.

GEORGE CRABBE

IT IS fortunate indeed that no tiresome busybody with a mission to tidy and destroy ancient "rubbish" ever laid hands on the records of the overseers of the poor, for they were kept in great detail, and are complete from 1619 until the old system came to its end in 1836. They complement the church rates in preserving regular lists of the inhabitants. They give an account of every aspect of the life of the necessitous poor, feeding, clothing, housing, sickness and death. Next, as the only sources of revenue for communal purposes were the church and poor rates, we find the money raised being used for incidental expenses such as the upkeep of gates and fences on the common lands, the apprehension of wrongdoers, maintenance of stocks, lock-up and pound, and many other occasional causes. As the same people were called upon to pay both rates, and the overseers were under the control of the churchwardens, it was often a matter of indifference from which fund payment was made for purposes not directly concerned with the church on the one hand or the poor on the other.

The study of these precious records takes us some way towards constructing a picture of the life of a rural community during more than two centuries. It may be said at the outset that though the life of the poor in this village as elsewhere was hard, there is revealed little evidence of inhumanity, and a great deal of compassion. Doubtless there were overseers who were mean and callous, but their traces are rarely obvious, and it must be remembered that such an inhumane practice as "badging the poor" was legally required. Further, the amount of charitable treatment bestowed on "strangers", sometimes at much expense, is remarkable, and must often have gone beyond what was required by law.

POOR RATE AND RATEPAYERS

Figure 11 shews the expenditure of the overseers every tenth year per head of population (estimated

before 1801). It illustrates the startling increase which began with the nineteenth century. No small part of the growing burden was the cost of disputes about the parish of settlement of poor persons (p. 107).

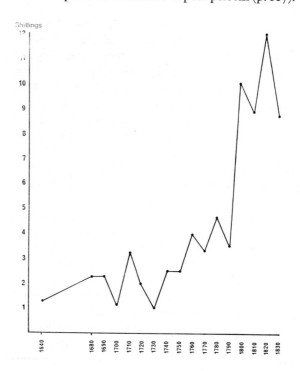

Note: Not corrected for changes in money values

Population before 1801 estimated

Fig. 11. Expenditure of the overseers
(per head of population)

Other charges which the ratepayers had to meet were a county rate which, beginning in 1740 as £2 2s 11d, was £16 2s in 1800, and in 1830 £86 16s 7d; and the maintenance of the families of men serving in the militia, or of the substitutes serving for them (p. 113).

Until 1660 one rate was collected for Batheaston and S. Catherine and it is not possible to determine the amount spent in each place, so the calculation is adjusted accordingly; thereafter the records apply to Batheaston only, the other set being lost, if they ever existed. The number rated cannot be counted exactly, because of erasures, alterations, and sometimes uncertainty about persons of the same name, but, fifty-two in 1620, the number fluctuated around that figure, without constant increase, until 1770, when it rose to about sixty-two, and approximately ninety-four in 1800. It seems that the overseers inclined more and more to leniency, for between 1660 and 1800 the population probably trebled.

It is difficult to estimate the prevalence of poverty at different periods because of the many and varying occasional payments in money. If the number having weekly relief is expressed in relation to the population it averages 2 % over the whole period, without constant variation. Women outnumber men in the proportion of about two to one. The relief given in the seventeenth century was usually less than a shilling a week (that being about a labourer's wage for a day's work). It was half a crown to three shillings in the last years of the system. It is not easy to relate the purchasing power of money at different times. In any case, these figures are not very helpful, for they take no account of other resources of the recipients, and large sums were paid out separately for rent, clothing, and in time of sickness and death.

HOUSING

As far back as the seventeenth century the parish owned houses on "the parish ground" or "the waste", paying token rents of fourpence to sixpence a year. They were occupied by the parish poor, but some lived in hovels elsewhere, for entries appear among the overseers' payments such as:

1642. Sarah England rent for year   8s 6d

Widow Stockes rent for half the year   6s 8d

An obvious means of helping those unable to be self-supporting, there are many entries; up to £1 a year was paid at the end of the seventeenth century, an average of £2 10s in the middle of the eighteenth, and by the early nineteenth £4 5s.

The parish continued to own houses, and in 1750, alarmed by Ralph Allen's claim to the right to grant leases as lord of the manor (p. 20) the Vestry agreed that leases "Determinable on One, Two or Three

Lives as shall be thought meet shall be immediately granted to every Cottage holder who is willing to become Lessee under us, the Freeholders of the parish, at the yearly rent of sixpence each". The rent was to be paid in equal parts at Lady Day and Michaelmas! The sixteen leases which were taken are extant, and the expenses of the Freeholders when they met at Peter Salmon's house to grant them cost the parish 18s 3d. Parish houses were at Fordway (i.e. road to Avon), the Bridge, the Fosse and Hollies Lane, and the last two sites can still be identified (Map 1, 8, 35).

Entries for the repair of houses often appear:

1677. carrying 7 loads of straw to Wm
      England   7s 0d
     for thaching William England house 17s 0d
     for helm   12s 0d
     for nayls for Wm England   1s 5d

1724. for 4 Dozen and three Sheaves of
      Helme   5s 6d
     For thatching Spicks and Ledgers   18s 10d
     Carpenter Boards Nailes and work   8s 8d
     To the Glasier   4s 3d
     Plaisterer Lime and Laths   2s 7d
     Helm Workmanship and Spicks on
      Bety Fishers house   18s 2d

Sometimes parish houses were the cause of trouble. In 1776 the widow of Daniel Mayes sold one for sixteen guineas. The overseers regained possession, and the next year: "Danl Mays house to be Rebuilt on the Same Foundation and in the Cheapest Manner but Covered with Stone Tiles". This cost £17 10s 8½d.

There was more trouble in 1784, when Edward Trotman and Richard Angell were to be turned out of a parish house they had unlawfully entered after the death of the leasee. Getting judgement at the Assizes, the overseers promise that if Angell, who has "thrown himself on the mercy of the Parish" goes quietly they will not prosecute him for eight years' rent—a good example of rural patience! Trotman being ejected, "made forcible re-entry the same night". The promise to him is if he goes quietly before Michaelmas Day (twenty-four days ahead) to "forgive him all that is past". The bill for all this, Angell's trial at Wells, Trotman's at Taunton, and lawyers' fees was £43 10s 10d. No wonder the poor rate was becoming a burden.

A number of papers relating to the parish houses survive. Several were reported "fallen down", two were sold for widening of the Turnpike Road. The last eight, all in or near the Fosse, are shewn in the Tithe Map of 1840. Soon after, the sanction of the Poor Law Commissioners was obtained for disposing of them towards paying off the debt on the Poor House. Actually, the final sales were not made until 1892, when the relics were to be demolished: for some reason, one was spared and may still be seen, its original door and window filled in, re-roofed, and without its chimney (Pl. 45).

An Act of 1723 enabled a parish if it wished to set up a communal Poor House for the more economical management of poor relief, and to arrange for such employment of the inmates as was practicable, and within a few years Workhouses became common. A committee appointed in 1802 to consider the erection of a Poor House delayed so effectively that it bears the date 1821 (Pl. 46). It was to accommodate sixty persons in eighteen rooms and cost £761 19s 6d, besides £35 16s 0d for "Wm Hobb's Bill for his Plan of the Poor's House and superintending the Building of it, and for building the Garden wall making sewers etc". Daniel Cottle, a local carpenter, obtained the contract, and the house was built on the site of one of the parish houses. The money was raised by loans totalling £700, to which an organisation called the Old Club contributed £400.

The accounts for 1822 contain a list of the rents paid for poor persons, and noting some to be discontinued, suggesting an access of thrift, or perhaps severity, and some persons "gone into the Poor

Pl. 46. Poor House

House" or "to go in". From this time there were regular requests, not always granted, for admission. Others were "to be removed to the Poor House". Obviously it was proving useful.

Such belongings as they had accompanied the entrants, but items appear such as: "Three bedsteads, bed and carr. of Do for Poor House £3 1s 6d". "Bed and bolster, pair of Blankets and Rug for Judith Alpheus in the Poor House £2 8s". In 1827 an iron bedstead cost 12s, two chairs and a table 6s 6d and a fender 1s 6d. It is clear from the number of rooms provided that the inmates continued to live their own lives. There are no entries for provisions at this time, though they had often been bought in the past.

Though the wide upper windows of the Poor House suggest that such was the intention, there is no evidence that the residents were actually set to work; no materials were bought. John Angell was appointed superintendent at a guinea a year, and his wife earned 2s 0d a week attending the sick. In 1830 they were dismissed and Thomas White and his wife appointed. Life in the Poor House was rough. Isaac Bakehouse was committed "for disorderly behaviour in the Poor's House" and William Tiley "for a breach of the peace". There are significant entries: "Paid a Man for destroying Buggs at the Poor House 4s 0d" and "distroying Vermin at the Poor House 10s 0d". Occasional entries record such events as "sweeping the chimneys", "repairing the pump",

Pl. 45. Last standing Parish House

"stopping up the Lock up room window", and "a slipper Bath for the Poor House £1 10s 0d".

The New Poor Law of 1834 established Parish Unions under Parish Guardians; the Bath Union, of twenty-four parishes, was set up in 1836, and the new Workhouse, now S. Martin's Hospital, built. In September of that year the delighted Guardians sent an address to the Home Secretary extolling the immediate success of the new system.[1] Among the benefits listed were the reduction of paupers receiving outdoor relief from 1758 to 875, and of cost from £10,311 to £5,360. They were at pains to claim that these remarkable figures were achieved, not by harshness to the deserving poor, whose pay, they said, was actually increased "in about 100 cases", but by offering the Workhouse to paupers considered too idle to work; and they noted with relish "favourable symptoms of returning industry and good conduct, even amongst those who formerly appeared to be incorrigible".

In Bath Reference Library is preserved an interesting and informative document, the Guardians' accounts for 1859, setting out, besides statistics for the participating parishes, the expenditure on the Workhouse, the diet for various classes of inmate, and the bulk prices of all the ingredients supplied. Of interest for the present study are the following figures:

Batheaston — average expenditure 1833–1835, £627, 1837–1839 £287.

S. Catherine — average expenditure 1833–1835, £114, 1837–1839, £38.

The further history of Poor Law administration scarcely concerns a local study.

So the Poor House of Batheaston was used for its intended purpose for a mere fifteen years. Its later history has been one of variety. According to "J.W.", writing in the parish magazine in 1899, it was used as a leather factory, as a carpenter's shop, and as a Mission Hall to serve the labourers building the railway, who were said to be "an orderly and attentive congregation". At one time the building was occupied by the Agapemonites, a sect founded in 1859, which led a life in community. At present it is owned by the Congregational Church.

CLOTHING

Naturally, the overseers' accounts contain many entries for helping the poor with clothing, an interesting record, and therefore quoted at some length. Representative entries have been chosen; some others are included in the account of the parish apprentices (p. 109). By no means all of the recipients were on regular parish relief:

1619.	Payd for Apperell for Thomas Gasted	
	Payd for A dublet	2s 8d
	Payd for A peare of breches	4s 4d
	Payd for A shirt and A peare of showes	3s 5d
	Payd to William Hoyam for making his apperell	1s 2d
1669.	To Joyce Lacey for Rudman's maide att our Ladeyday 1669 for her deyett and Clothes	£2 11s 8d
1688.	for A paire of Showes for Simons maid & mending	2s 0d
	for 2 Shifts 2 quayfs 2 neckcloths for Simmons two maids	5s 1½d
	for canvas & triming & Stockins for Lansdons maids cloathes	4s 0½d
	for trowsers for Jam cannigs	2s 9d
	for a paire of Shows for Lansdons children	4s 0d
	for making Ann Lansdon 2 coats	9d
	for sarge to make Lansdon britches	2s 1d
	Pd for a Shirt & stockins for James Cannings	2s 9d
	for making James Canings coat	1s 0d

The Rudmans, the Simmons, the Lansdowns long struggled on the edge of destitution. Why, it is not possible to say, among the manifold causes of defeat in the battle of existence.

1708.	For a pettycoat for Hannah Davis and Cap	3s 0d
	For a Canvas garmt and makeing for Wid. Thomas	3s 6d
	For a pair of Breeches for Nath. Bigs	6s 0d
	For 2 Caps 2 Neckclothes a pair of Stockings and Shoes for Salmons Children	4s 3d
	For a Gown Lineing and makeing for Joan Thomas	11s 2d
	For a Wastcoat Cloth pair of Breeches makeing and trimming for old Tyley	14s 4½d

For a Cloth Wastcoat for Nathaniel
Biggs 2 yds ¾ at 3s per yd
trimming and makeing   10s 5d
For a Gown and makeing a pair of
stayes for Salmons Child   5s 7d
For Whale Bone & for mending
S. Childs Coat   6d
For a Frock for Thomas Fisher of
Holliers Lane   4s 0d

There is no other reference to buying whalebone and
making stays for a poor child. Perhaps this one
suffered disease or deformity in addition to her other
misfortunes.

About this time a Mrs Cottle was supplying
material, and in 1711 a series of payments were made
to her:

4 Ells of Canvas at 16d pr Ell   5s 4d
3¾ ells of Flaxen Cloth   3s 5½d
3 ells of cloth for 2 Garments for Frank
Salmon   3s 6½d
Flannen to bury John Pearce   3s 0d
1 Ell of Cloth Flannen & Blanketting &
Treacle for holloways Child   3s 6½d
2 yds of Crape for Mary Webbs boy   2s 6d

These are just representative items from the list.
What little tragedies of humble life they illustrate!

A pathetic set of entries for James Lewis in 1754
reads:

a Shirt 4s 2d, Stockins Showes and Bridges 5s 6d
a Cap 7d

Other expenses on his account include Spanish bags
(for his bed) and "Clenin"; finally, "for Berin of
Jeames Lewis 16s 6d."

A little later, the overseers had responsibility for
a little creature, born in 1758, always referred to as
"Vinings Bastard":

1759. Mary Vinings Bastard Leading
Strings   1s 3½d
Stockings   2s 4½d
Cap and other thing   3s 10d
two Pair of Stockings   1s 2d
Shoes and worsted   1s 3½d
Bed Gown   1s 1d
Shoes   1s 2d
1767. a Gown Coat Stockings Shifts
Aprons Handkerchiefs etc for
Vinings Bastard   18s 11½d

1768. Choak Strangs & Handkerchief
Vinings   1s 9d
Stockings Vinings Bastard   1s 5d

The expenditure on leading strings (a unique entry)
is a puzzle. Throughout the accounts, single pairs
of stockings at long intervals for individuals appear,
and handkerchiefs are regularly bought, which seems
a lavish equipment in a poverty-stricken home. The
parish paid two shillings a week for the support of
Vining's Bastard for the first ten years of her life, and
intermittent sums afterwards, and her name was
included in a list of persons for whom clothes were
bought in 1772.

A few other entries may be quoted:

1768. For a Swanskin Choak & Canvas for
Bullocks child   2s 1d
1771. For Sunday clothes for the poor £1 5s 9½d
1778. A Coat and Breeches John Weston 11s 0d

By the end of the eighteenth century bills for clothing
are often quoted without detail—there were so
many—and entries appear such as:

1800. Mr. Godwin's Bill for making and
mending shoes for half a year £4 17s 2d
1807. G. Gay's son going to service
clothes   £1 2s 3½d
Abbey Jones girl going to service
clothes   £1 1s 9d

(Abbey Jones' bastards were a constant expense to the
overseers.) In 1815 is a rather touching entry:

A pair of Breeches and shoes for Geo. Pyatt
going to his sister for the winter   14s

He was a little before given 16 shillings from parish
funds as "sick and out of work".

As the old system of parish relief drew to its close
items of clothing were entered less and less often;
presumably the poor were expected to clothe themselves with the money allowed them. Prices were
rising fast; in 1822 "a Frock Pin-before & Stockings"
for a child cost 6s. The price of shoes was
heavy; in 1824 10s 6d was paid for a pair and in
1835 9s.

Thus ends a sketch of the clothing provided for the
poor of Batheaston during two centuries. The
illustrations chosen, it must be remembered, are a
very small fraction of the whole. The complete
record is of the greatest interest, and a most valuable
survival.

FURNISHING AND PROVISIONS

From time to time the overseers' accounts contain entries for household necessities, usually bed and bedding:

1641. Anne Mille a coldron	3s 0d
a coverlett and blankett	15s 10d
1753. 4 Spanish baggs	4s 0d

Spanish bags, in which wool was imported, the cheapest covering for the beds of the poor, were often bought during the next half century.

1786. To a Bed Case for Jas Weston	8s 6d
To makeing Do	6d
Bed cord	1s 10½d
To a Bed & sheet	11s 6d
To a Bed & sheets for Eliz. Farrow	15s 8d
„ Makeing Do	1s 0d
„ a Bedstead, Cord & Matt for Do	6s 0d

Bed cord was, of course, stretched across the frame to support the mattress.

It was usual for the poor to obtain their own food, except sometimes in sickness. About 1710, however, the overseers evidently thought to save by buying food in bulk and reducing money payments:

A cheese that weighed 10 lb and ¼	2s 2d
A peck & ½ of wheat	2s 6d
5 pecks of malt	5s 3d
¾ lb of bacon	5½d

Huge amounts of cheese were bought in the following months.

From time to time life was harder than ever, and extra help was needed; in 1766, weekly pay was increased "in Consideration of the Dearness of provisions". On 2 February 1784 is recorded: "At a vestry held in ye Church for ye purpose of relieving ye Poor during ye Severity of ye weather & dearness of Provisions Resolved that every person (during the severity etc) Receive in good brown Bread at 9d wk, half on Monday, half on Th. at noon. Tickets to go to the baker who will engage to deliver good brown Bread without taking out of ye Grist any other than ye Bran". An entry later in the year states:

Pd to Mrs. Harford for bread for the poor last winter	£1 3s
2 bushells 1½ pecks of Pease for the Poor	11s

In 1795, after the first of a series of bad harvests, was issued, under the signatures of E. Davies, Minister, and other leading residents, an appeal for funds to supply sixpenny loaves to the poor for threepence, "The Kingdom at large being under an Apprehension of a Famine of Bread". Unfortunately, there is no record of the response. Further, in 1799, on 31 December, a subscription was opened "because of the inclement weather and high price of provisions— to be Disposed of to the Poor in soup." Again, the outcome is unknown.

It is suprising to the modern mind that when nourishment was doled out to the sick poor it was likely to be alcoholic; in 1795, Betty Skrine, who had been on parish relief continuously for years, benefited by "A Pint of Brandy 1s 9d". In 1802 appears the following:

A bottle of Port for Rd. Pryer			3s 6d
2½ veal	„ „	„	1s 10
mutton			1s 11d
Half a Pint of Gin & Mutton for Prior			3s 1½d

Shortly after he died.

Rarely, money was paid out for coal, just a sackful usually. The small amount supplied would be of little use in a hard winter or a long illness to supplement what fuel was available.

1633. To Agnes Somerell to paie Toby Pearce for sackes of Coole	1s 0d

In 1663, a single sack cost a shilling.

SICKNESS

Through the seventeenth century there is little to be learned about attempts to deal with sickness, in any medical sense. From time to time small amounts were paid out to named persons, often for dressing a leg or foot, usually probably an injury or a varicose ulcer. The first entry indicating treatment appears in 1659:

Mathew Sandell for Cures done to Joane Rudman and her Childe	6s 0d

A set of entries in 1706 yield a vivid picture of sickness and its outcome:

Thomas Fisher in his Wife's Sicknese in Money & Ware	5s 10d
for Treacle Nutmeggs & Cordial in her sicknese	6d
for Apothecaries Stuff and Ware	2s 5d
for Laying out of Joan Fisher Carying her to Church and going on Errands	7s 6d
for Bran and the Coffin	5s 6d
for White Lyme and Whiteliming Thomas Fishers house	1s 4d
Pd for the Death of Joan Fisher	14s 6d

The whiteliming was an attempt to contain an infection, quite likely smallpox. Treacle was a term for medicine, not necessarily syrup.

At about this time, one Rebecca Bletchley evidently won a reputation for her skill in treating sickness:

1712. Rebecca Bletchley for Curing Wm
       Tyly's legg, Wm White's head
       and Salve for Susan Lewis   £1 1s 6d

Payments for the nursing of the sick are regular items. In 1692, for instance, John Stibbs, almost the last sad member of a family which had been prominent in the village for at least four hundred years, was nursed for 21 weeks at 6d a week, and then buried by the parish. It fairly often happened that an attempt must be made at the cleansing of some sick wretch, and for that extra payment was given, appearing in such terms as:

1691. Paid to tobey for washing a man   1s 0d

The bonesetter was able to charge a considerable fee for his services. In 1737 Henry Davis was receiving 1s 6d a week from the parish. These entries appear:

Aded to Henry Davis in the time of his
    sickness   6s 0d
Pd for Linen for Henry Davis   6s 11d
  „ Thomas Amsbury for fetching the
     bone Setter   1s 6d
  „ for Setting Henry Davis Thigh Bone £1 11s 6d
  „ funerall Expences for Henry Davis   5s 6d

In 1749, it was Doctor Palmer who set Henry Aust's leg and supervised his after-care, and earned two and a half guineas for doing so. This Palmer, who came from Bradford on Avon for the purpose, was the first professional man to be regularly employed in the treatment of the sick poor, and his name appears regularly for the next twenty years earning up to £10 in the course of a year; the last entry was £3 16s 0d "for curing Betty Morris' Arm & Geo Knight's boy's fractured Jaw". From this time on, it was the practice to employ a salaried parish doctor; Mr. Goldstone's salary was ten guineas in 1799, Dr Watkins' in 1803 fourteen, a considerable sum.

The building of the General, or Mineral Water Hospital, began in 1737. Reference to it in the Batheaston records begins in 1745 with the entry:

Pd to the Hospital at Bath during John Davis's
    stay there which is to be returned   £3

The payment was probably a security for good behaviour, for treatment was free to all *except* inhabitants of the city of Bath. In 1793 the Vestry agreed to pay to the Hospital an annual subscription of two guineas. In 1796 Bacchus' wife was taken to Bristol Infirmary at a cost of 13s, and two others were sent in 1799, though there were already other hospitals in Bath.

References to the treatment of syphilis with mercury are found in 1764, when Dr. Parry's bill for "salivating" Richard Hall was £4 18s 0d, Hall was allowed £5 16s 0d during eight weeks, when he died. In 1768 Dr Palmer "salivated" William Lewis at a cost of three guineas, and in following years there appear:

1776. Mr. Hooper for Cure of Ed Cable in
     the foul Disease   £2 2s 0d
1799. To Mr. Goldstone for Curing
     Fisher of the Venereal Disease one guinea

Some case of mental illness occurred:

1742. Carrying Ann Poringer a Mad
     Woman to Pottern   11s 0½d

1767. Samuel Shell was attended by Peter Cannings until he was sent to the Madhouse (at Laycock) where Dr. Jefferies was paid half a guinea "for entrance" for him. Shell evidently recovered, partially or completely, for he was about for many years afterwards, the parish supporting him. In 1799 straps for Butterfield's "st waistcoat" cost 1/-, and after a night attendant paid to look after him was unable to manage, he, too, was entered at Lacock at a cost of a guinea to the parish.

For a final picture, this sequence:

1803. Pd. a Letter from Laycock   4d
    „ journey to Do   3s 6d
    Turnpike and other Expinces   1s 6d
    for Horse and Cart to convey
     Geo. Fisher to Laycock   5s 0d
    3 Guards for Do.   6s 0d
    for Turnpike and other Expences
     for Do   5s 6d
    Entrance for Geo. Fisher at Do £1 1s 0d

For these poor creatures the rest is silence. At least the parish seems to have done its best for them.

A few other of the innumerable entries relating to illness are so suggestive as to deserve mention:

1715. Flocks for Tyly's Bed when in the
     Feaver   6s 0d

1771. Extra pay for laying out Nathaniel
    Jones, he being in a most nasty
    condition

1774. Tilleting for a Blister   2d
    Two Boxes of Jacksons Ointment for
    the Itch for Silverthorns Family 3s 6d

1802. Pd. for repairing Lucy Smart's Truss 10s 6d

The tilley seed contained a strong irritant, and would produce a fine blister, a favourite remedy. The Itch was scabies, and the ointment probably contained sulphur. The mention of a truss is a salutary reminder of the disastrous disablement of a hernia in the days before there was a possibility of surgery.

Always over the scene hung the menace of smallpox, and many entries relate to this scourge. The wise practice was to isolate infected persons or families in the charge of someone who had had the disease, and supply the necessary support in the form of money or goods. As for wretched vagrants wandering about, such as could travel at all were bribed to move on. Some of the earliest mentions of smallpox by name refer to these unfortunates:

1663. a man yt had ye pox   5s od

1715. A woman whose Child had the Small
    Pox   2s od

1725. Pd to a woman as had the Small
    Pox to Leave the Parish   1s 6d

A typical item for parishioners appears in 1729:

Mary Fisher and Henry her son when they
    had the Small Pox & for tending them &
    other necessarys   £5 5s 10d

In the next decade smallpox was more than usually prevalent, and cost a great deal of money. Again, in 1747:

Sarah Fisher for meat ale Small Beer &
    Cheese for Betty Rudman when her
    children had ye Smallpox   17s 3d

a pint of wine for John Rudman and
    Physick   2s od

There were two deaths in this family:

1766. Abraham Iles for ye care of Augusta
    Teads in ye small Pox   £2 2s od
    Thos Syms Family in ye Small Pox £1 5s od
    Jane Adams for attending Kite's
    Family in the small Pox 5 weeks 15s od
    Mr Street for attending Geo. Kyte's
    Wife in the Small Pox   7s 6d

The first reference to preventive treatment is in 1774,

when £1 5s was paid "for Inoculating Woodman's children". Mr Smith inoculated three children in 1786, and in 1788 was paid 3s. each for treating fifty-two poor people. An important decision was taken in 1803:

A Vestry held in the Parish Church to take into Consideration the Expediency of inoculating the Poor The Smallpox being in several parts of the Parish. Unanimously agreed that such a measure will prove highly beneficial to the Interest of the Parish and do further Order that Mr Watkin do perform the same after the rate of two shillings and sixpence each Person including proper Medicines for the said Purpose.

Strangely, the only subsequent entry was in 1816, when four children were inoculated. The practice of inoculating persons with fluid from a smallpox vesicle, introduced by Lady Mary Wortley Montagu about 1721, was popular in England through the remainder of the century. It gave immunity to the persons inoculated, but those in contact with them might develop the disease, with all its danger to them, and the risk of an epidemic. Vaccination gradually took its place after Jenner's work of 1796–1798, and inoculation was forbidden by law in 1840.

The epidemic of cholera when the disease arrived in England in 1831 visited Batheaston, where the overseers paid for the whitewashing of cottages "during the prevalence of the Cholera" (p. 60).

Information about childbirth yielded by the Poor Books is scanty. In 1747 the midwife earned half a crown for a confinement; in 1752, 5s. Mrs. Godfrey was paid a guinea in 1782 for delivering Elizabeth Goodenough, but the mother was nursed for eight weeks, and the child died, so the case was probably complicated. In the late eighteenth century Surgeon Grigg was evidently in repute as an accoucheur, and earned two guineas several times.

DEATH AND BURIAL

The cost of the last illness and funeral of persons on the verge of penury was obviously often too much for their families to bear, so besides burying the poor regularly supported by the parish, the overseers frequently entered payments on behalf of people not ordinarily classed as paupers. The evidence is not easy to interpret for another reason, the number of parish burials that took place elsewhere. For example, of eighty-four persons buried by the parish from 1720 to 1769 inclusive, only fifty-seven appear in the register of burials, and there is no reason to suspect its accuracy. The explanation must be that many, if not all of them, were living in other parishes with the approval of the overseers of both parishes.

However, it is possible to work out some figures bearing on the incidence of destitution at life's end. Burials at the cost of the parish were not many in the seventeenth century because the number "on the parish" was small. From 1720 to 1739, 259 persons were buried in Batheaston (excluding bodies from Bath and elsewhere—see p. 58); in these years the parish paid for sixteen burials, fewer than one a year, but six of these are not in the register. From 1740 to 1769 there were sixty-eight burials by the parish, an average of more than two a year. The data for these observations comes from the overseers' accounts.

Between 1784 and 1790 the clerk entered the word "pauper" against relevant names in the register of burials, so here is independent evidence. In these years there were 131 burials, omitting those from elsewhere, and they included thirty paupers, that is, nearly 23% of all burials; and that takes no account of burials of poor persons elsewhere. The finding, of course, only reflects the well known fact that the burden of poor relief rose fast at the end of the eighteenth century (Fig. 11). In the six years 1806 to 1810 the parish paid for 31% of 101 burials, a higher rate than ever.

The early custom of entering the cost of a funeral in detail has preserved evidence of the practice of associating feasting with the disposal of the dead, perhaps considered a proper recompense for the parish's footing the bill.

1695. Payd for bering of Mary Davis &
        Ringing the bell   2s 6d
      Payd for bred & bear & Chees   5s 1d
      „   „   her shroud & making &
                3 yds of Ladis(?) and
                A ¼ of tobacco   4s 7d
      „   „   tow womens Afidavid   1s 0d
      „   John Jefery for ye tax of bereing   4s 0d
      „   Joan Lacey for tending her   1s 0d

The "afidavid" was the legally required evidence that the corpse was not buried in anything "other than what is made of sheep's wool only" according to an

Act of 1678, designed, of course, to protect the wool trade. The penalty for breaking the law was £5, half of which went to the poor of the parish, and half to the informer. When it was decided to break the law in order to use a linen shroud, it was quite usual for one of the family to inform, halving the real cost of the fine. Thus, the overseers record:

1681. Recd of Will. Blanchard for Bury-
         ing his Mother Mary Blanchard
         in Lining   £2 10s 0d

The Blanchards were a wealthy family, and could well afford the luxury of wearing linen in the grave. The Act was not repealed until 1814, but it seems long before to have been defied with impunity, and the affidavits have quite a short vogue in our records.

The burial tax was granted by Parliament in 1694 for five years to finance the war with France; though as it did not apply to paupers it is not clear why it was paid for Mary Davis.

Here is another example of funeral junketing, one of many:

1711. for a cheese at the Burying of Mary
         Webbs Child   1s 0d
      for 2 Doz of Beer at the Burying   2s 0d
      „ a Loaf of Bread   1s 0d
      „ the Affadavit   1s 0d

The shroud was always an expensive item. In the same year it cost 3s 6d and 4d for making for Thomas Webb—and 3s 0d was paid also for ale at his burial!

The vestry in 1748 "Agreed that from henceforward no more than fifteen shillings shall be allowed for the burial of any poor person (that is to say) ten Shillings to the Clerk for a Coffin and Burial and Four Shillings and sixpence for a Shroud and Two shillings in ale to persons who shall Carry the Corpse to Church but if a Child only five shillings to the Clerk".

A little later 16s 6d was regularly entered as the cost of a burial, and this figure was continued for many years. The price gradually rose and by 1826 averaged £1 10s;

Usually there is no clue to the cause of death, but records of accidental death and consequent inquest are not infrequent:

1792. Twelve jurymen paid 8s 0d for the inquest on the Body of Mary Bolwell's Infant Bastard Child, and William Cannings 1s 6d "for takeing up and Burying Do". Peter Vezey earned 10s 6d fetching the coroner from Wells. (It was no rare thing to fetch the coroner from Wells.)

1804. "Received from Mr Lye a fine imposed by the Coroner on account of his Waggon going over the Body of a Man which caused his Death 5s 0d".

1826. Hannah Brown killed by a cartwheel and a deodand of 5s 0d paid. Deodands were abolished in 1846.

1827 and the two following years parishioners, three in all, were drowned in the river and the inquest charged to the overseers.

SETTLEMENT

The long and dismal history of the effects of the settlement laws on a rural village and its inhabitants is of importance to require consideration in some detail. The theory on which the laws were based was the logical one that everyone belonged somewhere, and that some parish was ultimately responsible for his maintenance in case of need. A person's settlement was ordinarily the parish of his father's settlement, usually the parish in which he was born, and so it remained unless he "gained a settlement" elsewhere. The idea in its developed form was the cause of such a burden of expensive squabbling, in and out of the law courts, on the part of parishes, and misery on the part of the poor wretches dragged hither and thither, backwards and forwards from parish to parish, as would be thought impossible, had it not actually happened.

In Batheaston's records the cloud on the horizon is seen first in 1647; in the Poor Book under that year is the entry:

The humble desire of these inhabitants is that your worships bee pleassed to send by this bearer a warrant to remove Mauris Sparks and Anthony Chap from this p'ish they being intruders contrary to the Statute.

Legislation from 1662 onwards laid down conditions for "gaining a settlement". A newcomer could establish himself if he rented a tenement at £10 or more, paid the poor rate, served a parish office, an apprenticeship, a year as a covenant servant, or resided forty days in the parish after giving written notice; or had written evidence that his parish of settlement would take him back should he be liable to become a charge on the parish of his adoption. A married women took her husband's settlement.

Bastard children had a settlement in the parish of their birth; later, their mother's parish during infancy.

References to the expulsion of "intruders" are few before 1700. There is evidence, however, that outsiders would go to considerable lengths to establish themselves. From the records of Bridgwater Sessions 11 July 1671:

Order for the removal of Edmund Jones with his wife and family from Bathe Easton to Itton co Monmouth ... as it appears that he formerly intruded himself into the parish of Bath Foord, when he was removed to Itton, but shortly returned with a certificate by the minister and inhabitants of Itton owning him as an inhabitant of their parish, which certificate he burnt, and that he afterwards intruded himself into the parish of Bathe Easton, where he was disturbed but remained in hiding so that no warrant could be served on him (but his wife was removed and soon sent back).

There is no clue to why Edmund Jones was so desirous to establish himself in these parts. The overseers' accounts for 1708 contain two entries foreshadowing what was to come:

Pd for Beer with the Churchwardens when they met and warned Ingram out of the Parish	1s 0d
Lodging Sarah Buckle and carrying her to Mambury (Malmesbury)	5s 9½d

In 1712 orders to remove five "intruders" were obtained, and £6 4s 11d paid for "Charges and Expenses in Tryall at Wells Sessions with Bathford about Mary Webb's settlement".

The Poor Book records the examination at a petty sessions held at Batheaston in 1725 of thirty-one "intruders" concerning their settlement. Among the parish papers, too, are preserved examinations taken from time to time on oath before two magistrates, sixty-nine in all, between 1720 and 1795—later ones are lost. These documents are of interest and importance not only as illustrating the working of the system, but for their evidence on the histories and occupations of humble folk. Some could claim a settlement in Batheaston; those who could not were usually allowed to stay so long as they could support themselves, in the safe knowledge that they could legally be sent to their own parishes if they were judged "liable to become chargeable"; after 1795, only if they were actually chargeable. Two examples of these examinations are given in Appendix 6.

These were the fortunate ones. There are also among the parish archives the records of removals, 138 during the eighteenth century, and there were doubtless others. There is an example in Appendix 7. These include paupers moved out of the parish and those received from elsewhere, the former somewhat outnumbering the latter; whether this indicates that Batheaston held special attraction for would-be settlers or had specially vigilant overseers it is not possible to say. The load of misery concealed in these purely factual records can scarcely be imagined; it must be remembered, too, that almost every removal involved not an individual but a family. The cost to the ratepayers was enormous, the largest item legal fees, the dispute not infrequently going to appeal at Quarter Sessions. The chances of expensive litigation and removal costs largely account for the fluctuations in the sum the overseers had to raise from year to year. For example, in 1774 legal fees on a successful appeal which "fixed" a pauper at Exmouth cost Batheaston £82 11s 7d.

The following account of a removal is representative:

> 1726. Pd Mr Pearce of Bath for Carrying William Bolwell and his family to London   £1 5s 0d
>
> Pd the Waggoner to maintain them on ye Road   £1 17s 0d
>
> Expenses in delivering Bollin and his Family to the Overseers in London   5s 2d
>
> Pd for three Quarters of a year's Rent for Bolling   £1 2s 6d
>
> Pd for an Order and a Coppy thereof for Bolwell and his Family   3s 4d

This sad little family party consisted of Bolwell, his wife, and four children. They were sent to S. Giles in the Fields because Bolwell took his settlement from his father's settlement in that parish.

Year after year the law, cruel if logical, weighed upon poor and ratepayers alike. Perhaps the extreme of tragic absurdity was reached in 1809, with the affair of the Widow Kite, quoted here in full to emphasise the remorselessness of the system. The grounds of the dispute, and why it was necessary to take the poor woman to and fro in the course of resolving it, are not recorded:

	Journey to Marshfield with Wid Kite & also to Bath in the same business	3s 0d
	2 Journeys to Bath abt Kites business	2s 0d
Ap 6	Coach hire for Overseer & Wido Kite to London	£3 10s 0d
	Expences on the Road	11s 6d
	Carriage back for Wido Kite & expences	£2 1s 0d
	Expences in London for Do and Overseer	8s 0d
Ap 8	Journey To Epping and back to London	£2 4s 0d
Ap 9	Overseer in London	5s 0d
Ap 10.	Coach hire to Chelmsford	18s 0d
	Expences on the Road	3s 0d
Ap 11 & 12	Expences at Chelmsford	19s 6d
	Attorneys fee at Chelmsford	13s 6d
	Coach hire from Do to London	18s 0d
	Expences on the Road	3s 0d
Ap 13.	Expences in London	5s 0d
	Journey home	£2 1s 0d
	Carriage for Wido Kite & family to London	£6 0s 0d
	Paid Do for expences on the Road, and to take them from London to Epping	£2 14s 0d
	Overseer out 9 days at 2s 6d each day	£1 2s 6d

Logical, and probably a good bargain for Batheaston, to be rid of Widow Kite and her family for £25 2s 0d, but how hard for Widow Kite!

One consequence of a parish's undertaking to receive back anyone having a settlement who could not maintain himself in the parish of his adoption was the practice of sending money to such persons to prevent their becoming paupers, and the overseers used this device quite often. The lengths to which it could be carried are seen in the history of the

Fisher family, living about twenty-five miles away at Dursley, Gloucestershire. The story begins in 1734, when £1 10s 0d was sent to William Fisher while his family had smallpox. In 1739, his broken leg cost Batheaston £4 5s 0d, and from then on he received partial support, on and off, until in 1762 the bill for another broken leg was £7 6s 8d. William then disappears from the record, but in 1771 Giles was helped until he was buried at the expence of Batheaston. Mary Fisher then took up the tale, her rent paid at £2 a year, and 2s a week or so sent her until 1804, when presumably she died. This family, then, received almost constant help for seventy years! Many letters were sent to Dursley at a cost of threepence each, but there must have been other means of conveying regular sums of money.

Certificates of settlement and orders for removal are dated until 1864. The next year Villier's Act transferred settlement problems to the Union; removals from Union to Union continued into the present century, but no longer directly concerned the parishes.

PARISH APPRENTICES

Three sources yield evidence, considerable but tantalisingly incomplete, about poor children apprenticed to learn a trade, almost invariably in a neighbouring parish; a useful device, for apprenticeship gave a settlement after forty days and so relieved the overseers of further charge. There are the Poor Books, in which may be entered the child's name, the master's name and parish, the premium paid, and details of the outfit supplied by the parish. Secondly, there is a bundle of forty-one apprentices' indentures, dated from 1687 to 1794, preserved among the parish archives. These give, besides the child's name and occasionally his age, the name and parish of the master, the trade to be taught, and the term of the contract, but only "until he shall accomplish his full age", of twenty-one or twenty-four, of twenty-one or until marriage in the case of a girl, but without agreeing a date, an omission which one would think conducive to wrangling towards the end of the contract. Many but by no means all of the children appear in both records. Finally, the age of the child can sometimes be established from the parish register; though, of those identifiable by Christian and surname, and with regard to obvious pitfalls, about a

third were not baptised at Batheaston, indicative of how often fathers with young families "gained a settlement" in a new parish, they or their children becoming later "chargeable" to the parish of their adoption.

Of the seventy-five known apprenticeships, none later than 1823, only nine date from the seventeenth century, the earliest: "1629. For Water Jones with Tylye by the appoyntment of Mr Lee (the vicar) and the parishioners £1". The familiarity of the reference to Tylye suggests apprenticeship within the parish; but of fifty-three children whose destination is recorded, only four went to masters in Batheaston.

A horrifying story can be told of the sending out of little drudges by parishes only anxious to get rid of them, under the pretence of their learning a trade; but it is good to record that no evidence of fictional practices can be found in Batheaston. A favourite device of overseers was to apprentice boys to "husbandry" and girls to "housewifery"—possibly genuine, but doubtless often an euphemism. However, it is rather surprising that only one Batheaston boy was apprenticed to husbandry, and he to a widow! and four girls to housewifery, one of them to a relative and one to Henry Walters, the unofficial Squire of the village. Admittedly, children were thrust out into the world painfully young, as was the practice of the time, and a suggestively impersonal air appears in the early nineteenth century, when the poor rate was a grievous burden, and the entry was invariably brusque: "Minty's boy" and "Kite's girl".

The trades to which children were apprenticed are shewn in Fig. 12. No details are available for earlier and later periods. It will be seen that the cloth trade leads easily, though it only appears once after 1762, when the trade was declining. A fair variety of other trades is represented; the single recruit to "writing" was George Aust, the bright boy whose interesting career is noticed elsewhere (p. 91). The premium paid was usually about £4 or £5, less with older children.

The age of thirty-one children is known; nine were twelve, six eleven, three each ten and thirteen; eight were younger, including two mites of seven. One of two boys of fifteen had recently come into parish care and possibly the other also. Seventeen only of the total were girls; there is no record of their being sent out before the age of twelve, except one who went to a relative. Probably the usual practice was to put the girls into domestic service locally.

Four children, mostly of tender age, were certainly placed with relatives, and there were probably more where the name does not give a clue. The master who in 1765 took two little brothers, aged ten and seven, on the same day to the distant parish of S. James, Bristol, to learn the trade of a rough mason, was probably related to them. Some others were, however, apprenticed exceptionally young, especially in the cloth trade, where it is supposed that they could do some simple task; for instance, three Godwin brothers were sent in 1760 and the two following years, aged eight (two) and seven to different masters in Bradford on Avon to learn broadweaving. Perhaps the parish was reluctant, among its obligations, to support three of the same family. In 1776, the Vestry ordered: "The poor children of a Sufficient Age to be put out apprentices" without specifying further, and it is rather curious that there was only one binding that year, and none the next.

Two examples of early indentures are given in Appendix 8. Two typical outfits sent by the parish with apprentices may be of some interest. In later years details were rarely given:

1664.	Paid with Rudmans boy to bind him apprentize and for a wascote hat stockings and bands	£9 6s 3d
1731.	paid John Workman of Winslow for taking John the Bastard son of Betty Fisher Apprentice	£2 10s
	paid for his Indentures	3s 9d
	Shoes Hatt and Stockings for him	6s 0d
	John Bletchly for Clothes for him	9s 9d
	For making two shirts	8d
	Wm Russell for making his Clothes	3s 6d
	For a pair of new Breeches	3s 0d
	more Expences about him	4s 6d

An attempt to trace some of the parish apprentices in later life has been quite without success. In several instances it was possible to consult the register of the parish to which they went, but no entries were found, nor were any of them noticed to return to Batheaston, except one girl who was married. The overseers paid the cost of nursing a boy with smallpox in his second year of apprenticeship; and that is all.

Cloth: Broadweaver	14
Burler	1
Shearman	1
Clothworker	1
Housewifery	4
Tailor	3
Mason	3
Baker	2
Butcher	2
Husbandry	
Writing	
Carpenter	
Bandbox maker	
Basket maker	
Tiler and plasterer	1 each
Quilter	
Breeches maker	
Shoemaker	
Tallow chandler	
Ropemaker	

Fig. 12.   Trades to which parish apprentices were put, 1688 to 1794

DISCIPLINE

The special discipline to which the poor were liable was the wearing of the hated badge—"upon the shoulder of the right sleeve of the uppermost garment a large Roman P together with the first letter of the name of the parish . . . in red or blue cloth". This iniquitous humiliation was required by Act of Parliament of every pauper, his wife and children. Several references appear in the Batheaston records:

1749.	One Weeks pay deducted from Ann Aust and Bolwell "they appearing without the Badge".	
	Peter Salmon for 13 badges	10s 6d
1776.	The Vestry resolved that "the Poor be obliged to wear their Badges".	
1779.	Persons seen at any time without the badge to be struck off for one month.	
1787.	Pay to be stopt immediately for not wearing the Badge constantly & Neglect bringing their Family to Church at our Meetings Monthly.	

No further references to the badge were made, but in 1774 and again in 1795, it was ordered that "any Person keeping a Dog shall have no Relief Whatsoever". It seems a harsh provision, but understandable when poor relief was costing the parish so dear.

1802. "Ordered that every Pauper receiving Weekly Pay should attend the Monthly Vestry & to receive their pay for the Current Week of late shamefully disregarded. Pay for the week to be witheld unless excused for illness, infirmity or distance of Residence".

EMPLOYMENT

No reference to unemployment occurs before 1741, when Meredith and Mayes were paid £1 1s 6d for "mending the highways when they had no work". The same year, J. England had 1s 6d when he was out of work. It is fair to conclude that the able-bodied of Batheaston usually found work, for it is into the nineteenth century when the entry "no work" often appears. Thereafter matters deteriorated, and the number of unemployed rose fast in the bad times which followed the Napoleonic wars.

In 1817 Cornelius Button was set to work on the highway, and paid 9s a week. Three years later, 17s 6d was spent on hammers "for the use of men out of employ to break stones on the Highways", and again, £1 12s 6d on "repairing hammers for Labourers on the Turnpike Road". The years that follow contain frequent entries for the making and mending of hammers. In January 1829 it is noted that six men and one boy were out of work, and the next month labourers "out of employ" were paid £5 1s 9½d for working on the roads. In 1833 three breast ploughs were bought at three shillings each. This seems very late for the use of such a primitive implement.

Payments to the support of "able-bodied paupers requiring work" appear to the end of the record, £9 7s 0d for the June–September quarter 1835 being an average sum.

Very little other evidence about employment for the poor can be gathered from the Poor Books, and none of deliberate policy. Rarely, special help was given, such as:

1782. A spinning tarr   4s 0d
1803. Elinor Trotman for Teaching Mary
          to spin   5s 0d

1809. A loom for Thos Woodman   £2 10s 0d
1810. Thread for Cox's Wife to make lace   2s 8d

ILLEGITIMACY AND THE OVERSEERS

A parish was, of course, keenly interested to avoid as far as possible the burden of supporting illegitimate children, so it is not to be wondered at that it was often at much trouble and expense to bring about the marriage of any poor girl found to be pregnant. Among "forced" marriages recorded are the following:

1745. Pd the Revd Mr Hall for marrying
      John Iles with Martha Kerton £1 14s 6d
1760. John Noyes apprehended in
      Bastardy, for a licence and
      getting him married to Ann
      Godwin   £4 13s 4d

In 1785 Betty Woodman was forcibly married to David Mead of Road. Mead received from Batheaston parish three guineas with his wife, £1 15s 6d for a licence and 15s 9d, the fees of the minister and clerk at Road. These entries follow:

To Tythingman Time keeping the Man
  in Custody 7 days and 6 nights   13s 0d
To an Assistant to Road   2s 0d
To Horsehire   6s 0d

Forcible indeed! There was a similar episode in 1789, when Alex. Mortimore was married by licence to Mary Box at Walcot, and given a guinea with his wife. The ring "and other expences" cost 18s 0½d and the tithingman was paid 3/- for keeping the bridegroom in custody for two days.

In 1804, when Mary Weston "swore her Child to Jas Rose", the writer of the account expressed his feelings thus:

Gold ring   4s 0d
Church Fees   13s 0d
The Young Lady's Fortune   1 guinea

Bastardy was not a serious problem for the overseers before the later eighteenth century, for only three children are recorded as regularly supported by the parish up to 1770. It was not until 1733 that the law required that any man charged on oath with being the father of a illegitimate child should be apprehended and committed to prison until he undertook to indemnify the parish from expense. The possibilities for abuse are obvious. In 1776, "John Wood Esq's Butler" paid £2 towards "a Bastard

Child upon Bette Cottle in her Lying In". Five years later it is ordered that fathers of bastard children behind with their pay are to be prosecuted.

It was the custom to allow the mother of an illegitimate child £2 for her lying-in, and of course the overseers extracted this sum from the father whenever they could. In 1788 James Mayan paid the curious sum of £4 15s 3d "in full clearance to his child by Lydia Loveday". The amount required was soon increased, however, and from 1806 it cost the father £26 to indemnify the parish of his bastard. In 1807 John Cottle signed a receipt for £26 for a pregnancy, "none to be returned if the child is born alive and dies before it is capable of supporting itself".

At the turn of the century a regular bastardy account appears in the Poor Book, six mothers receiving from 1s 6d to half a crown a week, obtained from the father, of course, when possible; but even when the father was known and could be pressed, he did not always pay up, and entries were made such as "Ballance against the Parish on the whole of the Bastardy Account £3 6s 8d".

By 1813 there were ten bastards on the list, two women, at least, being promiscuous, with five between them. Perhaps Elizabeth Gay—the name seems oddly apposite—did even better, for in 1830 three men were paying to the support of her three children!

There is a quaint suggestion of social snobbery in 1824, when Miss Chubb and Jane Gray were "examined concerning their settlement being advanced in pregnancy".

Prices were rising, and in 1826 £50 was paid to release a father from the charge on his bastard. In 1831 Mister Baynton paid £15 for arrears of maintenance. He was evidently quite unwilling or unable to perform his duty:

1834. Coach hire and expenses going to
      Cheltenham and Cross to appre-
      hend Mr Baynton   £2 5s 0d

There is no record of the outcome of the enterprise.

STRANGERS

It has already been noted (p. 52) that during the seventeenth century many entries in the churchwardens' accounts record the bestowal of a few pence on an endless procession of "travellers", "passengers", soldiers, sailors, men, women and children, and the abundance of these entries related to the fact that an important road traversed the parish. From about 1700 the evidence on the relief of vagrants and other poor persons not of the parish is found in the Poor Books; and it is found in great amount and wide variety. The instances that follow are chosen as representative; they could be expanded and multiplied many times. The miseries endured by these wretched wanderers are obvious, as is also the generosity accorded to many of them.

1694. A traviling woman that was delivered.

1717. To a Woman with Child to send her
      away   1s 0d
      To a man whose wife was hurt by a
      wagon   5s 0d
      for his lodging and house room   7s 6d

1720. A great Bellyed Woman   1s 0d

1734. Martha Kerton for one nights
      lodging ye poor Woman   6d
      Saml Fuller for ale for her   2d

1746. Reliefed a Corperals Wife & 4
      children in her return from the
      fatal battle of fontenoy   1s 6d

1747. Lodging for a woman & her 2
      children from Flanders   2s 0d
      Gave to a Soldiere that was in ye
      Battle of Culloden & to some
      others   2s 2d

1786. To Dr. Attending and Medicine to
      Sarah Higgins of Godstone in
      Surrey taken Ill on the road   £1 7s 6d

1794. A Poor Man taken Ill on the Road   2½d

1798. Expences at the Public House one
      Night for a stranger found ill in
      the road & attendance on him
      all night   6s 2d

1810. A Sick Man at the Lamb all night   1s 6d

1821. A stranger ill at the Lamb   2s 6d

In 1823 a stranger lay ill at the White Hart for seven weeks at a cost to the parish of £8 15s 4d, and in 1832 Dr. Davies was paid £5 19s 9d for attending persons ill at the White Hart.

In the earlier years sick strangers were invariably nursed at the Lamb, which also received the bodies of persons who were killed or found dead and accommodated the inquest; in the last years of the system, for some reason unknown the White Hart took the place of the Lamb in the reception of sick strangers. Doubtless many of the strangers taken ill and unable to proceed were journeying to Bath to avail themselves of the supposed medicinal qualities of the waters, and the free accommodation provided for them at the Hospital. In this respect, the experience of Batheaston cannot have been typical.

The overseers were never free from the necessity of relieving such as "travellers with a pass", that is, on journeys sanctioned by a magistrate or parish officer, and "distressed families on the road", the sums paid out amounting to a considerable burden. Always it was expected of the overseers to get strangers out of the parish, if possible, before they expired, or gave birth to a child who would thereby gain a "settlement" in the parish and might become a charge upon it. Nevertheless, it was no uncommon thing for them to have the disposal of a corpse:

1694. Burying a Strangwoman that died
in ye Street   3s 0d
1717. To the Grave & Bell for the travelling Womans Child   1s 6d
       Shroud, Coffin and other Expences   5s 0d
1741. Going after the Coroner for the
poor woman who died in the
Foss   12s 6d
       Paid the Coroner   13s 4d
1793. Body of James Doran of St.
Thomas St, Bristol found Dead
on Bannadown & bringing said
Body to the Lamb Inn Jan. 25th   3s 4d
       To Tythingman fetching the Coro-
ner from Wells on Do.   10s 6d
       12 jurymen said Body   8s 0d
       Coffin and Shroud for Do.   13s 6d
       Clerk & Expences Carrying Do. to
Church   6s 0d
       Laying out Do. Cleaning Cloths
etc.   4s 0d
       My own Expences   2s 2½d

If James Doran's own parish repaid Batheaston its expenses on his inquest and burial the fact is not recorded. A mere three months later, another dead stranger was carried to the Lamb cleaned, laid out, and buried.

An entry for 1787 reads: Pd Daniel Cottle for Frame of a Sheet for the Instruction to Restore persons to Life when Aparently Drowned. Hanged up in the Lamb Kitchen 1s 0d. In 1797 appears:

To paid for a cart to bring the Corpse of a
stranger Drowned in the River near the
Mill to the Lamb   1s 0d
To Mr. Creaser the Surgeon's Fee for
endeavouring to restore life   5s 0d
To Expences at the Public House for
Flannel Brandy fumigation etc.   12s 6d

The usual items for fetching the coroner from Wells, the inquest, and the burial follow. By fumigation probably is meant the burning of feathers to provide ammonia as a stimulant. Clearly, every effort was made to resuscitate this poor stranger.

THE MILITIA

Previously, the duty of providing armed men and their mounts for the defence of the country was laid upon men of substance, but from 1757 the responsibility was placed on the parishes. A man chosen by lot had either to serve in the Militia or to provide a substitute. As in the former case the support of his family was likely to fall upon the parish during his absence, so it was often considered the better bargain to contribute to the cost of a substitute, though the advantage of so doing was not always obvious when the substitute's family in turn needed support. The first reference to the Militia appears in the Poor Book in 1777 when John Pyatt and Francis Smith each received four guineas to match his own contribution. In 1782, however, the family of F. Smith's substitute was paid a shilling and sixpence a week for 46 weeks!

George Sendall proved exceptionally expensive, for in 1795 the family of his substitute cost ten guineas, and in 1799 £10 was paid for their support to the overseers of Nunney. Besides this, in the same year the support of five other families cost the parish £36 1s 0d. The following years saw frequent payments of £3, "the parish bounty", and in 1804 it is noted hopefully that £25 4s 0d is to be repaid by the county. It was, of course, the time of the napoleonic wars, and the threat of an invasion was pressing. Evidently the parish did not fully meet its obligations to provide militia men, for in 1805 a rate was levied to raise £80 "for Fines for defective men under the Defence Act". One of the parish officers journeyed to Wincanton to pay the fines, and was out for two days at an additional cost of a guinea. In 1808 it was ordered that the names of persons liable to be drawn for militia men be taken down. This was the occasion of the establishment of the "Local Militia", not replacing what was thereafter called the "Old Militia", but adding a larger force of men who were to serve locally except in actual emergency. With the fall of Napoleon, of course, the danger to the country receded, and thereafter only occasional entries relating to the Militia appear in the Poor Books.

VERMIN

Payment for the destruction of animals really or reputedly inimical to husbandry was long a feature of country life. There was legislation for the killing of specified birds, and payment at 2d the dozen, in 1533 (24 Hen. 8 c 10), and it was the churchwardens on whom the burden of payment was laid. In Batheaston the early pages of the accounts record payment for foxes' heads, 1s each, one or two in most years; and an occasional shilling for a gray's (badger's) head. Hedgehogs first appear in 1683, when 18 were paid for, 2d each. In 1694 the churchwardens paid also for 3 foxes, 8 badgers and one polecat at 3d. The account is summed up: "disbourst in all for ye destruction of such vermin £1 1s 3d". The whole of their expenditure for this year amounted to £3 2s 1d.

In 1738 the Vestry decided that money would be paid for "greys and poles heads" only if taken in the parish or within two miles of the church"; they do not say how they proposed to prevent cheating, but from that time payments declined, and from 1750 the official hunt against "vermin" was off for the present. There is no further entry until 1772, when a $\frac{1}{2}$d was to be paid for every rat's tail and a $\frac{1}{4}$d for every sparrow's head—both creatures mentioned for the first time. This resulted in a bill for 60 rats and 388 sparrows, and the thrifty Vestry repealed the order the next year.

By 1834, however, sparrows were evidently causing much damage, for the payment of a farthing a head was authorised. From then on, numbers rose fast, and one to two thousand and even more sparrows were slaughtered each year until 1856, when it was agreed that the item for sparrows be continued. Nevertheless, payments ceased, without further remark, and no more profit was made from the destruction of wild life.

The only other creature for which payment was made was 26 "vipers" at 3d each in 1835. The record tells nothing of the methods used against the proscribed animals; nor why the attack was at one time concentrated on foxes and badgers, at another hedgehogs, then rats, later sparrows, and finally the 26 "vipers".

Chapter 9

Education

DATA on literacy, as judged by the ability to make a signature, are necessarily scanty before the mid-eighteenth century. Such evidence as there is comes mostly from the holders of parish offices, who tended to be the better educated and more prosperous inhabitants. It was quite common for the overseers to signify with a cross. The churchwardens usually signed; the last to make his mark was Henry Fisher in 1810. He was a substantial tiler and plasterer, and an owner of property.

King Edward's School in Bath was founded in 1552, and it must have been possible to obtain some learning in Batheaston before there was formal provision for it. At a visitation in 1615, for instance, it was reported that "James Duport is a very poore man and teacheth skole without licence".

From 1754 couples marrying were required to sign the register, or the equivalent, and so it provides valuable evidence. However, it must not be forgotten that by this time the village contained a number of educated people not of local origin, and that the standard required to count as literate was no more than the ability to scrawl a few letters which the officiating minister could accept as a signature.

In Fig. 13 may be seen the fruits of this analysis.

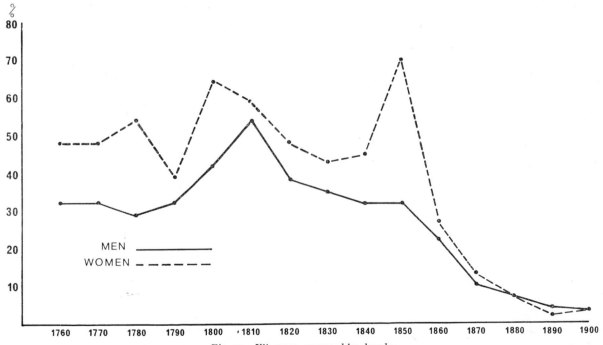

Fig. 13. Illiteracy, averaged by decades

It is an unexpected finding that women were not much less literate than men. The rise in illiteracy, common to both sexes, in the early nineteenth century, was the sequel to hard times to which both bad harvests and the Napoleonic wars contributed. W. P. Baker[1] found a similar trend in East Yorkshire. The great but unsustained rise among women at 1850 looks like a distortion due to necessary reliance on small numbers, especially as illiteracy among their men was falling steadily. The census analysis (Fig. 10) shews what a large proportion of these women were born elsewhere. To this time the fruits of the elementary education offered by the National School were not impressive, but the position soon changed; the last person to make her cross was a widow of fifty-three in 1903.

The history of education in Batheaston begins with John Hellier, vicar, who by his will, proved 20 February 1817, left an endowment for the education of poor boys of the parish in reading, writing and arithmetic. The bequest was £100 for the education of eight boys, to be followed by £80 for six more boys on the death of one of his beneficiaries, and the residue of his estate for a further ten boys, twenty-four in all. His trustees were the incumbents of neighbouring parishes, but the churchwardens' accounts for 1793 record that the vicar of Box "taking the active part and dying insolvent", only £120 remained for the charity. His son-in-law repaid this sum to the parish, and it was invested in £178 8s 9d of 3% Consolidated Stock in the names of Henry and Thomas Walters.

The number actually taught on the foundation was eight. No other light on its early years remains. One Morris, schoolmaster, paid the highway rate on a single occasion, in 1745, and Thomas Russell, the clerk, filled the office in 1784. It is likely that more than one parish clerk acted as schoolmaster. Where they taught, whether in their own home or in church, and how much time they gave to their duties, no one knows. Probably the school included other boys whose parents paid something for their education.

It was well into the nineteenth century when, under two impulses, a recognisable parish school came into existence. The National Society for the establishment of schools in which the principles of the Church of England were to be taught was founded in 1811, and the vicar, J. J. Conybeare, was eager to build a school for the children of the parish. His enthusiasm and generosity made possible the establishment of a National School, and a building was erected in the churchyard in 1818. It consisted of a single room, and the archway which gave access to a flight of steps into the churchyard may still be seen in the churchyard wall.

At this point it is necessary to look back at the Sunday School movement to provide elementary education for the poor. According to the notes issued to the Mayor of Bath's guides, Mrs. Elizabeth Montagu, the Blue Stocking, stayed in 1740 with her sister, Mrs. Sarah Scott, who founded a Sunday School in Batheaston; no local record of it has been discovered. In 1789, in response to an appeal for schools on a national scale, a Sunday School was established. The appeal proposed not less than four hours attendance, divided into two sessions, the pupils to be over six years of age, and a teacher to every thirty, who should be paid 1s to 2s a Sunday. Religious Observance of the Sabbath and Improvement in virtuous Habits should be taught; strangely, neither Writing nor Arithmetic, though reading the Scriptures and spelling were to be used "as a Preparative", and Alphabets or Spelling Books might be taken home. It is good to learn that teachers were to "check wanton Cruelty towards Animals".

In response to a local appeal, £46 6s 0d was promised by forty-one persons, all but two as annual subscriptions. The record from which these notes were taken continues for several years, the London Society contributing £10 8s 0d in 1791, and there is no doubt that the Sunday School was in being until the establishment of the National School, in which it was finally merged. A note attached to the report on the School made in 1821 (below) reads: "Garraway the School Master obtained the first Prize for the best Sunday School in the Archdeaconry in 1822".

The Rev. H. Harvey Marriott in 1821 reported thus on the National School:

The lower department is backward in reading and more so in religious knowledge. This may be attributed to their early age and the instruction being only that of a Sunday School.

The senior classes read in a plain and unaffected manner, and quite free from the monotony so frequently apparent in Village Schools. Religious knowledge bears more than a proportionate improvement to . . . junior classes.

The Master appears very zealous and attentive in his office. . . . I was sorry to perceive an omission on the Master's part which is of essential consequence to the childrens' progress in the practical and daily duties of Religion. The progressive series of instruction had not been observed, and tho' the senior children are many of them well able to answer questions the Master's attention does not appear to have been employed in the way prescribed for giving them the form of prayers.

I cannot but express the pleasure I experienced in the orderly and respectful conduct of the whole school. There was an appearance of decency in their manner, and a cleanness in their persons and cheerfulness in their countenances, which speaks more for the progress of many of the material parts of a Charity School Establishment than any other external Test.

The report concludes with a recommendation that as the school was necessarily confined to one room, it should be divided into boys and girls, and the observation that the senior class appeared to consist almost entirely of girls. It seems to be the earliest explicit record of the school that has survived, save for the Report of the Commissioners concerning Charities the previous year. It is there noted that the annual dividend of five guineas was regularly paid to the schoolmaster, who educated for it eight poor boys in reading, writing and arithmetic. The nomination of boys was with trustees, who had always selected from the poor of the parish. The same person was master of the Sunday school and the day school, but gave particular instruction to the eight boys for the particular consideration. They added that the vicar visited the school and "sees that the master does his duty". There is no record of the names of Hellier's boys.

In 1834, under the guidance and with the financial aid of the vicar, Spencer Madan, who also obtained a grant of £50 from the National Society, the school was enlarged by an upper storey. There were then three rooms, the girls' and infants' rooms above, the boys' below, the remainder of the ground floor divided into two compartments euphemistically labelled in a surviving plan W.C. The roof was of slate, the rooms of good height, the building, of course, of stone.

Among the early archives of the school is a small book of accounts and notes, which records that in 1837–1838 there were forty-nine school weeks and an average attendance of thirty-four; in 1839–1840 of forty-six. The increase was probably due to the influx of labourers and their families, noted in the census of 1841, for the building of the railway. It is therefore unexpected to find that the earliest remaining Log Book opens with a list of 226 children on the register on Lady Day 1840, and that according to the census return of 1851, 324 of the 397 children between the ages of five and fifteen, and many younger ones, were solely "scholars"! They were able to attend either day or Sunday school, but most in theory did both. Study of the Log Book alone enables the deduction that for many children school was a rare penance or pleasure, according to their point of view, but it has no figures to show how tiny was the fraction actually present; it is clear, however, that the average records the sparse attendance of a large number of children. Yet there were children, not a few, who really attended school to the age of thirteen and fourteen—greatly to the credit of poor parents.

It is not possible to discover how many Batheaston children at this period had no formal education; the children of the professional classes, the younger ones especially, were mostly taught at home, and of course there were schools in Bath, and perhaps in Batheaston, too. The repeated entry "Gone to Miss Haywood's" tells that there was at least one "dame" school in the village. The census of 1851 provides additional evidence, fifteen women and girls being there registered as schoolmistresses.

The Log Book is a valuable document for the study of social history in Batheaston. It gives the parents' names, residence, occupation and "principles"; the children's date of birth, place of baptism, date of admission, date of leaving, and a generous allowance of space, often informatively used, under the heading Remarks. The pupils were almost exclusively of the humbler sort, the children mainly of labourers and gardeners, a few tradesmen and a rare farmer. Of the parents' "principles", all were "church" except a few families of "dissenters", one "papist" an Irish child, and four whose "principles" were lacking, or in some category unknown. The Methodist Church dates from 1797, and the small number of "dissenters" suggests that many of them were educated privately; or perhaps the "Chapel School" mentioned in the Log Book in 1869 was already in being. The great majority of the children were baptised at Batheaston or S. Catherine.

The staff in 1840 consisted of William Coles, a local man, previously a shoemaker, his wife, and at times a female assistant. The Log Book preserves a list of the books received by them annually as gifts, religious themes predominating, with occasional titles such as *Zoology*, *Mother's Help* and *Manners and Customs of the East*. Children might be "entered" at any time after their first birthday! When they actually came is not stated, but from the age of five each child who attended gained a book annually, the titles all entered— *Railway Cripple*, *Swearer's End*, *Obstinacy* are examples—even when the report was far from satisfactory. Reports range through Good, Well Conducted, Middling (many of these), Inclined to be saucy, Inattentive and impertinent, Very saucy, Bad boy, to Very bad boy. The telling word Irregular stands against many of the names, and obviously some children attended only occasionally and for a short period. It is not possible to say how far the curriculum reached beyond the basic "Three Rs" and religious knowledge. William Coles' own hand, seen in one of the enumerator's books of the 1851 census, is that of an accomplished practitioner of the copper-plate style.

A slip of paper, preserved by chance, gives a glimpse of the treat provided at Christmas 1845, for "270 children, infants included". It contains the account for puddings; Mrs. Cook, who made them, appropriately, earned 5s and the same sum was charged for baking. The main ingredients were 11 pecks of flour at 2s 8d, 44 lb of suet at 7d, 41 lb of raisins at 7d, and 11 lb of treacle at 5d.

A report on the school in 1857, written by the vicar, gives interesting information. The boys' master was John Harrison, aged twenty-three; a newcomer, he had been apprenticed as a pupil teacher in Leeds, obtained a certificate after a course in a training school lasting nine months, and had two years' teaching experience at Ledbury. The mistress of the girls was Harriet Yates, probably about to leave, "when we hope to obtain a certificated mistress". The girls were often to suffer frequent changes of not very competent teachers.

Expenditure on the school for the previous year was £107 1s 4½d, the chief items being:

Teachers' salaries	..	..	£90	9	6
Assistant's salary (infants)		..	3	9	6
Books and apparatus	..	..	4	2	7½
Fuel and lights	..	..	..	3	0	7

No hint of lavishness here! The corresponding income was:

Endowment (Hellier's Charity)	..		8	0	0
Voluntary contributions		..	69	7	0
School pence	..	..	42	9	2
Balance from previous year		..	2	11	1½
		Total	122	7	3½

The weekly payments were a penny for one child, a penny for the next two, fourpence for a family, whatever its size.

As the need for education became more fully recognised, facilities were extended. In 1836 a school was established to serve the growing hamlet of Bailbrook and in 1855 had fifty pupils. Before 1858, also, the generosity of the Hon. Emily Strutt provided for S. Catherine a school which she maintained at her own expense. This latter school never came under the wing of the National Society, but continued its independent existence until 1919.

Batheaston School was now growing fast, and in 1858 the urgent need for extension was recognised. The average attendance was 81 infants, 58 boys and 47 girls at the day school, 76 boys and 75 girls on Sundays. Another difficulty was that the Government would not provide funds for a school built on consecrated ground, and the need of help was becoming imperative. The bishop decreed that it was not illegal to pull down the present school, which, he said, ought never to have been built in the churchyard.

Plans for a new school were prepared by Davies and Tew of Chesterfield, boys', girls' and infants' departments, each to hold ninety children, and a master's house. The foundation stone, brought from the old building, was laid on 15 November 1858, and the *Bath Chronicle* reported the event at length. After a service in church, and a procession to the site, enlivened by the ringing of the bells, "Mr Walters then proceeded to lay the stone, which he did in a most skilful manner, with the aid of a beautiful trowel". So the familiar school came into being, and was opened on 24 June 1859. The cost was £2,237 13 1, the parish raising £900, and the Government granting the same sum. Melmoth Walters, the last of his family to exercise a benevolent despotism over the village, gave half an acre of land costing £80, £100, and the promise of a like sum if needed.

In a collection of notes and newspaper cuttings recalling the restoration of the church and the rebuilding of the school an unnamed joker has left this:

THIS TABLET IS ERECTED
IN GRATEFUL REMEMBRANCE
OF THE REV JOHN JOSIAS CONYBEARE
AND THE REV SPENCER MADAN
FOUNDERS OF THE OLD PARISH SCHOOLS
ALSO
OF MELMOTH WALTERS ESQUIRE
WHO PURCHASED AND PRESENTED
THE SITE OF THE NEW SCHOOLS
THE CORNER STONE OF WHICH WAS LAID
NOV 15 1858
ALSO
OF THE REV T. P. ROGERS AND CAPTN
THOMPSON
WHO BULLIED CHRIST CHURCH OUT OF
£50
THE PRIVY COUNCIL OUT OF £900
THE DIOCESAN BOARD OUT OF £50
WITH CONSIDERABLE SATISFACTION
ALSO
OF SAMUEL BOND QUARRYMAN
WHO WITH MUCH DIFFICULTY AND
ILLWILL
WAS FORCED TO SUPPLY THE STONE
ON REASONABLE TERMS
REQUIESCANT IN PACE
THE STONECUTTER WHO ENGRAVED
THE ABOVE
LIVES AT   & REQUESTS THE
PATRONAGE
OF ALL INTELLIGENT PEOPLE

Internal evidence reveals more than a probability that it was the vicar who thus relieved his feelings!

THE MELMOTH WALTERS PRIZE

The sum of £58 3s 6d, subscribed as a testimonial to Melmoth Walters when he resigned the office of churchwarden, was given by him for the foundation of a school prize. A Vestry minute records in 1868:

"It is proposed that the money, less the costs, shall be invested in the purchase of 3% Consols, in the name of the Official Trustee of the Charity Commissioners, to the intent that the Dividends shall be remitted yearly before Christmas, to the Vicar or Officiating Minister for the time being of Batheaston, who shall thereout purchase a small pica octavo BIBLE, of the authorised version with marginal references, and bound in strong calf with red edges, and a BOOK OF COMMON PRAYER AND THE HOMILIES OF THE CHURCH OF ENGLAND to match, and shall during the week next after Christmas present the same books, with the residue of the Dividends, as "A Prize", to the boy in the Parish School who, during the preceding year, shall, in the opinion of the Vicar or Minister, have excelled in learning and good conduct: but if the boy who shall stand first in the order of merit shall have received the Prize in a former year, then it shall be given to the second in order, and so on".

The prestige of the Prize was such that the bible and prayer book are cherished in many households in the parish. A note by the vicar in the parish magazine in 1891, explaining the principles on which he acted in awarding the Prize ends thus:

"I hope that a knowledge of these rules will prevent the keen disappointment a boy must feel in not receiving so great a prize, for which he might otherwise consider himself eligible".

Since 1939 the prize money has been added to the school prize fund.

A set of Log Books, complete from 1862, would enable a later history of the school, of much interest, to be written. Here only a condensed account can be given, choosing such features as may help a reader to construct in his mind some idea of the development of a village school during most of a century.

In early days especially, the master's constant anxiety was to get many of the children to school at all. There was no compulsory attendance, and the habit of regular school-going was formed neither in parent or progeny. School pence had to be found, too, except for Hellier's boys, and poor parents were deprived of the small earnings of children sent out to work. So we find John Harrison constantly lamenting "desperately poor" attendance, children kept away—for potato planting and harvesting, fruit picking, bird scaring, gleaning; for minding the home, as "mother is in the hayfield", even for "picking up acorns, which they sell for 3d a peck". Attendance was usually low on Wednesdays, when children were "taken to market to mind the vegetables".

This matter of attendance held extra importance, because these were the days of "payment by results", of government grants calculated on the number of children who passed the annual examination in Reading, Writing and Arithmetic for which the master anxiously groomed his pupils, writing up, daily at times, the results of his tests. Having an endearing habit of confiding his musings to the Log Book, he wrote in 1865:

"It is very trying, and seems to take away one's energy entirely. I think there are few who have such difficulties to contend with. It cannot be avoided, there is such a demand among the market gardeners for juvenile labour".

In the classroom he was of course handicapped by the need to go over the work again and again, as children strayed in and out of school. A natural optimist, he was jubilant when a class worked a few sums correctly, or were persuaded not to count on their fingers (as this, he noted, was no longer to be allowed), or could work as well on paper (an innovation) as on slates; only to be downcast next week when his charges seemed to have forgotten everything so laboriously taught.

Kindly as well as hardworking, he hated corporal punishment, writing hopefully that he was now in the third week of avoiding it, having "adopted the plan of detaining disorderly children after school"; but the plan failed and the significant letters C.P. followed by two or three names appear without comment at the end of later reports. Another time this lovable man confided to the Log Book:

"I invariably find that stopping lessons for a quarter of an hour and singing a few lively tunes will restore order and cheerfulness much better than punishment".

It was the custom to employ pupil teachers to help with the work of instruction, and also monitors, who received a small payment in return for simple duties in the classroom. The work of teaching the former, out of school hours, was an additional burden on the master; if they did well enough, they went on for training as professional teachers.

In 1871 the school managers decided that the salaries of the master and mistress (Mrs. Harrison) should be fixed at the average of the last five years, instead of varying with academic success; the sum was £134 8s per annum, raised in 1886 to £150. In 1876 there was a severe financial crisis, subscriptions being "utterly inadequate", and a deficit of £71 to be made up on the year's expenditure of £371. An urgent appeal went out for increased subscriptions, the alternative being the establishment of a government School Board and a compulsory rate. The accounts were brought into balance more by a larger government grant than by increased subscriptions, but the crisis was resolved, though another appeal was necessary in 1881, in order to keep the National (Church) School. The children's fees were now twopence a week. In 1886 they were raised to threepence, except for infants, the extra penny to be returned for everyone making 350 attendances, sickness to be taken into consideration. In 1891 the managers abolished fees, and agreed to provide the children's books and slates.

Evidently some attempt to compel attendance followed the Education Act of 1870, and an attendance officer made his appearance in 1877, "causing some alarm in the village", a few summons and fines, but by 1882 Harrison was troubled because "the visits of the attendance officer at such long intervals is perfectly useless".

There is no doubt that during John Harrison's mastership, as well as under later heads, by the standard of the time Batheaston School did well. The report for 1876 is typical:

H.M.Inspector: Mixed School. The Children are in good order, the exercises smartly done, and the work throughout careful and accurate, the large proportion of Children presented in the upper standards being very creditable. There is still some weakness in the Arithmetic of the Third Standard, and the division of Syllables wants attention. The Singing was good. Another set of reading books is wanted.

Infants' School. The Infants are well and carefully taught, and the general condition of this department is very satisfactory.

Diocesan Inspector: Religious Knowledge, discipline, tone and repetition all very good. Full, ready and intelligent answering from all the children of all the classes. Quiet and orderly. An excellent School in all respects.

This year the average attendance was 145.

Harrison entered the close of the school year in the Log Book in July 1885, and three weeks later his successor took up the tale, without comment by either. According to uncertain local memory, Harrison "went elsewhere". He deserved well of Batheaston.

George Harding, too, was a humane and conscientious man, and followed the lines laid down by his predecessor. He introduced certain innovations, among them a School Concert, and an enthusiasm for drawing, the proceeds of the former being applied to the purchase of materials for the latter. He had other progressive ideas, and in 1886 recorded with delight that on Ascension Day, after taking the boys to church as usual, they proceeded to Solsbury and used for the first time the means of playing cricket, provided with a subscription raised by the curate and some of his friends.

It is important to remember how large a part was taken by the parish clergy in the conduct of a National School. On 23 Feb. 1888, Harding wrote "Our beloved Vicar died suddenly last night. In him the Schools lose a daily visitor; the children a kind teacher, and myself a genuine friend". Another occasion for grief was the death from diphtheria of a little lad of whom he thought well, in the course of an epidemic which seriously disrupted school work. Outbreaks of children's ailments were, of course, a commonplace of school life.

The Inspectors' reports were mostly favourable during his mastership, and in 1890 the government grant was 20s 6d per head—the highest possible. He resigned in 1891, because of the continued ill-

health of his wife (it was still a joint appointment), writing in the Log Book "We have spent six very happy years here, and have much cause for thankfulness for the many kindnesses and sympathy in our work shown us by the Managers". Thirty-five years later, he attended the farewell presentation of one of his staff.

His successor, William Crossman, is still remembered as an excellent teacher and a strict disciplinarian, with no scruples about corporal punishment. In 1896 the Diocesan Inspector reported "The teaching and tone of the school deserve much praise" and H.M. Inspector "The children attending this school are very orderly and attentive and are receiving very careful instruction. Their progress in all subjects reflects much credit on their teachers". Not only was the maximum grant gained, but the school was exempted from examination the following year. This master demanded effort not only of the children, who were daily exercised in a mental gymnastic called "Long Tots", which they, especially the girls, found difficult, but his time-table of study for the pupil teachers, each day from 7.45 to 8.45 a.m., might intimidate any but the most devoted.

He went from Batheaston to West Twerton and was succeeded by Alfred Wilson, from Boston, Lincolnshire, in 1898. He wrote, "Just before the close of this afternoon's session, the children and teachers presented me with a very beautiful spirit-case. 'Tis with great regret that I now finish my work here, after seven happy years".

The rest of the story is familiar to senior residents of the village, and may soon be told. Yet another capable and well-liked master ruled this school, and saw great changes in the pattern of education. The Act of 1902 set up local education authorities and a system of secondary education, and it was not long before Batheaston children who were successful in examination were continuing at Bath Secondary School. The Hellier Charity, having lost its original function with the abolition of fees in 1891, and disposing of the income with certain additions to it, encouraged this trend by giving two scholarships of £5 each for two years from 1909. Yet as late as 1924 the master recorded sadly in the Log Book that it was difficult to persuade parents to allow children to enter for the examination for free places

Pl. 47. Upper Standards, c. 1902

because of the difficulty in reaching the school. Among other changes he remarked the first medical inspection in 1914, and the first visit of a dentist the next year.

By this time out-of-school activities were becoming more common. In 1918, evidently as a patriotic gesture, the children picked 2½ cwt. of blackberries! What became of them is not recorded.

On retiring, Alfred Wilson wrote that he left after more than twenty-six happy years. The next master, John Beake, came from Norton Fitzwarren School, and set about introducing progressive ideas, such as educational visits, a school garden, "houses", sports day, and obtained the use of a field for football. Early in his reign, also, the Hellier Trustees gave a grant of £5 for a school library.

In 1930, there was a reorganisation, and senior children were admitted from elsewhere, sixteen from Swainswick, sixteen from Bathford, but in

1937 another change restricted the school to infant and primary departments. In 1941 extensive reconstructions were carried out in the parish at a cost of £1,600, with the help of grants from the Diocese and the National Society; but the requirements of the 1944 Act were too much for local enthusiasm to provide. At a public meeting in 1948 the Rev. Mercier, vicar, after recollecting with gratitude the help generously given by the Free Churches to maintain the school, continued that it was listed as desirable to be maintained as a Church School; but required improvements and additions which were to cost £23,000, of which the managers must raise half. This was considered a burden too great to be attempted and the meeting passed unanimously a resolution supporting the proposal of the Managers of Batheaston Church of England School to apply for Controlled Status. Thus the future of the school was determined, and so it is.

In compiling this short account of the history of the school it is intended to convey admiration for the service given by the succession of devoted masters and their assistants, and the inestimable benefit the school has given and still gives to the village.

To complete the account of education in Batheaston requires a few words on the private schools of the later Victorian period.

Avon House Academy, a "Middle Class Boarding and Day School" was in being by 1858, and lasted until about 1892. At first conducted by William and Harriet Coles, son and daughter of the parish schoolmaster, by 1864 the proprietor was John Dingle, later assisted by his son.

Several times a "Ladies' School" made a brief appearance in the Bath Directory. In 1899 was entered for the first time Fairhaven School, under the Misses Herbert. This one prospered, and is still remembered in its later years, when Miss Frances Herbert was the mistress. In 1915 the Directory entry was changed to "Girls' School" a concession, presumably, to changing *mores*. Its last appearance was in 1917.

BAILBROOK SCHOOL

Written inside the cover of a book of accounts is the following:

Rules of Bailbrook School begun Aug 29th 1836.

1. Each child to bring a penny every Monday.

2. Any child absent more than a week exept(sic) from illness, to pay a fine of a penny the first, and a halfpenny each succeeding week before being readmitted.

3. All above six years to attend the Sunday school.

4. Any child habitually absent at Morning Prayer to have *no* reward. School to open at 9 A.M. and close at 5 P.M.

5. Those who obtain a ticket each Month for regular attendance at Sunday School to have an extra reward of 2s 6d.

6. Religious instruction to the elder children from ten to eleven each morning, till half past Eleven spelling, Arithmetical Tables etc till Twelve writing sums etc. Afternoon working and knitting.

Always under a woman teacher, work with the needle was prominent in the syllabus. The completion of a sampler was noted with triumph; even more, the little maid who finished a stocking and was rewarded with a case of needles "for her perseverance". There was the usual trouble with truant and troublesome children, rude and difficult parents. Once an appeal went out asking for children not to be sent before the age of three, as the noise they made interfered with the reading!

Bailbrook School continued until about 1920, when the few children attending were transferred to Batheaston School or S. Saviour's, Larkhall. The last mistress is still remembered affectionately as "Govvie" Haynes.

Chapter 10

The Highway

It is in life as it is in ways, the shortest way is commonly the foulest, and surely the fairer way is not much about.
FRANCIS BACON

THE pattern of roads and lanes is certainly ancient. The Romans must have built their Fosse Way, essential for communications, soon after their conquest of the south-west about the middle of the first century A.D. As for the lanes, there is visible evidence of their antiquity, deeply hollowed between their banks, especially on the hillsides, by centuries of wear and weather, a process arrested now by metalling. They probably date at least from the Saxon settlement, and some may be far older, taking their origin in tracks used by prehistoric man, who left so many traces hereabouts (p. 6).

From Saxon times responsibility for the upkeep of roads and bridges rested on landowners. In the Middle Ages, too, bridges were often built, and sometimes endowed, as acts of charity. The whole system was haphazard, and dependent on goodwill which was often lacking. Roads were usually deplorable, scarcely recognisable as such to modern eyes, and bridges frequently ruinous; both often dangerous and even impassable.

Nothing is known of the upkeep of roads in Batheaston before the seventeenth century, except that the monks of Bath, interested in communications between their house and their grange at S. Catherine, almost certainly built the paved causeway which until recent years ran through the village and into S. Catherine's valley, some of which remains.

An Act of 1555 required parishes to maintain every public highway, and to this end they were to provide the free service of one or more Surveyors of Highways each year, whose duty it was to decide on the necessary work, and coerce their neighbours into doing it; the more prosperous were required to provide horses and carts too. So the Surveyors (also called Waywardens), became parish officers, and "statute labour" one of life's disagreeable necessities. Originally defined as eight hours work on four consecutive days each year, it was not long before the more well-to-do were paying to be excused their duty. In 1654 the levying of a rate for the repair of the highways was made legal.

Batheaston was ahead in this, though, for the surveyors' accounts from 1651 to 1825 are complete save for the years 1697–1704, a rare year omitted by neglectful officers, and the year 1816, excised

Pl. 48. Paved Causeway on the Batch

after completion, during a time of angry disputes with the Turnpike Trustees, as will appear. Until 1765 the Vestry met in church to appoint the surveyors and pass the accounts on 25 December! Afterwards they met on 25 September.

Though in many, if not most, parishes, statute labour was scandalously neglected, often only attempted at the insistence of the justices, the Batheaston Highway Books record an expenditure of labour and materials which would be incredible were it not written there. Even allowing that the entry "done work" may sometimes be an euphemism, that at some periods little was done, and that the wretched paupers employed on the roads in the nineteenth century were probably neither able nor willing to do a hard day's work, the sheer mass of materials shifted and used is certain evidence that a great deal was done, however inefficiently, for the upkeep of the roads.

The first rate preserved, levied on "the inhabitaintes of the parrish of Batheston for repayring theire hywayes the 10th of May 1651", assessed some fifty persons in sums ranging from £1 to the 4d of the eighteen cottagers whose names complete the list. The rate amounted to £8 11s 6d. How many performed their allotted work, and how many chose to pay the equivalent is not recorded, but a note at the foot states:

It is Further agreed and concluded by the inhabtaneds Afore sayd that if any person or persons shall neglect or willfully refuse to do theire worke being summoned theare unto or pay theire monie as they are assesed or taxed whereby the service is not performed betwixt the tenth of May and the twenty four of June thus then the survayors shall make returns of such defaulters at the next qtr session that the offenders may be proceded againste as the bench of sessiones shall order in the behalfe of the Commonwealth whereunto wee have subscribed our names the day and yeare before written.

A note in 1653 reads:

"All have performed theire service or pd theire monies for as much as wee doe know exeipt Mr Button and Tho. Thunstall. Mr Button is in areares for the last yeare 7 lodes. Tho. Thunstall is in areares for the last yeare and this yeare 2s 7½d."

In some years the surveyors listed separately those who were credited with work and those who preferred to pay the equivalent in cash. In 1671, for instance, fourteen persons "dun worke" to the value of £3 11s, and twenty-nine paid £3 9s for their share to be done by hired labour. The practice of commuting the obligation into a money payment grew, and a "composition" was the rule from about 1750 onwards.

An attempt to "farm" work on the roads was made in 1674 in the following terms:

An agreement Maade the 20th of Aprill 1674 Beetweene Jerom Richmond of ye one party and And (sic) all the Rest of the Inhabytants of Batheston Concerning the Highwaies as foloeth That ye sd Jerom Richmond Baring no other parish Offis is to Maintaine and Ceepe the Highwayes of Batheston from ye daat above writen untell ye Full End of seven yeares if the sd Jerom Richmond Doth Soo Long Live provided that the sd Jerom Richmond shall have Full powre Every yeare to Make a Raate And gather 5s a yard land and 4d a Cot Betweene The first of May and the 21st of May during the abovesd Terme and Likewise to Receive and gather such Mony as Is beehind of the last Suparvizeres and if any parson shall Refuse to pay His Mony (or doo his worke according to statute—interpolated) hee shall bee proceeded Against According to Law at the parish Charg soo that the said Jerom Richmond shall bee at No Charg nor Trobell about it. Only to gather the Mony and doo the werke and the said Jerom Richmond doth promise that Hee will pay at the end of every yeare unto ye Overseares One pound Ten shillings to bee disposed as the parish shall Thinke fit. Notwithstanding if any parson shall Refuse to pay his Raat and Retain it untell the end of the year and the Law bee not Trydd Nor the money Reseved by the said Jerom Richmond that then it shall Bee Laafull for the said Jerom Richmond to Retaine And Ceepe backe somuch out of the one pound and Tene shillings untell The Law bee Tryed, and the said Jerom Richmond doth farther promise that if the aforesaid High waies shall be presented at sessions by his Neclect That it shall bee Taken of at his Oyne Charg. But in Caase thare shall any presentment happen by The defat of any of ye Inhabitants as by the Anoyance of ye high Wayes with soyl dichis fries goutes Backes or and other aNoyance that May Caues

Charg it shall fall one hee or them and not On the sd Jerom Richmond in witnes heareof whee have heare unto set our hands.

The agreement evidently came to naught, for there is no record of the payment being made, and in 1677 Richmond's name appears among "those that have not pd this yeare neither don their worke", though with "worke don" later written in and the debt cancelled. He was a substantial parishioner, perhaps a clothier, and in 1693 was buried in the chancel under a slab bearing an unusual design, and entered in the register as "gentleman".

The assessment of labour due according to the occupation of land in terms of yardland, ploughland, later shortened to plough, or by the annual value of premises was the practice as long as the record continued. By 1750 a ploughland was assessed at £1 10s, while property was usually charged on a sixpenny rate. The categories assessed in the last years were ploughs (at £1 5s), carts with two horses (17s 6d) carts with one horse (12s 6d), and "occupiers under £50 per annum" (6d in the pound). The monetary value of the rate increased nearly tenfold during the eighteenth century, reaching £94 13s 8d in 1790. At times, nevertheless, the roads received practically no attention, the supervisors conniving at almost complete neglect. The nadir was reached with a page inscribed thus:

Phill Webb and Simon Bustard served the office in ye yeare 1718 but gave no a Count.

Below, in a large copybook hand:

Simon Bustard recived 7s 6d And paid him Self with The same for the los of His Time.

It is difficult to form a mental picture of the roads during these centuries, and the work done on them by the parishioners or labour hired in their behalf; the vast amounts of stone quarried on Banner Down, or picked from the fields, to be broken up with hammers and flung on the roads, the ruts being literally levelled by ploughing! A few typical examples may encourage belief in the almost unbelievable:

1656. 170 loads of stone
1705. 294 „   „   „
1752. 405 „   „   „
1815. January and February 1054 loads
        May 352 loads

Even allowing for small carts and meagre loads, the amount of material was huge, and the question what became of it baffling; pulverised by cart wheels and horses' hooves, then blown off by the south-west winds which constantly torment Batheaston, or carried away by the process called "shovling up the Dirt", it seems impossible that it could be entirely removed. Yet the usual Batheaston lane is a deep hollow.

Some attempt at keeping paved causeways, especially the ancient route up the valley (p. 124) is shewn in references to "pitching" stone and "mending the pitching", but it must have been rapidly broken up, for repair work was constantly needed. Stone, too, was used for covering the primitive drains known as fries. A typical account, kept by John Bullock and William Lacy, surveyors in 1669, may help the imagination:

Laid out for work in bathway	5s 0d
for work don in ye Street	4s 0d
Pd to Rich Harford for caring of stones	4s 0d
Pd to John pearce for caring stons	11s 0d
Pd to Willm Blatchley for carrying stons	£1 6s 6d
Pd for ye carsway at lugbrok	4s 6d
Pd for mend ye gutter in ye Street	6d
for worke in hollos lane	2s 0d
for making ye fry and other work in gooce lane	2s 0d
for mending ye cas way at ye bridg	8d
Pd for ye carsway in ye Street	5s 0d
Pd for mending ye fry & skowering ye gutter in ye Street	1s 0d
Pd for keeping ye accompt	6d
Pd for writting in ye booke	6d

The Street was the Roman Road, Hollos Lane (originally Hollows—significant title) is now Hollies Lane, Lugbrook crosses Northend in a culvert below the church. Goose Lane has not been identified; the name persisted at least until 1730, when masons were paid half a crown for mending Goose Bridge. Elimination of other possibilities leads to the suggestion that Skeway may for a time have borne this name. Richard Harford and his associates were no humble labourers, but substantial parishioners carrying out work by contract.

Before leaving the seventeenth century, the plaintive entry on the last page of the first book may be quoted as a reminder of the troubles that were the lot of those serving the unpopular office:

An a Coumpt hoo is Bee hind for worke for ye yeare 1692: wee Required 4 dayes worke.

Mr John Fisher Behind 10 dayes worke according

to ye Justis order for one plow

Wm Harford to dayes worke behind with one plow

Thomas Henesly behind for one dayes worke with one plow

John Dolling to dayes woorke behind for parsonal sarvis

Wm Woodward one dayes woorke behind for parsonal sarvis

It is noteworthy that the only workers who received free beer, occasionally, were "ye plowmen".

The duty of keeping the parish bridges in repair also fell to the surveyors; maintaining a passage over the numerous streamlets which crossed the roads on their way to S. Catherine's brook or the Avon. Work done on the footbridges at Lugbrook, Swinbrook, Goose Lane and Dyehouse Lane (Map 1, 24) is often recorded. At this last the labourer earned an extra sixpence "for working in water". Batheaston Bridge, which carries the main road over S. Catherine's brook at Stambridge (the name derives from Stone Bridge), though often repaired by the parish, was actually a county bridge.

The unsatisfactory state of roads and bridges often led to complaint and legal action; bridges were especially notorious. In 1666 an order was made at the Quarter Session "to compel the treasurers and surveyors of Bathford, Bath Easton and Swainswick Bridges to pay the masons who were appointed to build them their arrears, in accordance with an order made at the last Bridgewater Sessions, which they have hitherto disobeyed". The year 1666 happens to be among the few for which the surveyors of Batheaston left no account.

In 1751 the Quarter Sessions received a petition from the inhabitants of Bath shewing that certain county bridges, including Stambridge in the parish of Batheaston (Batheaston Bridge) were in decay, and four of the justices were to examine the truth. The same year the parish was indicted on not repairing the ford across the Avon to Bathampton. The record runs: "On Trying the Traverse on the Indictment of the Ford over to Hampton the same was discharged —not having ever been repaired by this Parish", and adds laconically: "n.b. This Cost £17 2s 8d".

With the eighteenth century came the turnpike roads. An Act of 1707 provided for the turnpiking of all the main roads into Bath:

"... and being all of them ancient Roads for Coaches, Carts Waggons and other Carriages, by reason of the great and many Loads and heavy Carriages of Goods and other Things, which are weekly drawn thro' the same ... and being almost in every Place in the said several ways very ruinous and impassable, insomuch that it is become very dangerous to all Persons, Horses and Cattle, that pass those Ways ... neither are the Inhabitants of the several Parishes, in which the said ruinous Places of the said several and respective Roads do lie, in any wise of Ability to repair the same, without some other Provision be had or made for putting the same into good and sufficient repair."

The Justices were to appoint "sufficient and able Persons residing in or near the respective ruinous Places of the said Roads to be the several and respective Surveyors." Labourers and owners of carts, teams etc. (other than those performing statute labour) were to be paid according to the usual rate of the country. No person could be compelled to travel more than four miles from his dwelling, nor to work more than two days in any week in seed-time, hay-time or corn-harvest.

The London Road was turnpiked in 1707–8, the Fosse Way in 1756–1757. Local farm or mill traffic was exempt from tolls. Coaches, chaises etc. with one or two horses paid sixpence, if more than two a shilling; waggons or carts on four wheels 1s. The toll for a horse was a penny, for sheep, lambs or swine fivepence a score, oxen tenpence a score. Returning tolls were not charged on the same day. An amusing concession was the return in full of return fares for persons taking the air or recreation!

Most of the local gentry were trustees, and undoubtedly the roads were much improved under the new system. Some trusts, however, defaulted on repairs, and the Quarter Sessions had to intervene. Roads could still be villainous, and ours must have been bad, for according to *The Gentleman's Magazine* for September 1754: "that great road from London to Bath errs and blunders in all its forms; its strata of materials were never worth a straw; its surface was never made cycloidal; it hath neither good side ditches, nor footpaths for walkers; no outlets were made for water that stagnates in the body of the road; it was never sufficiently widened, nor were the hedges ever cleared—of course it is the worst public road in Europe, considering what vast sums have been collected from it".

Pl. 49. (a, b, c).
Stambridge.
So – what next?

(a) *About 1800, from a sepia by Mrs. Sophia Walters*

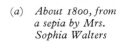

(b) *About 1910*

(c) *1969*

Perhaps this condemnation contributed to stir the trustees into action, for in 1757 they set up a body of gentry, mostly of Batheaston, to control "the separate care of the London Road", and from their minute book it appears that the Banner Down Road (Fosse Way) also was put under their surveillance. At their first meeting they resolved that "the entrance into Batheaston" was very narrow and should be widened, as well as the road from Batheaston Bridge to Bathford; that the road ought at once to be effectually repaired and that its upkeep was a great expense from its not being properly made and drained; and that the Surveyors were to "send notice to the Landowners to open and scour their Ditches, lower their Hedges and shroud their trees". The London Road certainly was improved about this time, and on 2 August 1784 it carried the first of John Palmer's mail coaches from Bristol to London.

Details of the remaking of Banner Down Road in 1760 survive; it was to be stoned 22 feet wide (later altered to 21 feet), 18 inches deep in stone in the centre to 6 inches at the sides, and the cost was 2 shillings a running yard.

Though the upkeep of the turnpike roads was partly paid for by the tolls, the burden on the parishes through which they passed was heavy, and constantly increasing. In Batheaston since to about 1740 some of those liable chose to do work on the roads rather than pay a highway rate, so expenditure for this reason cannot be exactly counted; by 1750 all were paying. In that year the roads in all cost the parish £26 17s 2d; in 1780 £61 4s 9d, in 1810 £191 1s 5d.

The next development took place in 1810, a proposal by the Turnpike Commissioners that the parish should undertake the repairs of the London Road in return for a weekly sum which was finally agreed at £6 14s 7d. This seems to have been a bad bargain for Batheaston, for according to a statement written in the Highway Book "because of the great accumulation of Dirt and the very neglected state, the expense for 67 weeks beyond the weekly allowance was £400, defrayed by extra rates. The London Road gets all the Travelling from the Bradford, Devizes and Chippenham Roads, and the parish can get no better material than the bastard-freestone from Banner Down. The indifferent and perishable nature of the materials, so soon reducible to dust, and occasioning a heavy expense in the scraping up and conveying away is not one of the least disadvantages". The statement continues that the parish has 12 miles of parish road and more than a mile of stoned footpath to keep in repair, and cannot continue without further aid. The Turnpike Trust, like so many others, was much in debt. The parish obtained Counsel's opinion, which was that it must keep the roads in repair or risk indictment. In spite of this, in 1814 it gave notice that it would no longer repair the turnpike roads. Dissatisfaction was general at this time in neighbouring parishes also (as may be read in the *Bath Journal* for January and February 1814.) Eventually the Commissioners agreed to pay Batheaston 8 guineas a week; but this was far short of the amount needed, for in 1815 the parish received £436 19s 11d and spent £676 8s 2½d on the turnpike roads and a further £202 10s 11d on the parish roads —a tremendous burden on a rural parish. The accounts for the following year must have contained matter of interest to the historian, for they have been excised, and are lost! When they recommence, the parish was again refusing to repair the turnpike roads, a rebellion which was resolved by the Commissioners agreeing to pay £13 a week. At this time, much pauper labour was used on the roads.

The turnpike gate long stood opposite Batheaston House. In 1829 it was replaced by a tollhouse at Bailbrook Lane (Map 1, 3), with "a Turnpike Gate and Weighing Engine across and upon London Road, with Gate and Bar across entrance to lane, to be attended by same Collector".

Statute labour was abolished in 1835, the upkeep of parish roads thereafter falling entirely on the local rates. By this time, owing to the work of Telford and Macadam, roads were greatly improved, but the turnpike era was approaching its end. Locally, the railway was opened in 1841, and long-distance road traffic soon declined. The last stage coach ran from London to Bristol in October 1843. The system, too, was in chaos, most Turnpike Trusts sunk in debt, and all heartily disliked by the people, who hated paying the tolls. As the century advanced, there were riots, and a number of tunpike gates were destroyed by mobs. One after another, the Turnpike Trusts were dissolved, and by the 1870's the system was practically obsolete. The Bath Trust was wound up in 1877; its records are deposited at the County Record Office. As the Trusts surrendered the roads, they returned to the care of the parishes through which they passed, many of which had by this time amalgamated into Highway Boards. The direct responsibility of parishes came to an end in 1889 with the formation of County Councils, which took on the upkeep of the highways. Footpaths have remained in the care of Parish Councils.

The names borne by parish lanes have taken various forms through the generations, often referable to the proprietor of adjacent land. A good example is (Map 1):

1835. Partridge Lane

1836. Stallard's Lane

Mid 19th century. Angell's Lane

Late 19th century. Waterworks Lane

1967. Seven Acres Lane

"Angell" lingers in old memory, and Partridge in the form "Parsonage" (p. 19) is only just forgotten.

Until 1872 the crossing of the Avon between Batheaston and Bathampton was by the ford (p. 127) and a ferry, both below the weir. In that year the toll bridge was built by Messrs. Hickes and Isaac. It cost about £4000, and the leasehold with toll rights and the toll house was sold for ninety-nine years to a Bath gentleman for £1750. When the lease was offered for sale in 1908 the gross receipts were said to average £223 per annum. To-day the bridge is one of the few remaining toll bridges in the south of England, one penny for a pedestrian, sixpence for a motor car, and no return tickets.

Chapter 11

Agriculture

Only a man harrowing clods
In a slow silent walk
With an old horse that stumbles and nods
Half asleep as they stalk.

THOMAS HARDY

THE HISTORY of agriculture in England is a large subject, and much of it obscure. The study of a single village discovers evidence of ancient cultivation in features on the ground, and of practice in recent centuries in written records—manorial rolls, parish and state documents, private deeds. An account based on them can only illuminate momentarily an ever-changing scene. Here an attempt is made to sketch the probable story; but the gaps are large and long, and the main emphasis lies where chance has preserved the most.

Until comparatively recent times the people of Batheaston and S. Catherine, of course, lived off their land. Evidence of cultivation in three periods, prehistoric, mediaeval and modern is still clear to the eye. The "celtic" fields of the Iron Age settlers, at present time defined by low banks, have received mention (p. 8, Fig. 4). They are always small —rarely exceeding an acre, many smaller—and rectangular. Sometimes the rectangles are elongated, and experts think that this shape belongs to fields of the Romano-British period[1] (H. C. Bowen, *Ancient Fields*, British Association for the Advancement of Science, 1961, p. 24). These fields were ploughed and used for corn-growing, with stock grazing on them during the fallow periods necessary to restore fertility. It is not known how fences were managed to keep animals from the growing crops. The remains of fields of this type are here confined to Charmy Down: there may have been others, now obliterated.

The next oldest relics of ancient cultivation are the strip lynchets or terraces that are so conspicuous on the hillsides, usually more or less following the contours; they are a common sight throughout the district (Fig. 4). Much discussion has gone into the theory of the making of these terraces: they

seem to result from a combination of the turning downhill of the slices cut by the plough, and the arrest by a barrier—which might be no more than uncut turf—at the lower edge of the unploughed area, of soil washed down the slope. In time a "flight" of terraces could build up, and the "steps" between them could be remarkably deep, eight, ten or more feet. There are good examples on Map 2, B67, 78 and in Chilcombe Bottom. The field called Oldlands (B78) recollects this period, and has a good set of lynchets.

It is believed that in the thirteenth century the population grew to such a size that hilly land previously neglected or used for grazing had to be taken into cultivation, and that the strip lynchets date from this time. When they became "fossilised" under grass is not known, but the giant catastrophe of the plague of 1348–1349 is usually cited as the cause.

Some enclosed terraces have a rectangularity and a uniformity which suggest that they were once units in the common fields of later times; an example is seen at C62–64, where a steep step continues the line from the angle below the lower hedge, so that three units are clearly indicated, the highest one, at the north, of double size, as would result from the union of two strips. Identifiable sites to the north and south of this complex were arable land in the common field in 1625, so it was almost certainly included therein. True, it may have developed from the strip lynchet of an earlier period, but the regular shape and the hedged boundaries distinguish it from the haphazard appearance of earlier work.

The third piece of evidence belongs to the period of enclosed fields. Wherever a field boundary on sloping ground is of some antiquity, and the land adjoining has been cultivated, a lynchet develops, and the process is still at work. There is no sign of the ridge and furrow pattern so common in the midland counties.

COMMON FIELDS AND ENCLOSURE

Open field cultivation, probably introduced by the Saxons, and common to the whole of midland England, was the practice in Batheaston. There were two fields, documentary evidence dating from 1291, when the Prior of Bath granted land "in campo orientali" and "in campo occidentali", in the east field and the west field. The later formula was "the east or Banner Down Field" and "the west or Salisbury Field". A crop was taken each year from half the arable land, the other half being fallow and the farm stock getting from it what sustenance it could. The lord owned the land; his underlings, the villeins and cottars of Domesday, were obliged to work that part from which he took the produce, and they, the villeins, at least, were allowed to cultivate the remainder for their own sustenance. Their descendants probably became in the main the copyholders of later centuries.

Communal ploughing was inevitable when tillage required teams of eight beasts, quite beyond individual resources. The practice was to allocate strips, either permanently or annually, according to that rigid regulator "the custom of the manor". Extant manorial documents do not tell us what the local custom was. There is also a long interval, of which we know scarcely anything, between the time when the lord was paramount and the conditions depicted in seventeenth century records, by which time the manorial system had broken up, and the land was tilled by a community of freeholders and their tenants. A little is known of the process by which this great change came about; some acquired freeholds in 1594, when Sir John Harington sold the manor of Easton and Catherine to William Blanchard (p. 18), and there are titles, both in Batheaston and S. Catherine, which derive from that date. Other freeholds were sold at the final dissolution of the manor of Batheaston in 1667 (p. 14). It is not always possible to tell which men owned their freehold; the seventeenth century was certainly a time when prosperous families, Fishers, Pantons and Walters especially, were buying up holdings as opportunity arose.

Doubtless men were glad, whenever they could to make into compact holdings, by exchange or otherwise, the land in which they had rights, and from this it was a natural step to enclosure, with corresponding loss of rights in the common fields. The process took place early in Somerset. John Leland, antiquary to Henry VIII, wrote: "Most part of all Somersetshire is in hedgerows enclosed". It was not altogether true of Batheaston. Written in the Poor Book is an agreement of 1620, which shews that although enclosure was already proceeding on an agreed basis, and more was intended, the completion of the programme would leave the greater part of the arable still in open field.

And wearas wee the Inhabytants of Batheaston have Allwayes heare to for kept 100 shep to A yardland within ye pishe and we did Abat five shep for every Acre Inclosed out of our fealds. And nowe wee the Inhabytants of Batheaston doth All agre to kepe 80 shep to every yard land and to Abat for Every Acre Inclosed out of the feald fower shep.

Further wee doth All Covenant and do Agree to hayne our feald from the 26 of feabruary untell the 25 of March.

and wee doth Allso Agree As wee doth kepe 80 shep to every yard land and to Abat for Every Acre inclosed out of the feald fower shep so we doth All Agree that for Every shep of Any mans within our pishe that shalle in the fealde Above the rat Aforsayd that he shall pay unto the Overseers for the us off the por within our pishe VId being lawffully demands of them.

And we doth Allso Agree that upon Every yard land within our parish from the 25 of March shall kept in the feald 16 Lames ontell the 30 of Aprill next fowlowing and After that day Every Lame shall go for A shep in our fealde and for Every Lame of Any mans within our parish that shalbe in the fealde Above the rate Aforsayd that go on shep shall pay unto the Overseers for the use of the por six pence being demanded of the(m) and not payd we doth Agree that it shalbe lawfull for the Overseers to Impound Any of our Cattell untell pay be mayd it. In witness hearunto we hav put to our hands this 10 of december and in the year of or lord god 1620. Signatures of: John Fisher, Thomas Blanchard,

Anthony Townsend, William Lewis, Thomas Lideard, John Lewis.

Marks of: Richard Ponting, John Murford, Walter Simonds, James Webe.

In this district a yardland was twenty acres.

With the agreement is a list of thirty-six names, relating to a total of forty-two rights, with no indication who was a freeholder and who a tenant. Against each name, except one for whom the figures are lacking (that of a "small" man), is the number of acres in each field it was intended to enclose and the number of sheep that might then be kept in the common fields, according to the new stint of four sheep to each remaining acre of the share. It can be calculated that they proposed to enclose at least 291½ acres, leaving 781 acres in common, on which there might be kept 3,124 sheep! This, of course, was in addition to any sheep they had in the new enclosures. It is clear from the preamble to the agreement that part of the intention was to reduce over-stocking. It would be a satisfaction if some of the enclosures of this date could be identified in fields still bearing names that appear in the list, but though there are several such, in none does the acreage quite fit.

Five years later, when John Fisher's land was recorded, (p. 76), besides cottages and smallholdings he owned six substantial properties, five of them farmed by tenants. About half of the land was enclosed, and his arable, except three acres, all lay in the common fields, in many "parcels"; one area, at Banner Down, however, amounted to 20 acres. A number of the sites can be more or less exactly identified, from a knowledge of field names; they shew a distinct tendency to area grouping, evidently a stage in the production of compact farms, and it is even possible to hazard the ancestry of some of the farms of today.

A terrier of the rectory of 1709[2] states that the Chancel Land (p. 25) was in the common field until twenty years before, when it was enclosed "with the lands of Richard Harford".

In 1719 a deed defining grazing rights was executed by those having an interest in the common fields; again, the number happened to be thirty-six. Briefly, it provided:

1. The right to graze two sheep for each acre held in the common fields, a proportionate deduction to be made for each acre enclosed in the future. Certain persons having rights in the commons but not in the common fields might graze one sheep for each 3s paid to the Poor Rate when the rate was £24 16s. These rights could be let or sold.

2. There was no common in the cornfield between Michaelmas and Michaelmas, i.e. while the crop was on. The fallow field was hained (closed) from 10 December to 25 March.

3. The common was always to be opened on 3 May, fed and rested for two weeks alternately from then until 9 August, when it was closed until the breaking up of the stubble. How long a rest preceded the spring opening is not specified, probably from early in the year. (At Chipping Norton the common was hained from 13 February to 2 May.)

4. A hayward was to be chosen at Christmas, and had the right to a small levy for his services, including two-fifths of the fairly stiff penalty for exceeding the stint of stock. The other three-fifths went to the poor. A lamb counted as a sheep from 3 May. Stock found "trespassing" was to be detained in the Common Pound, the enclosure still standing on Pound Hill (Map 1, 32).

5. Trustees were elected to ensure the carrying out of the deed.

From this document it is not possible to determine the extent of common field remaining, but it was obviously considerable. It is noteworthy that it had been found necessary to reduce the quota of sheep from four to two per acre.

At least 63 acres became enclosed arable between 1742, the date of Thorpe's map, and 1786, when Harcourt Masters drew his fine maps for the Turnpike Commissioners. These are the fields at the northern end of Banner Down (B43, 44, 45), and they probably included part of the down. Their straight sides indicate planned enclosure.

Further evidence on the late history of the common fields comes from a valuation of the rectory made by William Chapman in 1779.[3] He there states that there were 43 acres in the common fields "called Swanswick, Salisbury, and Baller (sic) Down"—a meagre remnant of the open fields of 1620. (The name Swanswick Field had become attached to the land to the north-west of Little Solsbury, B132.) Chapman added that enclosed arable was about 487 acres "the Greatest part very good Land".

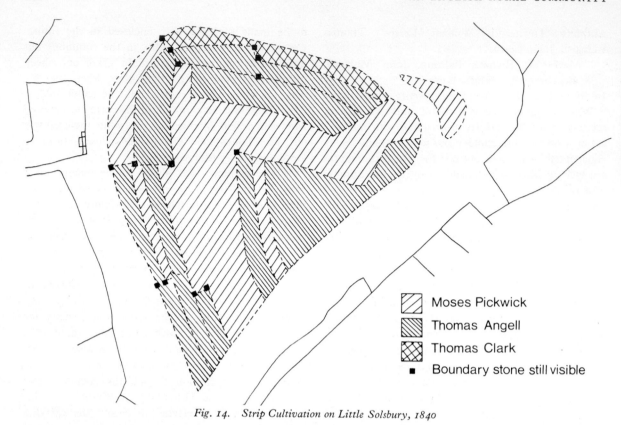

Moses Pickwick
Thomas Angell
Thomas Clark
■ Boundary stone still visible

Fig. 14.   Strip Cultivation on Little Solsbury, 1840

Pl. 50.   Aerial photograph of Little Solsbury shewing "fossilised" strips
(photograph by J. K. St. Joseph, Cambridge University Collection: copyright reserved)

Thomas Wyatt, making a valuation in 1800, estimated 55 acres in the common fields, 300 acres of enclosed arable, 700 acres of meadow and pasture, an estimate which does not well correspond with Chapman's. He added: "The state of cultivation in the parish is inexpressibly bad, and no advantage has been taken of the improvements in agriculture, except in the conversion of several acres of pasture into gardens and potato grounds".

When the Tithe Map of 1840 was drawn, there remained 20 acres of arable in strips on the plateau of Little Solsbury, where lynchets bounding the strips and some of the boundary stones are still be be seen. (Pl. 50.) About the same area lay open in Swainswick Field (Map 2, B132), now a field sometimes ploughed, sometimes in grass. At its southern end, several long, narrow gardens "fossil-ise" the strips of 1840. Finally, the map shews,

too, strips still demarcated in a few of the fields, but in single ownership.

Batheaston never had planned enclosure, much less an Enclosure Act, as had so many parishes. The ancient system of communal enterprise just died out, gradually.

Scarcely anything has been discovered about the common fields of S. Catherine. A deed of 1594 speaks of "the south-west field", and includes in it Map 2, C30, 59, 66.[4] C58 is still called Catherine Field, and so is B101. No reference to another common field has been found, and nothing is known of agricultural practice in the period of the open fields.

The strong move towards enclosure of the agreement of 1620 was undoubtedly for sheep pasture, as is known to have taken place widely during the seventeenth century. The calculations in Table 6

Table 6.   Land use

			Area in acres		
BATHEASTON					
Date	Source	Arable[1]	Pasture	Garden	Total
Before 1620	Agreement in Poor Book	1072			
1620	Agreement in Poor Book	781+[2]			
1779	William Chapman's Survey	530	623		1153
1800	Thomas Wyatt's Survey	460	700	95	1255
1814	Richard Crabtree's Survey[3]	572	768		1340
1840	Tithe Commissioners' Survey	571	780	115	1466
1866	Agricultural Returns[4]	769	846	no return	1615
1914	Agricultural Returns	125	1147	90	1362
1967	Agricultural Returns	62	733	89	942

[1]Includes fallow.
[2]One man's share not entered.
[3]Christ Church MS. 248.
[4]Probably includes part of S. Catherine.

			Area in acres		
S. CATHERINE					
Date	Source	Arable[1]	Pasture	Garden	Total
1840	Tithe Commissioners' Survey	221	679	0	1000
1866	Agricultural Returns[2]	115	271	no return	386
1914	Agricultural Returns	96	889	6	991
1967	Agricultural Returns	132	360	8	500[3]

[1]Includes fallow.
[2]Part of S. Catherine probably included with Batheaston.
[3]Rough grazing not returned.

are based on the figures given in that agreement. Chapman's estimate of 1779 makes it plain that the arable had further contracted during the intervening 159 years. (Wyatt in his report asserts that "the quantities stated by Chapman do not seem grounded on any regular measurement, and the property must really be greater in extent".) However, Wyatt and Crabtree in their turn underestimated the total of

for S. Catherine in 1967 is that the rough grazing was for some reason omitted.

In Batheaston the conversion to pasture of the seventeenth century continued, but more slowly, until with the twentieth arable farming sharply declined. Figs. 15 and 16 illustrate the contrast in a representative part of the parish between 1840 and 1965.

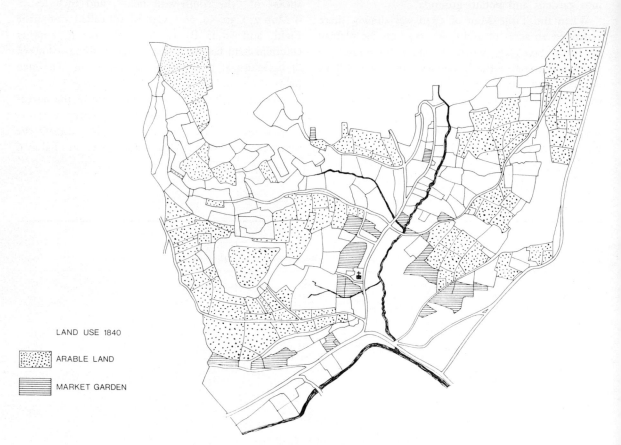

LAND USE 1840

ARABLE LAND

MARKET GARDEN

Fig. 15. Land use 1840. Batheaston parish

agricultural land, for the Tithe Survey of 1840 was made with great care, and is certainly accurate. Agricultural returns for parishes have been gathered since 1855, and here it looks as though part of S. Catherine was in that year returned with Batheaston. The year 1914 was chosen as the nearest not affected by the war of 1914–1918 to the half-century from 1866. The explanation for the shrunken area returned

Table 7 shews the area devoted to corn-growing, peas, beans and roots accounting for the remainder of the arable. The decline in Batheaston indicates a profound revolution in farming practice. In S. Catherine, however, that part of Charmy Down which is not under tarmac is mostly growing corn, whereas before 1940 it was grass.

In Table 8 is set out figures for the population

of livestock at different times. For sheep they are startling. The numbers for 1620 and after are based on the agreement already described, and comprehend the totals permissible, not necessarily used in full; but the reduction in stint effected by the agreement suggests that the flocks nearly if not quite reached that size. To them would be added, if they could be known, those pastured in enclosures made before

Smithfield market in 1795 was double that of 1710, reflecting the advances in breeding and feeding achieved by the pioneers of the eighteenth century.[5]

We do not know when the flocks began to shrink after the great conversion to pasture of the seventeenth century, a conversion well known to have taken place nationally. Our next evidence comes from 1803 when, during the threat of invasion by

LAND USE 1965

ARABLE LAND

MARKET GARDEN

Fig. 16. Land use 1965. Batheaston parish

1620. Besides the sheep in Batheaston, there was common for 1,050 on Holts Down (p. 18) in addition to the traditional flock on Charmy Down (p. 17), and such sheep as were kept privately in that suitable terrain. The sheep must be pictured as small creatures, most of them getting a scanty living in stubble field, fallow, and poor common land. It is reported that the weight of sheep and cattle in

the French, returns of resources were collected. Unfortunately for us, the unit was the tithing, and as Shockerwick was included in Easton and Amorel, the numbers are thereby a little inflated. Obviously, the picture was very different from that of two centuries before. There was no arrest of the decline in the sheep industry, and today a few sheep in a field are a sight almost rare.

K

Table 7.   Acreage of corn

BATHEASTON

Date	Source	Wheat	Barley	Oats	Total
1779	William Chapman's Survey				346
1800	Thomas Wyatt's Survey				437
1814	Richard Crabtree's Survey	120	110	20	250
1866	Agricultural Returns[1]	167	94	45½	306½
1914	Agricultural Returns	35	26	15	76
1967	Agricultural Returns	14	14	0	28

[1]Probably includes part of S. Catherine.

S. CATHERINE

Date	Source	Wheat	Barley	Oats	Total
1866	Agricultural Returns[1]	45	10	8½	63½
1914	Agricultural Returns	10	18	14½	42½
1967	Agricultural Returns	35	88	0	123

[1]Part of S. Catherine probably included with Batheaston.

Probably the herds of cattle had grown meanwhile to compensate, the city of Bath making increased demands for dairy produce. We have no data on the number of cattle kept in earlier times. The large increase in the total between 1803 and 1866 indicates a growing demand for beef, and the trend continued, with increase, too, in the milking herds, until 1914. Since then, numbers have fallen, but efficiency in the industry has so increased that total production has surely grown. Factory farming is still a threat unrealised.

The pig population stood very high between 1866 and 1914—and this probably does not include the cottager's pig. The small number at the present time can be attributed to the development of specialised pig farms.

The returns of 1803 gave 106 draught horses and 6 oxen; to-day there is no working horse. The 120 agricultural labourers of 1851 are represented by a few lads driving tractors. The School Log Book notes a truancy one December afternoon in 1863: "The inducement was a threshing machine"—perhaps the first piece of agricultural machinery the boy had seen.

To summarise: the evidence clearly shews that the area once under the plough is to a great extent converted

Table 8.   Population of livestock

BATHEASTON AND S. CATHERINE

Date	Source	Sheep 1 year and over	Cows	Total cattle	Pigs
Before 1620	{ Agreement in Poor Book,	5955[1]			
1620	{ and common of Holts Down	4174[1]			
1803	Preparations for invasion[2]	2671	168	271[3]	299
1866	Agricultural Returns	1935	176	532	677
1914	Agricultural Returns	363	354	760	699
1967	Agricultural Returns	15	290	546	82

[1]No figures for flock of Charmy Down.
[2]Includes Shockerwick.
[3]Includes colts.

to grass, a huge population of sheep has disappeared, and the land is practically given over to cattle.

MARKET GARDENING

According to Thomas Walters, leasee of the rectorial tithes in 1814, a few acres were converted to growing vegetables for the Bath market about 1774, and the practice had increased. In 1851 thirty-seven inhabitants, twenty-three of them "natives", called themselves market gardeners, mostly cultivating from one to four acres, but four amounting together to fifty-eight. The smaller ones must have had supplementary occupation. There was no market gardener in S. Catherine. Produce was taken to the Wednesday market, when attendance at school fell drastically! Nowadays the market gardeners, of whom there are about a dozen, cater to a considerable extent for luxury crops—soft fruit, strawberries especially, which do very well in the valley, and salads.

THE FIELDS

The present pattern of fields is shewn in Map 2. It differs little from the Tithe Map of 1840— a few fields thrown together, a few divided—except that many acres of agricultural land have meanwhile been lost to housing.

Readers are asked to use Fig. 1 as a reminder of the steepness of much of the ground, accounting in part for the irregular shape of field whose boundaries tend to follow the contours. Some fields may date from the early centuries of cultivation: many probably are the enclosures proposed in the agreement of 1620 (p. 132). The one numbered B85 certainly existed in 1625 when John Fisher's lands were described (p. 133), for the list includes an eighth of an acre in a small angle at the west of it —in quodam parvo angulo ibidem ex parte occidentali—an angle still to be seen. John Fisher, too, owned the nearby Seven Acres (B99). Stibb's Piece (B26) cannot be later than the seventeenth century, for the family died out in the village about 1700. A well-to-do family of the same period probably gave its name to Bailey's Wood (B102). We know from the terrier of 1709 (p. 133) that Water Leaze (B7) was enclosed about 1690. These are instances for which evidence happens to survive; many more fields must be at least as old. Where

the pattern is predominantly one of straight lines, however, later enclosure is probable, as Holts Down (1748), and the northern end of Banner Down (between 1742 and 1786).

The key to Map 2 shews the great age of some of the field names, in early days usually applied to areas in the open fields. Where an unrelated name appears, satisfactory evidence of identification has been obtained, the main source being descriptions in old deeds; it is not practicable to give the collected data in full.

Certain peculiarities of these fields names are noticeable. One is a tendency to acquire a terminal s, implying an imaginary proprietor: examples are Gatteralls, Stammers Leaze, Holdings and Oldlands, Chamburys and Nesles (C31 and B52, 78, 78a, 109, 114). In conversation Cowleaze can even become Cowley's. (In the same way, Henyard Lane, Map 1, 28, became Henyard's, or a variant. The name obviously comes from an area liable to be fenced (hained). Generations of slipshod speech often accomplish the loss of meaningful names: thus, Ramscombe becomes Ranscombe, Ewcombe Luccombe, Starveall Starfall; similarly, the lane appropriately called Skeway acquires the inane Steway. The surveyors of 1840 obviously had difficulty sometimes in getting a recognisable name at all from the semi-literate. Stencils (B150) was an inspired guess, but certainly wrong; the name probably originated as Teasles, either from the native plant or the species grown for raising the nap on cloth. Packs of teasles were among the goods of a man buried by the parish in 1720.

The quest for names in current use meets difficulties, especially where the old name is obsolete. Then the new one may be inconstant, depending on the fancy of the present proprietor. More than one name may be current; estate maps usually retain the old names which may have gone otherwise out of use. Newly-invented names are almost invariably without interest.

THE FARMS

The history of individual farms is exceedingly difficult to trace, though some have certainly been recognisable units from the seventeenth century at least. Hartley Farm (Map 1, 45), in the extreme north-west of Batheaston, is probably as old as the delineation of the parish. Grimes[6] suggests that it was never part of the common field system, and that Charmy Down Farm (Map 1, 37), too, may always have been a compact unit. The given acreage of farms varies, sometimes widely, between successive records. The owner, too, has changed often, the occupant more often; tenant farming has in the past been usual, and the tenants have not generally been local men, nor have families remained for many generations. In the census of 1851, only six of twenty-one farmers were natives of either parish.

Eleven of the farms there recorded remain today, having absorbed the others, chiefly the smaller ones. One quite large farm, however, Lower Northend (Map 1, 27) with 100 acres in 1851 has gone the way of Cold Bath Farm (Map 1, 18), dismembered in 1812, and completely disappeared.

An example from one farm may usefully illustrate some of these observations. Church Farm is chosen, because of its long history as the farm of the manor of Batheaston (p. 13), and because it is relatively easy to identify in lists, as it was known as "the Farm". The following are the facts brought to light:

Date	Owner	Occupier	Area
1620	William Button	Anthony Townsend	
1647	„	William Bletchley	
	„	Martin Button	
	„	John Button	
1662	Sir Robert Button	William Clay	
1671	„	John Bletchley	
1680	Charles Steward		
1704		William Bletchley	
1719	Francis Fisher		
1743	John Fisher		
1815	Dyer	Vicary	
1825	Alexander Grant	William Fuller	
1833	Messrs Cowdry	„	
1851	H. Walters Trustees	Edwin Aust	100 acres
1860	„	Horace Hamper	
1862	„	Candy	92 „
1869			45 „
1888		Edward Evry, Bailiff	
1898		James Stone	78 „
		Arthur Stone	
	W. A. Hick	H. Tayler	
	R. Tayler	Himself	223 „

Some of the ancient farmhouses are briefly described in the account of the notable buildings of Batheaston and S. Catherine (p. 90).

THE COMMONS

The essential distinction of common land is that persons, not being the owner, hold rights over it, the usual right that of grazing; others are the taking of wood (estovers), turf (turbary), fish (piscary). Common land was usually the poorer land of a manor, the least promising for cultivation; the owner, originally, the lord of the manor. Legislation as early as the Statute of Merton (1235) required him to leave sufficient common land for the grazing necessary to his tenants. The amount of human misery and deprivation caused over the centuries by enclosure of commons and extinction of rights must be enormous, but the picture is not altogether clear, and historians still debate. All that can be attempted here is an account of local custom, which was in some respects peculiar.

Common land was included in the term "waste", which denoted such land as was not in cultivation or otherwise used; "waste", however, did not necessarily carry common rights, and the term came usually to be applied to odd pieces of unenclosed land, often by the roadside.

Batheaston has two Commons, Banner Down (60 acres) and Little Solsbury (25 acres). The history of Batheaston Commons is unusual owing to the fact that legal ownership lapsed some 300 years ago with the extinction of the manors; from that time they have been effectively owned by the freeholders of the parish. Transactions in their name appear in the parish records, and it is noteworthy that the deed of 1719 (p. 133) assumes their ownership. The parish officers collected small rents from persons using parts of the "waste", built parish houses on it for the poor (p. 99) and from time to time disposed of portions of it:

1765 Resolved that the Wast or parish ground commonly called the Batch be Conveyed by the Churchwardens and Overseers unto Daniel Cottle Carpenter in Fee Simple at the price or sum of ten pounds in which conveyance shall be inserted a Covenant to prevent the said Daniel Cottle from ever erecting a Pigstye on any part of the premises under the penalty of forfeiting five pounds for the use of the parish.

1775 14 November At a Vestry held in the parish Church of Batheaston . . . Resolved that the Freeholders ever had an undoubted and un-interupted power of granting the Waste Ground to any of the parishioners for the benefit of the Parish in General which power they have ever executed and can prove in many Instances from the beginning of the Reign of Charles the 1st. And therefore Resolved that the said John Miller Esq. be immediately served with a Notice in Writing under the Hands of the Churchwardens and Overseers and other Freeholders to desist from any farther proceedings or pretensions to the Waste Ground he has been inclosing unless he will treat and agree with the Churchwardens and Overseers for the same.

(Next Page). In pursuance of the Resolution on the other side John Miller Esq. did treat and agree to pay the Churchwardens and Overseers of the poor half a Guinea Yearly on Michaelmas Day for ever as an acknowledgement for inclosing a peise of Waste Ground in front of his house.

The ground in question is that once known as Cloud Acre (Map 2, B3). A verse by William Hayley in the *Poetical Amusements,* p. 88, is an interesting reminder of this episode:

". . . Said —— the person I ask'd for had lodged
in her cot,
"But, alas! Such good luck was no longer her lot.
"For she quitted her roof where she oft had
respos'd,
"When yon great house was built, and the common
inclosed".

Distinction between "waste" as such, and "common" would be of little moment.

The deed of 1719 explicitly declared that rate-payers should have common rights regardless of whether they had land in the common fields. In time a somewhat amorphous body of "Batheaston Freeholders" grew up, its rights determined by a mixture of ancient custom and present consent. The 1719 deed was always invoked—and still is—as a foundation charter, and obviously there were ample opportunities for wrangling. A Committee of Freeholders, meeting in 1879 under the chairman-ship of the vicar, reported thus:

"That the right of common lands being so indefinite and various, depending rather on the custom of the place than on any legal grounds or principles, requiring so accurate a search of all parish documents and examination of so many living witnesses before any decided and satis-factory legal decision could be given, they have not felt themselves in a position to ask for such opinion.

They held therefore that as it appeared con-clusive from the deed of 1719 that the Freeholders did frame rules there seemed no reason why they should not do so now or at any other time. The burden of proving their action illegal would lie on those who might feel themselves aggrieved".

Accordingly, at a General Meeting of the Free-holders, 24 November 1880, a report of the com-mittee was adopted, its resolution being:

"That the custom having been established by Deed in the beginning of last century, and known to have been acted upon within present memory, of allowing each Freeholder, or his tenant by his authority, to pasture on the Common Lands two sheep, or one horse or beast, for each acre of his holding, and so in proportion for a greater or lesser quantity, the Committee recommend that the custom be now re-affirmed".

The rule soon lapsed, however, for as far as living memory reaches there has been no enforcement. Little Solsbury, where beasts are safely restrained from wandering by the fences of fields surrounding the Common has never ceased to be used. In the past Banner Down, too, was safely closed against straying, and there are plenty of payments by the parish officers such as:

1733 Hooks and Twists for Bannadown
Gate and making up the Wall   5s 6d
At some date unknown the gates were no longer kept in repair, and the Common has long lain open, not only by the approach lanes, but to the Fosse Way itself. At least to the end of last century grazing stock was guarded by children, who drove their charges up from the farms in the morning and back at night. Recollections of about 1880 were set down by the late G. P. Hobbs when ninety years of age:

". . . There were 4 of us lads on the hill, 2 with cows and 2 with sheep. There were not many bushes, just a few lower down all the rest was grassland from Fosse Lane to the (illegible) and both sides of the road to the Shire Stones. There was not much traffic on the road, only a few horses and carts, all we had to do was see the cows and sheep did not stray or get into other peoples fields. We let the stock all run together till the evening and then would part them, had we kept them apart every time they met there would have been fighting. Men were working in the quarries and the stone was used for building and for road making, in the summer the roads were inches deep in dust and in winter deep in mud. It was quite a change for me from London, the lovely hills and the birds. I was never tired of looking at the views and listening to the wind playing tunes in the grass and rushes. Sometimes we would eat all the food early and then one of us would go and buy a tin of salmon or lobster it was only 7½d a tin, sometimes we would find a hens nest of eggs and at other times we would buy some eggs and cook them in a tin, also we would toast some bacon over a wood fire and it would be as black as coal but we enjoyed it very much. There were many different kinds of birds on Bannerdown and men would come out from Bath with cages and decoy birds and catch them, after a time this bird catching was stopped. I was very interested in the peewits, they would pretend to be lame to get me to try and catch them and in this way lead one away from their nest of young. There were also corncrakes there and these made a noise like a saw rasping on something hard, these birds have now disappeared as they have been killed off by the mowing machines cutting the grass. . . . What I liked best of all was to lie down in the grass and rushes and see the changing colours in the sky, the light seemed to come in waves, it seemed to open and shut, I suppose it was because Bannerdown is higher than some of the surrounding hills. I was never tired of the beauty of it all".

The quarry on Banner Down has supplied the stone which built much of Batheaston, and the vast quantities used in mending the roads (p. 126). The Freeholders of last century had the privilege of buying for twopence a bushel the turf removed when the quarry was extended. It was in use until after the end of the century and an old resident remembers passing the time talking to the quarryman while minding stock there. Grazing on Banner Down has quite ceased within the last few years, and its importance now is as an open space.

At present the Committee of Freeholders consists of ten members, with five more nominated by the Parish Council. Besides anxiety about deterioration consequent on non-grazing and the advance of scrub, its chief tasks are fighting the twin menaces of dumped refuse and the literally ubiquitous motor car, both illegal. Under the Commons Registration Act of 1965 the Freeholders are the registered owners of the Common and it is hoped that legislation will shortly enable their proper regulation.

For common land in S. Catherine we are indebted to evidence given in a lawsuit about common rights in 1620 between William Blanchard and the copyhold tenants.[7] The common land was Holts Down, then 120 acres, lying to the east of Charmy Down, and separated from it by a wall which the commoners were bound to keep in repair at the rate of six score luggs (a lugg was 5½ yards) for each yardland (locally 20 acres) of their holding. Part of the wall existed until the airfield was made in 1940. The stint allowed was 100 sheep for each yardland. Blanchard claimed that the customary (copyhold) tenants had enclosed most of the arable land of the fields of Catherine and Batheaston, and some had extinguished their common rights by so doing. He lost his case.

Holts Down, then reckoned 132 acres, with grazing rights of eight sheep to the acre, was enclosed by agreement in 1748; 59 acres went to the Blanchard interest, and the rest was divided between seven holdings. On the map the fields catch the eye, their sides almost entirely linear except where they meet undulating high ground (Map 2, C20, 22, 23, 32, 32a, 33. Coates and Drewett were two of the original participants).

Here it is convenient to speak of Charmy Down, the other large space, most of which is in S. Catherine. Alternatively called the Lord's Down, it has never been common land, but supported a large flock of his sheep. "The ewe flock of Charmy Down" figures in records from the thirteenth century onwards. From the source above we learn that "the farmer of the manor farm used to find two washers and two shearers yearly to help wash and shear the ewe flock. All the tenants of the manor helped with washing and shearing. The customary shearers had meat and drink for their pains, the washers a penny loaf and a pennyworth of cheese, and beer". Sold off in the seventeenth century, early in the nineteenth it was ruled out into numbered fields. Since the departure of the Royal Air Force it is partly restored to cultivation, but a desolation of tarmac and derelict huts is a memento of its occupation.

Chapter 12

Mills and Industry

See you our little mill that clacks
So busy by the brook?
She has ground her corn and paid her tax
Ever since Domesday Book.

RUDYARD KIPLING

MILL SITES are often of great antiquity, and probably some of the mills about to be described are the successors of the mills of Domesday; the two manorial mills of recent centuries almost certainly are. Early references to mills are usually impossible to identify with sites. An example: about 1288 one Roger de Sokerwike rented for 2s from the monks of Bruton a mill at Batheaston, sold to them by Hilary de Campo Florido, who was doubtless related to Lady Matilda (p. 20). Much later, when parish records are in being, the evidence is tantalisingly incomplete. "For the mill" may be an entry in a rating list, but it is rarely possible to establish a sequence of millers or determine a site; millers might move, and did.

S. Catherine's Brook was well adapted to supply water power; of manageable size, with a fall of 280 feet in 3¾ miles, up to a hundred years ago six mills used it, one in Cold Ashton, two in Marshfield, two in S. Catherine, and one in Batheaston. With the last three we have to deal, and with one mill on the Avon.

The mill at Northend in Batheaston (Map 1, 25) was the lord's mill of the manor of Batheaston (p. 13). Apart from documentary evidence, which is convincing, its situation is just what would be expected—at the nearest spot convenient to the demesne farm (the present Church Farm). Its primary purpose, of course, that of all ancient mills, was the grinding of corn; but in cloth-making districts water power was used in the fulling or tucking of cloth at least from the fourteenth century, and it was common for part of a grist mill to be adapted for that purpose. In 1623 the Justices of the Peace for the hundreds of Frome, Bathforum, Wellow and Kilmersdon reported:

" . . . the people of the country (for the most part) being occupied about the trade of cloth-making,

spinning, weaving and tucking. Also we find that by reason of the trade of cloth-making, and the increase of people working about that trade, there have been very many cottages erected within our said division for them to work in, which have no means of working but about that trade."

It is worth noting that the surnames Woollen, Dyer, Weaver and Fuller are to be found in Batheaston records. Traditionally, wool was sent out for carding and spinning in the home and then for weaving, but the practice has here left no visible trace, such as weavers' cottages with large upper windows. The other source of evidence, the parish records, yield an occasional reference to weavers; a narrow weaver and a "sarge" weaver were among newcomers examined in 1725 as to their parish of settlement.

John Taylor of Castle Combe, "clothman", in 1553 leased from the lord of the manor of Batheaston for 53s 4d a year "a gristmill and tucking mill under one roof".[1] A Court Roll of 1565, the latest one to survive, records that Robert Tyler, lately the miller (probably the son of John), took out and carried away a gallery from the mill and a bolt from the door of the cloth mill. (There was at least one other mill on the manor then, for at the same Court Thomas Dymoke was presented for failing to pay 9s in rent for Dymoke Mill for twenty-five years!) In 1566 the lord's mill was leased to John Fissher of Hampton[2] and in 1620 it was taken by John Jones, husbandman.[3] This was the mill which John Fisher bought for £105 in 1665, "that grist and fulling mill in Batheaston known as the New Mill", when the manor was breaking up. Near by in 1670 he built Middlesex House (p. 75). Shortly before 1752 Thomas Drewett, a drugget maker of Colerne (p. 79) bought the mill and Pine House. His son, Samuel, also a clothier, had the mill by 1755, and in 1770 was rated for "the newly-erected house in the mill". This would be the present Mill House, a reconstruction of an earlier building.

About 1780 Charles Harford rented the mill of Drewett. His successor, John Bell about 1795, was in 1799 rated for a "factory"—cloth-making was becoming mechanised. John Bell was evidently well thought of, for in 1809, then "Esq", he was invited to give an expert opinion on Anglo-merino wool at the Bath and West. The next owner, taking over in 1811, was named Price, followed in 1821 by Thomas Sykes. The cloth trade was depressed, and in two years Sykes was bankrupt. The catalogue of his goods (*Keene's Bath Journal*, 20 June 1823) shews how completely by this time the making of cloth was mechanised. This was the end of the trade in Batheaston.

No other mill in the parish is known to have had any part in the cloth trade. Whether other Batheaston clothiers had used their premises for cloth-making, or whether they were exclusively middlemen is uncertain. Three of their trade tokens of Charles II's time are known, those of Richard Harford, James Pearce and Eldad Walters.[4]

For the next two years "void" appears against the cloth mill in rating lists. In 1827 it returns as "The New Factory", occupied by W. G. Baker, the Price family probably retaining ownership. This was the beginning of the silk industry—chiefly silk winding or "throwing". It was introduced into Somerset about 1753, and when hard times befell the cloth trade many mills were converted to work silk. The mill at Batheaston throve for a while; in 1836 John Price was assessed at £170, a considerable sum, as owner and occupier. Paupers, especially children, were brought in to work it. An item in the Vestry Minutes of Keynsham, dated 20 June 1833, reads: "That the Overseer provide Beds and Bedding for the Pauper Children who are employed by Mr Price at his Silk Works in Batheaston. Mr Price to return the same upon the children leaving his employ". Children were still being sent in July 1835. Even adults were ordered to Batheaston; in 1833 a Mrs. Stock, applying for relief, was to be employed at the Silk Factory. One consequence of the exploitation of these children was that the illegitimacy rate reached a record level when six silk girls contributed to it in four years.

In 1840 Price died, and the mill was offered for sale. There was no buyer, and the premises remained empty in the ownership of Price's widow, Sarah. Unemployment caused distress, and the census report of 1841 notes that 164 persons had left Batheaston "in consequence of the stoppage of a large silk factory".

The last episode in the long story began about 1856, when Thomas Dewdney rented the factory of Mrs. Price and made paper there. An entry in the Directory of Paper Mills for 1860 reads: "Mill No. 406, Bathesdon (*sic*) Mill, making Grocery Papers and Double Small Hands". It is found from entries in the register of Batheaston School that the employees were not local men, but migrants from diverse places; Bristol, Winchcombe, Market Deeping, East Malling are among them. The enterprise evidently met with little success, for Dewdney's name disappeared from the Bath Directory after 1860 and the factory never resumed work. It stood empty for many years, and was demolished sometime before 1870. Only a piece of walling remains, the scant reminder that a factory of six storeys once stood on the site.

The lord's mill of S. Catherine, though downstream from the demesne, probably stood on the site of S. Catherine's mill (Map 1, 40). Sir John Harington in 1594 granted it to Ellen Balman, widow. In 1673 (the change in spelling can be followed), Joseph Beaman was granted "the Custom Grist Mill in the occupation of one Salmon", and it remained in the family at least until 1840, when Thomas Beaman had it. Thorpe's map of 1742, however, called it "Leather Mill", and there is record of tithe paid in 1787 for "Part of the New Mill converted to a Leather Mill". The New Mill may have been the little building which still stands; there is the date 1741 on a fireplace in the mill house. The power was probably used for crushing bark for tanning. Something of the kind continued at least until 1851, when three men of S. Catherine gave their occupation as leather-dresser. The mill ground corn in a small way until about 1891; just within living memory ponies carried sacks up and down the steep narrow bridle way which leads to the lane through the valley.

The uppermost of our mill sites is clearly located in a document of 1626 (Chancery Proceedings C3 bundle 414 No. 159) when the miller was Robert Eeles; over several generations the name became

Yeels, and by this the mill continued to be known, though, confusingly, it was sometimes called S. Catherine's (Map 1, 48). Still partly a grist mill, in 1799 there is a tithe reference to "Huband at the paper mill". This use developed, employing migrant labour, like its neighbour at Northend. Five paper-makers were counted in the 1851 census, their places of origin Condover, Wolverhampton, Brixton, Chepstow and Wycombe. The explanation for this mobility of paper-makers must be scarcity of employment. In 1860 Thomas Cross was making "Brown Papers, Cartridges, Small Hands, Millboards, Box Boards and Engine Boards". There was evidently an interruption, for the census of 1861 counted cnly 84 inhabitants, compared to 135 in 1851, while the report on that of 1871 attributes the rise to 160 to "the re-opening of the paper mill"; but the end was near.

The demand of Bath for water was the ruin of the mills in S. Catherine's valley. In 1870 the City constructed a reservoir at Monkswood (Map 1) and took off a large part of the water from the brook; the mills were bought up. Joseph Hall, the last to work the Paper (Yeels) Mill, submitted an enormous claim, and actually received £5,300. He joined the Bristol firm of Mardon, Son and Hall, which still exists. S. Catherine's Mill received £2,100, and, as stated, continued for a while. Sarah Price was paid £400 as owner of the site of the silk mill, by this time entirely cleared away.

The mill sites now are derelict, indeed, almost obliterated. Besides the little building at S. Catherine, now a store, all that remains is a few sluices, at Yeels Mill not even that, only the name Paper Mill Cottages and a small building by the roadside that was probably a hoist. When these mills flourished it is difficult to imagine how the lane through the valley, steep and narrow, took the traffic that must have plied to and fro—wagons loaded with corn, hides, dressed leather, rags, paper, presumably coal, too, for the paper mill. Obviously, the ordinary rural traffic one imagines— farm wagons and animals—was only part of the scene.

The mill site on the Avon (Map 1, 4) is certainly ancient, for when an old mill was demolished in 1844 there were found built into it some portions of Norman columns and two sculptured stones, representing the martyrdoms of S. Bartholomew and S.

Pl. 51. Mill on Avon, burnt down before 1899 (from "Picturesque Rambles")

Lawrence, believed to have been part of the Norman Cathedral. They indicate, of course, the long possession of Batheaston by the church of Bath, and have been restored to Bath Abbey. There is nothing to suggest that this mill, called Batheaston Mill, was ever other than a grist mill, though for much of last century the millers combined a brewery with their activities, a building which now houses a factory making paper bags, the sole remaining industry in Batheaston. Bath paid £375 in compensation to the owner of the mill for a somewhat hypothetical loss of water, and corn milling continued until the last mill was burnt down in 1907.

One industrial misadventure remains to be chronicled. In *The Monthly Magazine*, Vol. 17, 1804, p. 507 may be read:

"It is intended to form a company at Bath, under the style of the Batheaston Mining Company, for the establishment and advancing of a mine for coals or other minerals; the works of which are to be carried on in the parishes of Batheaston and Swainswick, near Bath, under a lease for 99 years, granted by Thomas Walters Esq., subject to payment of the clear annual value of one-eighth part of the actual produce, and with power to renew for a further term of 99 years on paying a fine of £1,000".

William Smith, "Father" of English geology, supplied encouragement and expert advice, the shares were quickly taken up, and were at a premium. At first the venture promised well. Two shafts were sunk and walled to a depth of some 300 feet (GR 782677). A warm spring was tapped, and the flow at the Bath springs was said to have been thereby lessened. Accounts vary somewhat; what is certain is that by 1809 £12,000 had been spent and funds were running out, but there was as yet no coal. In 1809 an appeal was put out for a further subscription of £10,000 to enable digging through a further 30 yards of rock, where it was hoped that coal would be found. At this point records are deficient, and it is uncertain how much more work was done. *The Improved Bath Guide,* 1810, p. 119, spoke of "that laudable and spirited undertaking, the Batheaston Mining Concern". The date when hope was abandoned and the exact cause or causes of failure have not been established. Work ceased in 1812. The Company was wound up, and the only reminders of its existence are local tradition and the name Coal Pits Road. Perhaps Batheaston had a fortunate escape.

(This account has been compiled mainly from papers and cuttings in the Bath Reference Library.)

Pl. 52.   Drewett family at the Forge, c. 1906

Chapter 13

Charities

Sunt lacrimae rerum et mentem mortalia tangunt.

VIRGIL

THE earliest charitable foundation of which any record remains (in the Poor Book), is the bequest by William Blanchard of S. Catherine in 1631 of £5, "to the poore of Batheaston and Catterne to remaine as a stocke for ever and the benefit whariseth thereof to be every year distributed among them". The interest amounted to 8s., and was given out the year following among twelve persons, nine of them women, seven being widows. The record is incomplete, but it seems that about the same time John Smith (a John Smith was churchwarden in 1640) gave a similar sum and for some years the interest on £10 was distributed. However, by 1642 only Blanchard's 8s appears, and this only until 1642, in which year we are told:

In Anno domini 1642 the stock for the poore of this parish was fifteen pounds as followeth
in the hands of Anthony Townsend £10
and in the hands of Micaell Lee under
his hand on bond which bond is in the
hands of John Gay £5

Blanchard and Smith's charities never appear again by name. A possible clue to the fate of the principal is found in an entry of the same year recording the requirement of the trustees of Henry Smith's charity, about to be described, that the parish should obtain deeds "for settlement of the said sume of Ten pounds" at an expected cost of £5, with the resolution that the sum in the hands of John Gay be used. May it be that legal costs swallowed up the whole of the stock, and that the parish officers saw nothing improper in so using it?

SMITH'S CHARITY

One Henry Smith, of Silver Street, London, by his will, proved 23 January 1627/8, appointed trustees who were to distribute the rent of the manor of Longney in Gloucestershire among twenty-four parishes, seven in London, the others scattered about England, and one, Radnor, in Wales. In this vicinity, Calne, Chippenham, Stanton and Batheaston were each to receive £10, Newton S. Loe £30, only exceeded by Pershore, Worcestershire, which had £50. Why Henry Smith chose these parishes is quite unknown.

The following was written in the Poor Book during 1775:

An Extract from Mr Smiths Declaration of the Uses of the Above Mentioned Charity enrolled in Chancery and bearing Date January 26. 1626.

Churchwardens and Overseers of the Poor to Receive and distribute the Above mentioned Charity commonly called the Gift Money.

Church Wardens etc. upon entering into their office to Give a Bond to the Vicar, of Double the Value of each yearly payment for the just Distribution of it.

The Vicar to Certifie to the Governors of Christ Hospital London that such Securities is given. In Default of this, the Parish is to lose the Benefit of the Charity for that Year. This Money is to be given for the Relief of the Poor; the Marriages of poor Maids; the Apprenticing of Poor Chilldreen and the Deed recites what sort of Poor; viz: the Aged and Infirm poor Married Persons haveing more Children born in lawfull Wedlock than their Labor can maintain; Poor Orphans; such poor as keep themselves and Families to Labor; and put their Children apprentice at the Age of 15, the Churchwardens are to keep a stock of money in Readiness to set such Poor to Work as are Able to labor.

This Money is not to be given for the Relief of Drunkards, Whoremongers, Common Swearers, Pilferers, or otherwise Notoriously Scandalouse incorrigible and Disobedient Servants, Vagrants such as have no Constant Dwelling such as receive any inmate into their Houses; such as have not inhabited in the Parish for Five Years next before such distribution to be made; and such as being able refuse to work labour and take pains.

The Churchwardens are to meet once in every month in the Church; on Sunday after Evening Prayer; to Consider of the State of the Poor, and which of them have most need of Relief; on some Sunday between Easter and Whitsuntide the Churchwardens etc. shall enter an Account in a Book kept for that purpose of all their Receipts and Disbursments relating to this Charity for the Year preceding this is to be done in the Church after Evening Prayer, notice thereof being first given after Morning Prayer. This Account to be Publickly read in the Church on the Sunday following, after Morning Prayer. A Copy of this Account signed by the Churchwardens etc. is to be affixed in a Table to the Church Wall for 14 Days to the Intent that Any one may see it and make Exception if there be just cause. This Account signed by the Vicar, Churchwardens etc and such others as were present at passing it, is to be sent to the Governors of Christ Hospital London within 10 Days after the Expiration of the aforesaid 14 Days— for a Neglect in any of the foregoing Premises the Penalty is, a Forefeiture of the Charity Money for the ensuing Year, and the Benefit thereof is to go to the said Hospital.

This Charity Money to be expended in Cloth of one Color, with a Badge; or also in Bread Flesh or Fish; to be distributed publickly in the Church on Sundays.

The Manor of Longney etc. is vested in the Governors of Christs Hospital London; but leases are to be granted to such persons, and at such Rents as shall be Approved by the Churchwardens and Overseers of the Several parishes (before mentioned) under their Hands and Seals. Leases not to exceed the Term of 21 Years or 3 Lives. The Charity Money is paid by the Treasurers of Christ Hospital London.

N.B. the two Deeds, from whence these Extracts are taken, are in the Hands of Henry Walters Esq, of this Parish.

It follows almost as a matter of course that the deeds are now lost.

Statements of accounts for Smith's Charity appear often, but irregularly, in the Poor Books. Evidently the value of the estate fluctuated, for Batheaston's share in the seventeenth century was usually far short of the promised ten pounds, and in the eighteenth came to about eight guineas. The monetary value of the gifts is always shewn, but in what form the beneficiaries received them is not stated. The account for 1698, when £5 12s 3d was distributed among twenty-eight persons, is typical. In the eighteenth century such items as apprenticeship indentures were sometimes included, and other expenditure of the overseers almost, if not quite, within the terms of the bequest.

With the nineteenth century the value appreciated, a note in the Vestry Order Book in 1835–1836 recording that owing to repairs on the estate only £13 2s 0d was received. This was distributed in bread to 91 families comprising 375 individuals. The note continues that after this year the mode of distribution was altered, and refers the reader to Smith's Charity Account Book. This has not come to light, and no more is heard of the Charity until 1875, when "Church Rambler" wrote: "I afterwards saw a distribution of bread being made in the church, and on enquiry I learned that this is a weekly custom out of the funds supplied by Henry Smith's Trust. . . . From what appeared to superficial observation the pious founder's intentions are very well carried out". Next year, 1876, the accounts appear again in the Vestry Book, for the good reason, apparently, that the recently-instituted Charity Commission was beginning to take an interest, for on the page opposite the account for £18 12s 6d spent on bread for thirty recipients—evidently poverty had decreased in the parish—is pasted a printed statement: in accordance with the Charitable Trusts Amendment Act 1855, the Charity Commissioners order the Trustees of every Charity to keep books and render an account.

They also modified the uses of the money thus:

The Charity Commissioners approve not only of gifts of clothing or blankets to poor infirm old people of good character (the directions as to the colour and badges being dispensed with), but also of small scholarships or payments to well-conducted poor children during their attendance at school, or in subscriptions to saving clubs, coal, blanket and clothing clubs for the benefit of the resident poor of the parish.

The legal settlement of the persons relieved is not material.

Following the Local Government Act of 1894 it was ruled that Henry Smith's Charity is a parochial charity within the meaning of that Act, not an ecclesiastical charity, and from that time it has been administered by the Parish Council. The yearly value now amounts to at least £30, which is spent on gifts of coal.

According to an official statement circulated for the guidance of parishes interested in the Charity, Christ's Hospital refused to accept the conveyance of the estate, and has never had any concern in its management. This is not true, for the Batheaston records often refer to money received from Christ's Hospital for the Charity. When its responsibility ceased is obscure.

WEAVER'S CHARITY

William Weaver, a retired farmer who died in 1865 aged 88, left the interest of £100 in 3% annuities for annual distribution by the churchwardens. The account of it first appears in 1876; it was the custom to make gifts of half a crown to twenty-four persons. In due time this Charity also came under the care of the Parish Council, and its income is now combined with that of Smith's Charity.

OTHER CHARITIES

Miss Constantia Miller, of Batheaston Villa, by her will of 1920 gave a bequest to provide school prizes and towards the care of the churchyard.

Miss Laxton, of Middlesex House, who died in 1946, left £350 to the parish, the interest to be applied to the Nursing Association, and the upkeep of the chancel and family graves.

Appendices

Appendix 1

Manor of Easton and Catherine
Court of 23 April 1310

Names of tenants in the mercy of the lord for grazing in the pastures and the enclosures.

Walter le Wodeward
Agnes atte Broke
Thomas Bigge
John Wylteschure
William Ponkeput
Walter Kington
William Slofaunt
Walter Stubbe
William Ocford
John Golye
Richard Kington
Walter Cromhale
Roger Sturegges
John Upehulle
William le Fomel
Thomas le Yonges
Nicholetta Lines
Henry de Hertlegh
John Oddemed
Walter Hertlegh
The shepherd of the Lady of Bathenestone
William Boldebury
Richard de Hertlegh
John Chaumpneys

Roger son of William Uppehulle
William Foghel
Walter son of William Uppehulle
Thomas son of William Uppehulle
} fugitives

Walter Wodeward has John [18] William [16] Henry [10] Agnes [19] Matilda [13] and Marion [4]

John Wylteschure has Robert [21] William [18] Thomas [13] Agnes [23] Matilda [15] Alice [18] John [12] John [8]

John Stybbe has Thomas [21] William [18] Walter [16] Alice [12] Julian and John.

The homage present that William son of William atte Mulle Walter son of Nicholas Gouthwy Robert West Roger son of William Uppehulle otherwise Churchman William Foghel Thomas son of Henry Uppehulle bondmen of the lord and fugitives make default nevertheless let not the homage be amerced for them because they have made fine for them from of old. and nevertheless it is commanded that they shall be taken if they can be found in the lordship of the lord.

Item they present that in the wood of Hunterwyke 2 maples (mepell) and two ash trees are cut down to the grave damage of the lord by the collusion of the messor because he did not proffer an attachment therefore he is in mercy and the damage thereof is assessed at 6d.

Item they present that Robert Cooke has two foals depasturing in Hunterwyke where no one has pasture and because the messor did not attach him nor proffer any attachment thereupon therefore he is in mercy. And that damage is assessed at 2d.

Of the attachments of the messor as appears by the extracts 5s.

Appendix 2

Manor of Easton and Catherine
Court of 23 April 1378

All the homage present of a certain rent 9s. 7d. And because they did not present the said rent therefore they are in mercy. Of the works of the vineyard 11½d.

John son of John Wylteshure
John brother of the same
John son of John Ters
William son of John Wylteshure with William atte Mulle
John son of Henry Uppehulle
William son of William Fox
Robert West
} with the lord

Appendix 3

Names of those who paid the Exchequer Lay Subsidy 1325-1326

(E)Stone

De Waltero le Wodeward	3s	od
Willelmo Pukeput		7d
Adam Wilteshire		7d
Thoma Bromehale		7d
Rogero Stugrigg	1s	od
Thoma atte Brouke	2s	od
Waltero Felaghe		10d
Johanne Gulye	2s	od
Waltero Goys		8d

Johanne (W)alle	1s	0d
Thoma Bigge	3s	0d
Waltero Kyngton	2s	0d
Willelmo Eltent	2s	0d
Henrico Hilles	2s	0d
Waltero le Clerk	1s	0d
Willelmo Foghel	2s	0d
Henrico Uppehulle	2s	0d
Waltero Uppehulle	2s	0d
Henrico atte Townsende		9d
Henrico Gothewy	1s	0d
Sum	30s	0d

Aumarle Chaumflour

De Thoma Praggy		7d
Johanne Goys		10d
Willelmo Fabro	1s	0d
Johanne Haukyn	1s	8d
Willelmo Abbod	1s	0d
Johanne Creyde	1s	3d
Thoma de Kymynton		10d
Henrico le Hore	1s	6d
Johanne de Salso Marisco	2s	0d
Johanne Midewynter	1s	11d
Willelmo Midewynter	1s	8d
Matill. Cuperes	1s	8d
Andrea de Medstede	5s	0d
Henrico de Lynecombe	1s	0d
Johanne Betrich	1s	4d
Roberto Symenel	1s	6d
Thoma Hughes	2s	0d
Johanne Aldred	1s	4d
Henrico Holebroc		8d
Johanne Godebergh	3s	0d
Roberto atte Midle	3s	0d
Johanne Poyntel	3s	0d
Johanne Kyft		
Willelmo Castel	(torn off)	
Willelmo Sely		

The latter part of the entry torn off.

The other surviving entries for the Hundred:

Hampton	21 names	64s	7d
Cherlecoumbe	4 names	21s	6d
Freshford	7 names	8s	5d
Lynecoumbe	15 names	22s	0d
Weston	23 names	30s	0d
Forde	20 names	30s	0d
Walcote	11 names	10s	0d
Langerigge	20 names	43s	0d

Appendix 4

Lease of the manor of Easton and Catherine

26. September, 18 Hen. 8. (1526).

For £7 now paid by Alice and Thomas Lieuwelyn

the reversion is granted to Benedict, William and John, their sons. They are to pay yearly when in possession £10 for the manor, Farm and Rectory of Kateryn at the feasts of the Annunciation and S. Michael equally and 12 measures of corn and 20 measures of barley to be carried into the monastery between the feasts of All Saints and Easter. And for the farm of Charmerdone £7 10s and one calf worth 2s at the feast of S. Peter in Chains. And for the close in Hunterwyke 7s and for the dovecote 6s 8d and the tithes thereof. And they may take sufficient housebote, firebote, ploughbote, and hedgebote. They are to collect all rents of assize of our tenants of Eston and Kateryn yearly and pay to us and render an account without fee. They are to maintain and repair all houses on the site of the manor, farm or rectory except Brokynhouse and the house called Overhall which the Prior and Convent will support.

The last of them or their executors are to hand over and deliver up the flock of 400 sheep and rams healthy, whole and strong, not diseased or attacked by any contagion, or at least for each head 13d to be estimated and judged, according to the judgment of all the homage there.

Reversion of the manor of Eston and Catherine, 5 November 1534

Harleian M.S. 3970 m II d.

William Holewey Prior of the monastery and Cathedral Church of the Holy Saviour and Apostles Peter and Paul. Whereas Alice Herford of Kateryn widow of William Herford holds the manor or chief messuage, Rectory and farm of Kateryn called Katerynscorte with an annexed tenement called Brokynhouse, and our wood called Palmerswode and two groves called le Hanger and Toteneys grove and all demesne lands, fields, pastures and meadows as well in severalty as in common and one close or parcel of pasture of 12 acres in Hunterwyke and all tithes of grain and hay appertaining to the manor farm and rectory for her life. Remainder to Isabel her younger daughter, wife of Thomas Lieuwelyn; after her to Agnes, her other daughter, wife of John Bysshope of Marfeld.

Nevertheless, reserved to the prior and Convent the rents reliefs and all other services of all tenants of Eston and Kateryn with all the customary works, as appears in an indented charter between the Prior and Convent and Alice and William Herford dated 1 August 8 Hen. 8 (1516).

And whereas Alice holds one several hill called a Downe or several close of pasture called Charmerdon, and divers other closes, lands, fields, and pastures at Chermburye with two houses there called the Shepe-houses of Chermburye with 400 ewes and rams called the Eweflocke of Charmerdon the price of each of them 13d as valued by the homage of Eston and Kateryn, with wool, lambs and tithes, and all pastures in the fields of Eston and elsewhere within the parish of Eston and Kateryn, with the customary works of all our tenants of Eston and Kateryn, to wit, washing and shearing of all the sheep aforesaid and of all their lambs yearly. And certain houses and lands at Warleigh in the parish of Ford for the sustenance of the sheep from the feast of S. Michael the Archangel until the Morrow of the Annunciation of the Blessed Virgin Mary.

Further, the 12 acres of pasture at Hunterwyke enrolled at the Court held at Eston 26 September. 6. Hen. 7. (1490). And one dovecote at Kateryn with all the doves enrolled at the Court held at Eston.

Appendix 5

Will of John Stybbe

About 1530. Calendared by F. W. Weaver. (Wells Wills P. 7). The original is destroyed.

In churchyard of Batheston——church of Wells 2d ——ymage of S. John a bushell of barley——the same to our lady——S. Katherine and S. Christofer half a bushell of barley (each)——Nicolas, Water and Thomas my sons——Alyse and Johan my dowghters ——my eldest son, a wayn.

Residue——Johan my wyf.
Witnesses——John Humfrey, Will Smyth, Tho Skyrell.
Supervisor——John lytheryg.

Will of Thomas Stockes

In Dei Nomine Amen. The xxvth. daye of June and in the fortieth yeare of the Reigne of our Soveraigne Ladye Elizabeth by the grace of god of England France and Ireland Queene defender of the Fayth Etc, And in the yeare of our Lord God A thousand Fyve hundred Nyntie nyne. I Thomas Stockes of the parishes of Batheaston in the Countie of Somerset husbandman beinge of good and perfitt mynde and memory thankes be gyven unto the Almightie God, Do make and ordaine this my Last will and testament in manner and forme following. First I gyve and bequeath my Sowle into the hande of Almightie God my maker and Redeemer and doe hope to be saved by the death and passion of Christ my onlie savior and my bodie to be buried and interred within the parishe Churchyard of the aforesaide Batheston. Item I gyve unto the Cathedrall Church of St Andruse in wells foure pence Item I doe gyve unto the parishe Churche of Batheston foure pence Item I do gyve unto the

poore of the saide parishe a bushell of Wheate Item I I doe gyve unto my three kynswomen the daughters of John Stockes of Sutton the somme of twentie poundes to be equallie devided betwene them by equall portions and to be paid within one whole yeare after my death. Item I doe gyve unto three of my Servants a sheepe apeece All the rest of my goods moveable and unmoveable
not before geven and bequeathed, I doe gyve and bequeath unto my welbeloved wief Joane Stockes whome I doe make my full and whole Executrix of this my Last will and testament and to see my debts and all things else to be discharged Item I doe ordaine and appoynte to be my Overseers of this my Last will and Testamente Richard Smith and Thomas Smyth my Sonne in Lawes and to

see the same approved and towards their painestakinge herein I gyve to each of them a sheepe apeece and a Lambe Thomas Stockes marke witnesses to this my Last will and Testament Tho Briton vicar Thomas Harforde John Stibes Walter Symmons Jo Jeffrye.

Proved   22nd. September 1599

The Will of Alice Bletchley

In the name of God Amen the xviith day of March in the yeare of our Lord 1624 I Alice Bletchley of Batheaston in the County of Sommersett sicke in body but perfect of memory do make my laste will and testament in manner and forme followinge. First I bequeathe my soule to Almighty God my maker and my body to be buried in the churchyard of Batheaston aforesaid. Item I give to my sonne Thomas the bed and bedsted wheron I did ly a paire of blankets a paire of coverlets twoe bolsters and one sheet and one pilstowe and to his wife one coffer with what is in it, my best gownde my best peticote and wastcote. Item I give to the children of the said Thomas each of them a young lamb. Item I give to my sonne William one bedsted and bed a paire of blankets a bolster and coverlet and eight pound of woll in the loft. Item I give to William his sonne one yow with lambe. Item I give to Anna the wife of my sonne William one bocrum sheete one holland pilstow twoe pillowes one partlet one brassen candlesticke one skillet. Item I give to Idith Bletchley of Cullerne Widow my new red wastcot my best blew apron and a petticot for workinge dayes. Item I give to Jane Bletchley daughter of my sonne Robert in mony two shillinges my best hat my holland bodyes my weddinge kerchef my fierpann and tonges my litle settle. Item I give to Mary the daughter of Robert Sommervill iii.s. and holland Apron. All the rest of my goods and chattles not yet given or bequeathed my debts paid and my funerall discharged I give and bequeath to my sonnes

Thomas and William whome I do make myne executors. And for overseers to this my will and testament I ordaine my welbeloved friends James Bullocke and Thomas Pearce. In witnes whereof I have hereto put my hand and seale this day and yeare above written.

Alice Bletchley   +

In the presence of George Lee
                                 Thomas Pearce
                                 James Bullocke
Proved at Wells 4th. October 1625.   £13 18s.

Extracts from the will of the Rev. Mark Hall 1765

I Mark Hall Vicar of BathEaston in the County of Somerset being of Sound Mind but weak in Body most humbly implore the Mercies of God thro' Jesus Christ my Dearest Lord and Saviour And I do make this my last Will and Testament in Manner following.

It is my Will after my Death that I be kept four or five days if it can be before I am interred and be put into a plain Coffin Covered with Black Bays and be buried in the Grave of my Dear Wife. And it is my Will that no part of my Wive's body be removed but that my Coffin may rest upon hers and that I be carried to the Grave with only a Pall and no Pallbearers by Six Labouring Men that have been employed about my House and that they have half a Crown a peise given them a Cup of Beer and two or three glasses of Wine for their trouble And I order that the officiating Minister and Thos Russell Clerk of this parish have a Silk Hatband and Shammy Gloves upon the Occasion and what Wine they please.

And it is my Desire that my Executor herein after named will cause a handsome Blue Stone to be placed upon my Grave with a Short Inscription.
(Among legacies totalling £709, mostly to relatives)

Item I give to Sarah Neat my Maid Servant for her Carefull Attendance on me in my long Illness ten pounds.

Item I give to Thos Gane the Boy that lives with me Forty Shillings. Item I give to Sarah Fisher Widow four pounds. Item I give to those three poor Men Peter Morris, Giles Fisher, and Henry Webb twenty shillings a peise.

All my Manuscripts as well in Books as Sermons I give them all to my Nephew George Hall . . . with Liberty of publishing or otherwise disposing of them to the most Advantage as he shall be advised by some Judicious Clergyman.

Appendix 6

Somerset, to Witt
        The Examination of John Fisher the Younger Labourer taken upon oath the 9th of June 1738.

This Examinant Saith that he was Born as he have heard and believes in the parish of Batheaston in the said County, and that he did agree with Mr Thomas Atwood at the Black Swan in the Parish of St Michaell in the Citty of Bath to serve him for one year from Midsomer in the year 1736 at £6 15s a year wages, and went to London in his service about six weeks before Christmas following and coming home was taken ill of the smallpox and stayed at his Fathers three weeks or more untill he was Recovered, and then Returned to his Masters Mr Atwoods in the said parish of St Michaell in the said City where he served out the Remainder of the year and to near Michaelmass following, and that Mr Atwood paid him his wages, and further saith not.

Sworn the Day and
    year above written before us
            Hen. Walters
            J. V. S. Houlton   The mark + of
                                                        John Fisher

County of Somerset THE EXAMINATION of Charles Jefferys now residing in the Parish of Batheaston in the said County Husbandman touching the place of his last legal settlement taken upon his Oath before us his Majesty's Justices of the Peace in and for the said County the 7th Day of Febry 1783.

Who upon his Oath saith that he is about 50 years old and was born in the parish of Minety in the County of Gloucester as he hath heard and verily believes and where his Father George Jefferys then resided and was legally settled and continued to be settled during the time that this Examinant lived with him And saith that upwards of thirty years ago he this Examinant at a Market or Fair (commonly called a Mopp) held at Cirencester in the County of Gloucester hired himself as a Servant from that day until the Michaelmas following to Mr William Parsons of Charlton in the County of Wilts Farmer and in pursuance of such Hiring this Ext went into the Service of the said Mr Parsons and continued therein in Charlton aforesaid from the day of such Hiring until Michaelmas following, being one whole year or near thereabouts and received Wages for the same And saith that he cannot now recollect whether the said Market or Fair was held on the Monday before or the Monday after Michaelmas day but he is sure that it was held upon one of those Mondays and saith it is and was then usual in the Neighbourhood of Cirencester to hire Servants from the sd Market or Fair to the Michaelmas following and that a Service during that time is by the Custom of the Neighbourhood accounted as a Service for a year tho' it sometimes falls a few days short of a year That the sd Market or Fair is usually held in every year both on the Monday before and on the Monday after Michaelmas day And saith that since his leaving the Service of the said Mr Parsons he hath done no act whatever to gain a Settlement in any parish or place And saith he hath with him in Batheaston aforesaid Martha his Wife (late Martha Bacchus) to whom he was lawfully married in Batheaston aforesaid.

The Mark + of
Charles Jefferys

Sworn the day and year first
above written before us
H. Walters
W. Wiltshire
Philip James Gibbs

Endorsed: Settled at Charlton near Malmsbury Wilts.

Appendix 7

Wilts. To the Churchwardens and Overseers of the Poor of the Parish of Box in the County of Wilts. and to the Churchwardens and Overseers of the Poor of the Parish of Bath-Easton in the County of Somersett

WHEREAS Complaint hath been made by You the Churchwardens and Overseers of the Poor of the said Parish of Box unto US whose Hands and Seals are hereunto Set two of his Majesty's Justices of the Peace (Quorum unus) for the County aforesaid THAT Edward Gay Laborer and Deborah his wife late Deborah Salter and Edward his Son aged five years and Thomas his Son Aged near half a year lately Intruded themselves into your Said Parish of Box there to Inhabit as Parishioners contrary to the Laws relating to the Settlement of the Poor, and are there likely to become Chargeable, If not timely prevented; AND WHEREAS upon due Examination and Enquiry made into the premises upon the Oath of the Said Edward Gay it appears unto US and WE accordingly Adjudge, that the Said Edward Gay and Deborah his wife and Edward and Thomas his Sons are likely to become Chargeable unto the Said Parish of Box, And that the Last Legal Place of Settlement of the Said Edward Gay was in the said Parish of Bath-Easton in the County of Sumersett.

THESE are therefore in his Majesty's Name, to order and Require You the Said Churchwardens and Overseers of the Poor of the Parish of Box aforesaid, that You, or Some of You, do forthwith Remove and Convey the Said Edward Gay, and Deborah his wife and Edward and Thomas his Sons from Your Said Parish of Box to the Said Parish of Bath-Easton in the County of Somersett and them to Deliver to the Churchwardens and Overseers of the Poor there, or Some, or one of them together with this our Warrant or Order, or a true Copy hereof; Whereby they are Likewise Required in his Majesty's Name, and by

Vertue of the Statutes in Such Case made, forthwith to Receive the Said Edward Gay and Deborah his wife and Edward and Thomas his Sons into their Said parish and provide for them as their Own Parishioners GIVEN under our Hands and Seals the 23rd day of September Anno Regni Domini Nostri Georg II Regis Magna Brittannia Xr primo, Annoque Dom. 1727.

M. Smith
Wm. Northey

Appendix 8

This Indenture made the sixth day of November in the third yeare of the Reigne of our Soveraigne Lord King James the second over England Etc. Anno Dm 1687 Witnesseth That Jeremi Richmond & John Murford Churchwardens of the parish of Bath Easton in the county of Somsett & Mr. Eldad Walters and John Jefferis overseers of the poore of the same by and with the Consent of his majesties Justices of the peace of the said County whose names are hereunto subscribed, have put placed and bound and by these presents doe put place and bind Martha Cannons a poore Child of the said parish Apprentise to William Haselwood and Sarah his wife of the parish of Bath-weeke in the said County Broadweaver, with them to dwell & serve from the day of the date of these presents, untill the said Apprentise shall accomplish her age of eighteen yeares according to the Statute in that case made and provided, During all which said time and Terme the said Apprentise, the said William Haselwood & Sarah his wife Faithfully shall serve & honestly and obediently demeane and behave herselfe, And the said William Haselwood & Sarah his wife doe Covenant & Grant for themselves their Executors and Administrators that they the said William Haselwood & Sarah his wife, the said Apprentise in a decent manner shall Educate & breed up & shall and will during all the Terme aforesaid find provide and allow unto the said Apprentise meate drink Apparel Lodging washing and all other things necessary fit for such a Servant, And at the end of the said Terme shall and will make provid allow and deliver unto the said Apprentise double Apparel of all sort good and new, that is to say a good new suit for holy dayes and another for working dayes In witnes whereof the parties above said to these present Indentures interchangably have put their hands and seales the day and yeare above written.

Will Hazelwood.

Sealed and delivered
in the presents of
John Robins
Jo. Morris

We whose names are subscribed Justices of the peace of the said County doe (as much as in us Lyes) consent to the putting

L*

Forth of the abovesaid Martha Cannons Apprentise according to the intent & meaning of the Indenture abovesaid.

        Jos. Langton   P. Roynon

This Indenture made the six day of August in the fourth yeare of the Reigne of our Soveraigne Lord King James the Second over England Etc. Witnesseth that Henry Blanchard and William England Overseers of the Poore of the parish of Batheaston in this County and Jeremy Richmand & John Murford Churchwardens of the same parish, By and with the consent of John Harington Esq. and Sir Thomas Bridges Knite two of his Majesties Justices of the Peace for this County have by these presents put placed and bound Nicholas Lansdowne (a poore fatherless and motherless child) an Apprentise with Anthony Millgrove of the parish of Bathweeke Broadweaver and as an Apprentise with him the sd Anthony Millgrove to dwell from the day of the date of these presents untill he shall come to be of the age of 21 yeares according to the statute in that case made and provided By and duringe all which time and terme the sd Nicholas Lansdowne shall his sd Master well and faithfully serve in all such lawfull business as he shall be put unto, according to his power wit and abillity and honestly and obediently in all things shall behave himselfe towards his sd Master his wife and Children And the sd Anthony Millgrove for his parte promiseth to and with the sd Nicholas Lansdowne (sic) in the craft mistery and occupation the which he now useth after the best manner he cann or may shall teach and informe or cause to be taught or informed as much as thereunto belongeth or in any wise appertayneth And also during the sd terme to find unto his sd Apprentise Meat Drinke Linnen Woollen Hose Shoes and all other things needfull for an apprentice of his condition, and att the end of the sd terme shall provide and allow the sd apprentice two shirts of apparell one for workinge daies and the other for Holydaies In Witness whereof the parties above named have to these Indentures sett their Hands and seales the day and yeare above writne

The Marke of
Anthony Millgrove

Signed seled and delivered in ye presents of
Richard hew Lord
peter Canings

Wee whose hands are hereunto subscribed Justices of the Peace for the County aforsd doe as much as in us lies consent to ye placing of the above named Nicholas Lansdowne according to the Indenture above writne Given Under our Hands 14th day of August Anno Dm 1688

    Tho. Bridges   Jo. Harington

Appendix 9

Batheaston Vicarage: Advent, 1865

MY DEAR FRIENDS AND PARISHIONERS,

I wish to say a few words to you about our Parish Church. You know that we have had before us the question of enlarging and improving it: that an Architect has been called in: and that Plans and Estimates have been furnished, according to the instructions of your Committee appointed in Vestry, July 13th last. Before any further steps can be taken, these must be laid before a meeting of the Parishioners for their approval; and I trust that a Vestry will shortly be summoned for the purpose. But in the meanwhile I have wished to set before you a few thoughts on the whole subject, in order, if I may, to deepen your interest, and give you a clearer understanding what our wants are.

But first, I would say, let us keep steadily before us the principles on which the work should proceed. Whatever may be done, should be done, (*a*) in the best and most substantial manner: (*b*) in that manner which shall most conduce to convenience and edification. The most perfect community of worship, and the greatest facility of hearing, should be our two great aims. The thorough carrying out, with slight alterations, of the Plans prepared, would I think most effectually satisfy all these objects. The only difficulty is the largeness of the sum required, viz., about £1700. But if this should seem too great for us to raise at once, we might confine our attention for the present simply to the erection of a new South Aisle, leaving the other improvements to a future opportunity, or a future generation.

And now, as to our *wants*. I have no hesitation in saying that they are, and long have been, very pressing. Our Church is lamentably deficient, both in the quantity and the quality of the sittings provided. A simple consideration of facts, will I think prove this. The actual accommodation is as follows: For adults, 355 sittings, of which 110 are free; for children, 135: that is, total of 490 sittings for a population of 1700. Now, making every deduction for those who prefer other places of worship to the Church, I think we must confess that this is miserably below what ought to be provided for, and occupied by, such a Parish and population as ours. But here, some have said, "We see no crowding for seats—no urgent call from these classes for whom you plead". True,—but is not this very deadness as to God's worship the natural and inevitable result of such a scant accommodation as we offer? Are not these careless and outcast likely to become all the more careless and outcast, if they see those, who profess to value Church privileges, making no effort to bring them in,—but rather looking on their godless life as a matter of course? What must they think of religious services, that leave men simply satisfied with their own good things, without one active desire to share them with the lost and outcast around them? Why, if they think at all, it must seem to them very like Dives, faring sumptuously within, and closing eyes and ears to the wretchedness of the poor Lazarus without. Be sure, if we, as a congregation professing the love of Christ, make no effort to provide for them, they most certainly will never trouble themselves to demand provision for wants which they do not feel. We must bear in mind, that in spiritual things, the limit of demand is no law for the limit of supply but rather the reverse. Where there is least demand, *there* is most need for supply.

But again, look at the *quality* of much of the accommodation we offer. I take the case of one of our poorer population. As a child at School, he is placed in Church under a deep Gallery, where *hearing* to say the least is not easy even with attention:—where *kneeling*, owing to the crowding of the seats, is so difficult, that it has been deemed advisable not to enforce it. So, the boy is taught that kneeling is in no wise needful for prayer, or for reverence before God. But he leaves School: he takes his place, as a youth, in the free seats: these are so high, that he feels every temptation to play, or talk, or be inattentive: and here again the kneeling is very difficult, if not impossible:—besides that he has already learnt to *sit* during the Prayers. So, with this practical teaching—far more effectual than any words— what marvel if it never come home to him, that in God's house he is in God's more immediate presence? what marvel, if he grow up a hard prayerless, irreverent man? It is but the one in a hundred that can rise above these lowering and irreligious influences.

I plead then with you, dear friends, in behalf of these, that our Church accommodation should no longer be left provocative of carelessness and irreverence; but that it should be so remodelled as to invite to a lowly and prayerful spirit. And I plead also for those others, who seem now as the lost sheep of our Israel:—those, I mean, who do not care, or at best are not over-anxious, to enter God's house; and who, if only there is a slight hindrance, will be at no trouble to overcome it,—if there is any excuse, will be glad to adopt it. They say to us, when urged, "If we came, we should find no room." Are they sincere? I do not know and I do not wish to judge; but I do know, that they say only what is a fact; and I should wish to remove their excuse. And I do know, that if we are ever to win over these, it must be not by waiting till they show their eagerness to come by crowding round the Church doors. We ought to be able to go to them with the true Gospel invitation: "Come, for there is room: Come, for all things are ready." Till we can say this, I cannot but feel that we are even encouraging them in their present Sabbath-breaking and neglect of God's worship.

I trust then, dear friends, that we shall be found in this our day willing to face our difficulties: prepared to take a living interest in the work before us. . . .

Your affectionate friend and Pastor in Christ,

T. P. ROGERS.

Appendix 10

CHURCHWARDENS

1609	Thomas Peares	James Bullocke
1616	John Murford	Robert Sommerhill
1619	John Jones	William Lewes
1620	Anthony Townsend	Richard Harbord
1621	,,	John Stibbs
1622	Thomas Blanchard	Richard Ponting
1623	William England	William Blechley
1624	,,	Thomas Pearce
1625	Thomas Sallmon	Thomas Simons
1626	Thomas Pearce	Tobyias Pearce
1628	John Bullock	John Steebe
1629	Thomas Murford	Richard Hurward
1630	Anthony Townsend	Thomas Blanchard
1631	,,	Henry Sellire
1633–4	,,	John Gay
1637	Richard Ponting	Henry Canninge
1638	,,	Francis Doby
1639	John Blanchard	Thomas Dyer
1640	John Smith	John Bullocke
1642	Richard Harford	Thomas Simons
1647	Anthony Townsend	Thomas Simons
1648	Thomas Blanchard	Will Pointing
1649	John Fisher	Henry Blanchard
1667	Thomas Clement	John Fisher
1668	William Horsington	William Harward
1669	Richard Panton	,,
1670	Richard Pontin	John Murford
1671	Henry England	John Blechly
1672	Thomas Butler	,,
1673	John Lancaster	John Tyly
1674	Thomas Buttler	Matthew Cannings
1675	Arthur Lewis	Thomas Dolley
1676	Robert Harford	Peter Canings
1677	John Tyly ye older	John Jeffery of Northen
1677–9	,,	,,
1678		,,
1680–1	,,	John Tyly the younger
1682	Thomas Hensly	William Woodward
1683	Gabriell Fry	John Bullock
1684	Jeremiah Lewis	Ezra Lewis
1685	William Harford	William England
1686	Charles Panton	Robert Harford
1686–7	Jerome Richmond	John Murford
1689	Anthony Harward	Eldad Walters
1690–4	Peter Cannings	John Jeferies
1695	John Symons	Thomas Hensley
1696	Thomas Butler	John Bletchley
1697	John Fisher	Eldad Walters
1698	William Harford of Middlesex	John Symons

Year		
1699	Richard Fry	William Weston
1700	William England maltster	John Pinnell
1701	Thomas Butler	Abraham Amesbury
1702	John Fisher	Charles Harford
1703	William Fisher	,,
1704–6	Charles Cottle	George Bullock
1707	William Bletchley	William England
1708	John Fisher junior	William Bletchley
1709–11	,,	Samuel Henslow
1712		William Bletchley
1713–4	James Walters	
1715–7	,,	William Panton
1718	Walter Perry	John Bletchley
1719–20	John Fisher	Thomas Gunning
1721	William England	Walter Danford
1722–4	,,	John Bletchley
1725–7	Thomas Clement	Daniell Chanter
1728–9	John Fisher	John Skrine
1730–2	William Batterbury	Thomas Smalcomb
1733–4	John Harford	Samuel Fuller
1735	John Fisher senior	Rosewell Smithfield
1736–7	Joseph Cannings	George Bullock
1738–41	John Crouch	Giles Bush
1742–4	Thomas Parry	John Harford
1745–6	William England	William Pyatt
1747–9	George Bullock	John Pillinger
1750–8	Henry Walters junior	Thomas Parry
1759	John Bush	Charles Bullock
1760	,, (Died)	,,
1760–2	Thomas Bush	
1763–6	John Harford	Isaac Gale
1767	William Fisher senior	Richard Hooper
1768	Samuel Drewett	John Harford
1769	,,	,,
1770–4	,,	Thomas Parry junior
1775–6	William Morley	John Bristow
1777	John Hooper for the Cold Bath Farm	Daniel Cottle
1778–83	,,	Francis Fisher
1784–6	Thomas Bletchley	,,
1787–90	William Fisher	Thomas Cowdray
1791–5	,,	Thomas Bletchley
1796–		
1801	John Hooper	,,
1802		Thomas Walters
1803–5	John Harford	
1806	,,	Thomas Lewis
1807–9	William Dyer	,,
1810–11	,,	Henry Fisher
1812–3	,,	John Godwin
1814–6	,,	George Melsom
1817–28	Ambrose Emerson	,,
1829	William Fuller	
1830	Thomas Angel	,,
1831	John Hooper	
1832	Melmoth Walters	George Sainsbury
1833	,,	William Hale
1834–5	,,	John Price
1836–8	Melmoth Walters	William Fuller
1839–46	,,	John Hooper
1847–52	,,	Jeremiah Ford
1853–60	,,	George Rawlison
1861–5	,,	Thomas Bullock
1866–7	John Robert Miller	,,
1875	,,	Capt. Ralph Sadler
1876–9	Capt. Struan Robertson	Dr. Charles Harper
1880–1	Henry Batchellor Inman	,,
1882–3	Dr. Jardine Wyndowe	,,
1884–99	Henry Batchellor Inman	,,
1900–1	William Rich	Henry Dingle
1902–4	Col. Henry Sealy	,,
1905	John Savage	,,
1906–7	,,	Dr. Joseph Hinton
1908–9	Col. Henry Sealy	,,
1910	,,	William Bryant
1911–3	Capt. Wilfred Richardson	,,
1914–7	,,	Arthur Bence
1918–24	Theo Northover	Alfred Wilson
1925–7	,,	Harold Hamblin
1928–32	Edward Bromet	,,
1933–8	Alfred Cochrane	,,
1939–44	William Rich	,,
1945–9	,,	John Beake
1950	Henry Hyslop	,,
1951	Thomas Harris	Geoffrey Grey
1952	,,	Mrs Phyllis Townsend
1953–7	Benjamin Smith	,,
1958–9	Frank Taylor	,,
1960	,,	Benjamin Smith
1961–3	Col. Christopher Brady	Reginald Rhymes
1964–5	Arthur Edwards	,,
1966–7	David Duncan	,,
1968	Leslie White	,,
1969	,,	,,

Appendix 11

Parish clerks whose names are known

In office 1609	Anthonie Anlie
1654–1675	William Jefferies
1675–	William England
In office 1685	John Lewis
In office 1703–1711	William Russell
Before 1713–1738	John Simmonds
,, 1754–1776	Thomas Russell
1776–1805	George Baker, snr
1805–1834	George Baker jnr
Before 1836–1859 or later	William Bell
1862–	James Hallett
1876–1881	S. F. Saunders
1881–1885	George Saunders
1885–1923	Edwin Gerrish
1923–1956	Charles Gerrish

Glossary

The meanings here given are the sense in which the words are used in this book; not necessarily exclusive.

Agistment Grazing used as tithe.
Amerced Fined.
Attachment Arrest.

Back Ridge of land thrown up out of a ditch, upon which a hedge is planted.
Batch First rising ground above a river or stream.
Bay (of housing) Division between walls, usually 15 to 20 feet.
Bed cords Stretched ropes on which a mattress was laid.
Bordar Cottager.
Bouts rime's Rhymes given out for competitors to incorporate in complete verses.
Brake Thicket.
Breach Clearing, usually at edge of a wood.

Capite, in Tenure of land directly from the crown.
Chief rent Same as quit-rent. Rent paid by freeholders and copyholders of a manor in discharge or acquittance of other services.
Close Fenced or hedged enclosure; the modern field.
Colibert Tenant of Domesday manor intermediate between villeins and serfs.
Copyhold Tenure of land by copy of the court toll of a manor. Also tenure by custom.
Court leet Court held regularly in a manor or hundred.
Curtilage Yard attached to a house.

Deodand Object which had caused a person's death and was on that account forfeited to the crown for pious uses. Literally: must be given to God.
Dowlace A coarse cloth.
Drung Narrow passage or footpath.

Ell In England a measure of 40 inches.

Faculty Here an ecclesiastical licence.
Feet of Fines Lowest part of an indenture recording a transaction, that part remaining with the court.
Field (of housing) Division of a building made by a low wall. Also bay.
Frith Hedging.
Fry Brushwood drain.

Glebe Land a part of the benefice of an incumbent.
Gout Mouth of drain, sluice.
Grip Ditch. Also greep.
Ground Enclosure of dry land, usually under grass.

Haine, hayne To fence, sometimes temporarily.
Halmote Assembly of the tenants of a manor.
Hatch Half door.

Hayward Manorial or parish officer having charge of fences.
Helm Straw, stalks. Same as haulm.
Heriot Best beast claimed by lord of manor on death of a tenant.
Hide Measure of land, especially in Domesday; probably 100 to 120 acres. Also a unit for taxation of land.
Homage Here the tenants attending a manorial court.

Impropriator Lay person having obtained the right to tithes or other ecclesiastical property.

Ledgers, lidgers Scaffolding.
Linsey, lincey Coarse linen cloth.
Lugg Measure of distance. In north-east Somerset usually 15 feet.
Lynchet Slope between two pieces of sometime cultivated ground on a hillside.

Mark Old monetary unit, equivalent to 13s 4d.
Mear, meer Boundary landmark, bank, line of stones picked out of path of plough.
Mercy, in Guilty of an offence.
Messor Title sometimes given to the villein who acted as leading hand.
Messuage Dwelling with outbuildings and sometimes land.
Moiety Share, usually a half.
Mortuary Secondbest beast sometimes claimed by the incumbent on the death of a parishioner. (*See* heriot.) Supposed to be a recompense for unpaid tithe.

Nigg Ball of tough wood used in the game of Not. Each side, with bats, try to strike niggs into opposite goals.

Oblations Donations for pious use.
Obventions Offerings, tithes or oblations.

Perambulation Tracing the bounds of a parish at Rogationtide, originally in procession with the priest.
Palstave Bronze instrument fitting into a handle of split wood.
Pitching Flagged footpath or pavement of pebbles or small stones.
Ploughland Land able to be cultivated by one plough team. Comparable to hide.
Probatur It is proved.

Quayf Coif. Woman's headdress.
Quare impedit Form of writ requiring a defendant to state why he prevents the plaintiff from presenting to a living.
Quitclaim Relinquish a claim or title.

Rectory Benefice the holder of which is entitled to the "great tithes", usually corn, hay and wool, but variable.

Ruckle drain Primitive drain lined with stones.

Seisin The giving of legal possession.

Sequestration Period of vacancy of a benefice.

Settlement Legal establishment in a parish, entitling to poor relief.

Shag, shagg Cloth with a nap on one side.

Shroud (**of trees**) Lop

Simnel Cake made specially for Mid Lent (Mothering) Sunday.

Sizar At Cambridge an undergraduate who performed services in exchange for an allowance.

Spanish bag Bag in which wool was imported from Spain.

Swanskin Fine thick kind of flannel.

Tarr *The meaning of this word has defied discovery.*

Terrier Inventory of church property.

Tilleting Application of tilly seed to cause a blister.

Tithe Tenth part of produce of land, applied to the support of parish clergy.

Traverse (**legal**) Denial.

Valor Ecclesiasticus Survey of value of churches made for Henry VIII in 1535.

Vestry Meeting of parishioners, having legal status.

Vicarage Parish the great tithes of which are due to a rector. (*See* rectory). Also the residence of a vicar, and the extent of church property enjoyed by him.

Vill Unit of feudal times, usually a primary settlement. Roughly equivalent to village.

Villein Highest class of peasant in feudal times.

Virgate A quarter of a ploughland. Same as yardland.

Visitation Routine visit by an ecclesiastical officer to enquire into affairs of a parish.

Yardland A quarter of a ploughland. Area variable, in Batheaston 20 acres. Same as virgate.

Bibliography

Abbreviations used:
Button: Button Mss. at Somerset County Record Office.
Ch. Ch.: Christ Church, Oxford.
C.P.R.: Calendar of Patent Rolls.
C.R.O.: Somerset County Record Office.
P.R.O.: Public Record Office.
S.A.N.H.S.: Somerset Archaeological and Natural History
    Society Proceedings.
S.H.: Somerset House.
S.R.S.: Somerset Record Society.

General references:
Collinson, John: *History and antiquities of Somersetshire*,
    3 vols., Bath, 1791.
Grimes, W. F. *and others: Excavations on defence sites*,
    Vol. 1, H.M.S.O., 1960.
Lewis, Harold: *The church rambler: churches in the neighbour-
    hood of Bath*, Vol. 1, 1876.
Wheatcroft, Mrs. L.: *Picturesque village rambles*, 1899.

Chapter 1
1. Grundy, G. B.: *The Saxon charters of Somerset*, S.R.S.,
    1935, p. 215.
2. Margary, I. D.: *Roman roads in Britain*, 1967, p. 142.
3. Grundy, G. B.: *The Saxon charters and field names of
    Gloucestershire*, Bristol and Gloucestershire Archaeo-
    logical Society, Special Volume, 1935/6, p. 97,
4. Finberg, H. P. R.: *The early charters of the West
    Midlands*, 1961, p. 53.
5. Grimes, W. F., *op. cit.*

Chapter 2
 1. Grimes, W. F., *op. cit.*
 2. Falconer, J. P. E.: *Antiquary*, 1902, Vol. 45, p. 454.
 3. Dobson, D. P.: *The archaeology of Somerset*, 1931, p. 87.
 4. Peake, H.: Catalogue of Bronze Age metal objects found
    in the British Isles. *At the Society of Antiquaries.*
 5. Winwood, H. H.: Bath Field Club, 1895, Vol. 8,
    p. 147.
 6. Skinner, J.: *Diaries*, 1822, Vol. 49, pp. 184–190. *At
    B.M.*
 7. Falconer, J. P. E. and Adams, S. B.: *University of
    Bristol Speleological Society*, 1931, Vol. 4, p. 183.
 8. Dowden, W. A.: *University of Bristol Speleological
    Society*, 1956, Vol. 8, p. 18.
 9. *Bath and Wilts Chronicle*, 8 July, 1954.
10. Scarth, Preb.: *S.A.N.H.S.*, 1885, Vol. 31, Part 2, p. 7.

Chapter 3
1. Darby, H. C. and Terrett, I. B.: *Domesday geography of
    Midland England*, 1954.
2. Darby, H. C. and Finn, Welldon: *Domesday geography
    of South-west England*, 1967.

Chapter 4
 1. A cartulary of Bath Abbey, S.R.S., 1893, Vol. 7,
    Corpus Christi College Ms. 37.

1a. S.A.N.H.S., Vol. 22, Part 2, p. 114. Facsimile with
    commentary.
2. A cartulary of Bath Abbey, S.R.S., 1893, Vol. 7,
    Lincoln's Inn Ms. 385 (Hale LXXXVII, The Bath
    Abbey Cartulary).
3. C.R.O., Button, 315.
4. C.P.R. 788, 38 Hen 8.
5. Augmentation Office, Particulars for Grants, Hen. 8,
    No. 739.
6. A cartulary of Bath Abbey, S.R.S., 1893, Vol. 7,
    Lincoln's Inn Ms. 164, 165.
7. Liber Albus, Chapter of Wells, I, f. 104.
8. A cartulary of Bath Abbey, S.R.S., 1893, Vol. 7,
    Lincoln's Inn Ms. 124.
9. *ibid.*, Lincoln's Inn Ms. 656.
10. *ibid.*, Corpus Christi College Ms. 1.

Chapter 5
 1. A cartulary of Bath Abbey, S.R.S., 1893, Vol. 7,
    Corpus Christi College Ms. 63.
 2. *ibid.*, Lincoln's Inn Ms. 164, 165.
 3. *ibid.*, Lincoln's Inn Ms. 656.
 4. C.P.R.
 5. Year books, 19 Edward 3, p. 115 and 20 Edward 3, I,
    p. 398.
 6. Dugdale, W.: *Monasticon*, 2, 260.
 7. Additional Ms. 13765.
 8. Letters and papers of Henry VIII, Vol. 21, Part 2.
 9. A cartulary of Bath Abbey, S.R.S., 1893, Vol. 7,
    Lincoln's Inn Ms. 3.
10. *ibid.*, 52.
11. C.R.O., Button 318.
12. Wilkins, D.: *Concilia*, 1737, Vol. 3, p. 216.
13. Warner, R.: *History of Bath*, 1802, Appendix 66:
    Harleian Ms. 3970.
14. Exchequer Special Commission 3222.
15. Somerset wills from Exeter, S.R.S., 1952, Vol. 62,
    p. 114.
16. Symons, K. E.: *The grammar school of King Edward the
    Sixth, Bath*, 1930, p. 192.
17. C.R.O.
18. Mitchell, W. S.: Bath Field Club, 1870, Vol. 2, p. 329.
19. *Notes and Queries, Eleventh Series*, Vol. 12, pp. 1, 21.
20. Deedes, C. and Walters, H. B.: *The church bells of
    Essex*, 1909, p. 8.
21. Cocks, A. H.: *The church bells of Buckinghamshire*,
    1897, p. 53.
22. Walters, H. B.: *The church bells of Wiltshire*, 1929,
    p. 266.
23. Ch. Ch. Ms. 232.
24. Matthew, A. G.: *Calamy revised*, 1934, p. 62.

Chapter 6
1. P.R.O.
2. S.R.S., 1904, Vol. 20, p. 72.
3. S.R.S., 1889, Vol. 3, p. 82.

4. Harleian Ms. 594.
5. Dwelly, E.: *Parish records*, 1913, Vol. 1, p. 68.
6. *ibid.*, 1914, Vol. 2, p. 202.
7. *Bath Advertiser*, 7 January 1758.
8. Fuller, M.: *West Country Friendly Societies*, 1964.
9. *Bath and Wilts Chronicle*, 30 April 1938.

Chapter 7
1. C.R.O., Button 336.
2. Munk, W.: *Roll of the Royal College of Physicians*, 1861, Vol. 1, p. 408.
3. Collinson, *op. cit.*
4. C.R.O., DD/BR/bb, Box 5.
5. Green, M. E.: "Bath doorways of the eighteenth century", *The Architectural Review*, May 1905, p. 67.
6. *Bath Chronicle*, 18 June 1781.
7. *Bath and Wilts Chronicle*, 7 March 1962.
8. Toynbee, Mrs. P., *ed.*: *Letters of Horace Walpole*, 1903–5, Vol. 7, p. 54.
9. Hesselgrave, R. A.: *Lady Miller and the Batheaston Literary Circle*, 1927, p. 76.
10. Graves, O. R.: *The triflers*, 1805, p. 13.
11. Dobson, A., *ed.*: *Letters of Madame d'Arblay*, 1904, Vol. 1, p. 381.
12. *Bath Herald*, 7 March 1913.
13. Ison, W.: *The Georgian buildings of Bath*, 1948, p. 41.
14. Egan, P.: *Walks through Bath*, 1819, p. 29.
15. Meehan, J. F.: *The Beacon*, August 1905.
16. Tilley, J. and Gaselee, S.: *The Foreign Office*, 1933.

17. Dean, C. G. T.: *The history of the Royal Hospital*, 1950.
18. Murch, J.: *Bath celebrities, with fragments of local history*, 1893, p. 434.
19. Bath Field Club, 1889, Vol. 6, p. 144.

Chapter 8
1. Notes compiled by John Whittington Bush, Bath Reference Library.

Chapter 9
1. Baker, W. P.: *The Amateur Historian*, Spring 1962.

Chapter 11
1. Bowen, H. C.: *Ancient Fields*, British Association for the Advancement of Science, 1961, p. 24.
2. Ch.Ch. Ms. 213.
3. Ch.Ch. Ms. 215.
4. C.R.O., DD/BR/bb, Box 5.
5. Trevelyan, G. M.: *English social history*, 1942, p. 378.
6. Grimes, *op. cit.*
7. Chancery Depositions, Elizabeth to Charles I, Bundle 51/2.

Chapter 12
1. C.R.O., Button 327/8.
2. C.R.O., Button 331/2.
3. C.R.O., Button 339.
4. Bidgood, W.: *Trade tokens*, S.A.N.H.S., 1886, Vol. 32, p. 124.

Field Names

Number of field	Name 1840 (Tithe Map)	Other references	Present name	See notes
1	Avonlands	Yaverland 1555, Averland 1625	Quarter mile field	A
1a			Little Meadow field	
1b			Weir Field	
2	Ebland		Part of 1b. Name recollected	B
3	Home Field	Clodacker 1290, Cloud Acre 1779	—	—
4	Pigacre		Pigacre	B
5	Woollands	1773	Top Field, Corner Field, Bottom Field	A
6	Great Tyning		Twelve Acres	—
7	Water Leaze	1767	Waterleaze	A
7a	—	Chancel Land 1640, 1709	Part of market garden	—
8	The Cliff	Clifte 1625	Cliff	A
9	New Tyning		"No name"	—
10	Croft above the brake		Fowl House Field	—
11	Garden	Wyre Mead, late eighteenth century	—	—
12	Townsend	The Townesend 1625	—	A
12a				
13	Cocksham Meadow	Croxsum 1625	Croxham	A
14	Gatteralls		Gattrell	A
14a	Gatterell	Gaterad/Gaterand 1291	Garden	A
14b	Gatehill		—	—
15	Starveall	Starvall 1775	Starfall	A
16	Muckleaze	Muckley 1625	Hatchet	A
16a			Little Muckley	
16b			Big Muckley	
16c			Sam's	
17	Bubbling Well	1625	Bubbling Well	A
17a	Little Bubbling		Little Bubbling	A
18	Ucombe Piece	Ewcombe 1625	Luccombe	A
19	Lillyport		Lilliput	B
20	George's Ground	1878	Garden of Eden or Tom Baker's Garden	—
21	George's Muckleaze	1878	Darke's Field	—
22	Stew Way Ground		White's Ground	—
23	Down Penning	Banner Down Penning 1834	Stone's Ground	—
24	Porters Bush	1755	Beggar's Bush	A
25	Six Acres		Martin's	—
26	Stibb's Piece	Stibbs family only to circa 1700	Stubbs	A
27	Great Tyning		Tynings Gardens	B
28	Foss Tyning		No information	—
29	Cottle's Tyning	1878	No information	—
30	Millway		Millway Gardens	B
31	Jones Tyning		—	—
32	Upright Lays		—	—
33	Alder Head		—	—
34	Stambridge Meadow, E. and W.	Stambrygmede 1431	Waterside	—
35	Lower, Middle, Upper Cross		—	—

Batheaston—Key to Map 2

Number of field	Name 1840 (Tithe Map)	Other references	Present name	See notes
36	Green Street	Grenestrete 1291	—	A
37	Foss Piece	Barebones 1826	—	—
38	Barnett's Piece		—	—
39	Smith's Ditch		—	—
40	Pound Ground		—	D
41	Procession Way	1625	—	A
42	High Mead		No information	C
42a	Land	Hennyard 1900	No information	C
43	Comers or Tyning	Corner or Tyning 1878	Tyning	—
44	Tyning	The Tynings 1914	Tyning	—
44a			Five Acres	
45	Slates		Sleights or Skeway	B
45a			Shire Ground	
46	Twelve Acres		French Ground	—
47	Great Field		No information	—
47a			Eleven Acres	—
47b			Barn Ground	A
48	Broad Moor	Broadmore 1625	Broad Moor	A
48a			Alder Beds	—
49	Alder Bed		Alder Bed	B
50	Little Field	1914	"No name"	—
51	Patch		"No name"	—
52	Stammers Leaze	Stammerland 1625	Firs or Badger Holes	A
53	Gritton	The Gritton 1773	Gritton	A
54	Holly Bush		Holly Bush	B
55	North End Cowleaze		Cowleaze	B
56	Mead		Mead	B
57	Orchard	Oakhay 1826	North End Orchard	—
58	Bence's Cowleaze	1914	Cowleaze	—
59	Horseleaze		Horseleaze	B
60	Cowleaze	1625	Cowleaze	A
61	Great Ground	1914	Barn Ground	—
62	Radford	Rodovus 1426	Tump	A
63	Little Radford		Fairhaven Field	—
64	Whiteley Hill	Wytlazehulle 1291	Whiteley Hill	A
65	Five Acres		Whitely Hill	—
65a	Six Acres		Long Ground	—
66	Normead		Normead Gardens	B
67	Wakefield	Wakefield 1869	Wayfield	B
67a	Wagfield			
68	Market Garden	Stokes' Close 1683	Marigolds	—
69	Orchard	Scudhayes 1623, Scudges 1767	—	—
70	Tyning above Luckham		"No name"	—
71	Great Lye		The Ley	B
72	Little Lye		Garden	—
73	Hard Piece		The Rodneys	—
74	Home Farm		No information	—
74a			Seven Acres	—
74b			Ley, or Home Field	—
75	Witchen Tree Field	Witchen Tree 1774	End of Farm	—
75a			Part of 107	
76	The Moor		The Nare or Little Nare	—
77	Tyning	Upper Tyning 1910	Shed Field or Big Nare	—
78	Oldlands Mere	Holding Mare 1769, Oldlands Mire 1863, Oldland's Mere 1910	Oldlands	A
78a			Plough Field	—
79	Two Acres		Hooper's field	B
80	Harrod Piece		Harrod, or Plough Ground	B
81	Stallard's Tyning	1819	Easton Gardens	—
82	Upper Book Croft	1750	Bookcroft	A

Batheaston—Key to Map 2

Number of field	Name 1840 (Tithe Map)	Other references	Present name	See notes
83	Old Tyning		Ricketts	—
84	Short Piece	A ground cold shortt pett 1693	Nissen	A
85	Mark Mead	Markmeade, or Vernyclose 1625	Home Field, or Hay Barn	A
86	Home Close		Hill Field	—
87	Banks Close		Home Field	—
88	Home Field		Paddock	—
89	Holly Lane Tyning	Holly Lane 1914	Hollies Lane Tyning	B
89a	Hollies Lane Tyning		Garden	—
90	Jeffries		—	
91	Summer Leaze	Somerleaze 1625	Summerleaze	A
92	Dyer's Leaze	Innocke 1625	Innox	A
93	Princes Hill	Princell 1625	Princes Hill	A
94	Upper Innox		Hill Fields	—
95	Nibley	Ebley 1625	Nibley	A
96	Giles Ground ⎫		⎧ Giles Ground ⎫	
97	Bar Hill Ground ⎭	1914	⎩ Barrow Ground ⎭	B
98	Cowards	Coward 1625	Cowards	A
98a	Ramscombe	Rushy Patch 1825	Rushy Patch	A
99	Seven Acres	1625	Seven Acres	A
100	Ramscombe	Remmescumb 1262	Ranscombe	A
101	In Catherine Field	S. Catherine 1914	Catherine Field	B
102	Bailey's Wood		Bailey's Wood	A
103	Yarn Drove Wood	Yarngrove 1423	Yarn Grove Wood	A
104 ⎫	Between Hills	Wyderetherecumb, Narwretherecumb 1262	⎧ Horse Ground ⎫	—
104a ⎭			⎩ No information ⎭	
105	Hilly Ground	1892	Hollow Ground	—
106	Three Witheys	1868	Part of Reservoir	—
107	Alder Moor Ground		Market Garden	—
108	Willis' Wood	(William Wyles 1425)	Wood	—
109	Charmbury's	⎧ (Nicholas de Chembury 1262), Charmbury 1446, ⎫ ⎩ 1673, Charmbury's 1925 ⎭	Bushy	A
110	In Shapcroft	Sharpcroft 1756	Home Ground	—
111	Pensylvania		Part of 113	—
112	Chelcombe	1625, Chilcombe 1925	Chilcombe	A
113	Home Hill	Haulm or Home Hill 1910	Steppy	—
114	Nesles Croft	Nessell Croft 1756	No information	—
115	Home Hill Ground		Little Ground and Square Ground	—
116 ⎫	Winterley	Wynterlye 1291, Winterlye 1625	⎧ Stone Shed ⎫	A
116a ⎭			⎩ Horse Ground ⎭	
117	Groves	1625. ? Hermegnof 1291	Groves	A
118	Penlands	Lower Groves or Penlands 1848	Lower Groves	B
119	Long Leaze		End of Farm	—
120	Bean Field	Middle Groves or Bean Field 1910	Groves	—
121	Cottles Penning	1910	Cottles Penning	B
122	Salisbury Hill		Little Solsbury	A
123	Salisbury Yat	Salisburyes gate 1625	Garden	A
124 ⎫	Greenway	1625	⎧ No information ⎫	—
124a ⎭			⎩ Flat Ground ⎭	
125	Bletchleys Tyning		Keyeses	—
126	Sillers Tyning	East of Pigeon Field 1825	"No name"	—
127	Pigeon's Leaze	Pigeon Field 1825	Pigeon's Lea	A
128	Hagthorn	Hagthorne 1625, Hackthorn 1825	Hagthorn	A
129	Pitlands	Putland 1291, Pittland 1625	Pitlands	A
130	Three Acres		South Penning	—
131	Two Acres		North Penning	—
132	Swainswick Field	1779	Swainswick Field	A
132a	Good Wives Acre		Banks	—
132b	Swainswick Field		Lands	—

Batheaston—Key to Map 2

Number of field	Name 1840 (Tithe Map)	Other references	Present name	See notes
133	Short Wood	Shortewode 1425	Shortwood	A
133a	Pasture		Ant Hills	—
134	Nimbletts	? Empnete 1262, Nimlett 1756	Nimlett	A
135	Hanging Furlong	1757	Furlongs	A
136	Cherrywell Wood	1757	Cherrywell Wood	A
136a	Moon Leaze		No information	—
137	Leys		No information	—
137a	Cherrywell Tyning		No information	—
138	Customary Down		—	—
139	Hartley Down	Hertlegh 931, Horteley 1425	Hartley Down	A
140	Fatting Down		Fatting Down	B
141	Long Mead		No information	—
142	Foss Down		No information	—
143	Twelve Acres		Twelve Acres, Plantation	—
143a	Pasture		Eight Acres	—
143b	Hunterwick Wood		Hunterwick Wood	B
144	Home Close		Home Close	B
144a	Hartley Wood		Hartley Wood	B
145	Hunterwick Field		Hunterwick Field	B
146	Part of Little Plain		Little Plain	B
147	Part of Great Plain		Great Plain	B
148	Lime Kiln Ground		Lime Kiln Ground	B
149	Jacks Mead		Jacks Mead	B
150	Stencils		Tassles, Stassells	B
151	Clay Pool		Clay Pool	B
152	Great Field		Big Down	—

S. Catherine—Key to Map 2

Number of field	Name 1490 (Tithe Map)	Other references	Present name	See notes
1, 1a, 1b	Huntricks, Hunterswick	Hunterwyke 1378	Firs, Hunterwick, Tumpy Field	A
2	Bushey Hill	Bushay Hill 1825	Bushy Hill	A
3	Upper Crocker Field		Bath Ground	—
3a	Lower, Middle Crocker Field		Plough Ground	—
4	Whitely	White Haies 1594, Whitey 1777	White Leaze, Whiting	A
5	Calf Hay	1777	Calf Way	A
6	Great Mead		No information	—
7, 7a	Lower, Upper Snail Pit	Snell Pits 1673, Snow Pits 1825	Snarl Pit	A
8, 8a	Cripps, Cripps Wood		Cripps, Cripps Wood	B
9	Home Field		Home Field or Lower Combe	B
10, 10a	Lower, Upper Lillys	Le Leys 1262 (John Lylys 1377) Lyllies 1594	Lillys	A
11	Andrews Mead		Wash Pool Ground	—
11a	Andrews Hill Mead		Hanging Ground	—
11b	Andrews Hill		No information	—
11c	Andrews Wood		No information	—

S. Catherine—Key to Map 2

Number of field	Name 1490 (Tithe Map)	Other references	Present name	See notes
12 12a	Sturridge	(Roger Sturegges 1310, William Styrigg 1388) Sterge 1594	The Plain, Hendres Hill Sterridge	A
13 13a	Combe Field Combe Wood	The Combes 1673, Combe 1777	Upper Combe Combe Wood	A
14	Brownings with Sharp Croft	Sharp Croft 1756	Sharp Croft	A
15	Down Field		Down Field	B
16 16a	Summer Hill, Summer Hill Wood		Summer Hill and Wood	B
17	Six Acres		Six Acres	B
18	The Hills	Hill Ground 1777	The Hills	A
19	Little Down		Little Down	B
20	The Down		The Down	B
21	Lewis's Norridge		Norridge	B
22	Drewetts Down	Name dates from the enclosure of Holts Down 1748	Norridge	—
23	Sperrings Down		Norridge	—
24	Broad Mead	1756, 1925	Field at the top of the Brake	A
25 25a	Home Ground	Six Acres 1446, Home Ground 1756 1756	Home Field Saw Pits	A —
26	Jones's Leaze	1733. Jones or Ox Lea 1776	Five Acres	A
27	Willis's	(William Wyles 1425), Willowes 1546, Willis' 1756	Horse Field or Square Ground	A
28	Tyning or Middle Hill		Horse Ground	—
28a	Sandy Hill		Tump Ground	—
29	Ramscombe	Ranscombe 1594	Ramscombe	A
30	Yarn Grove	Iron Grove 1594	Yarn Grove	A
31	Gatteralls	Gaterad 1446, Gateratte 1546	Gattrell	A
32	Holts Down	La holtes 1263, Holts Down 1594	Holts Down	A
33	Coates Down	Coat's Furlong 1755	Coaches Down	A
33a	Coates Wood		Part of Cowleaze Wood	—
34	Norwich and Cow Leaze	Norwiche 1594, Norwich 1777	Norwich	A
34a	Cowleaze Wood		Cowleaze Wood	
35	Stilcombe		Stilcombe	B
35a	Stilcombe Wood		Stilcombe Wood	
36	Bean Close		Bean Close	B
37	Berdgham Orchard	Burghams 1596, Burjams 1777	Burgains	A
38	Moor	The More 1673	North Field	—
39	North Field	1594	North Field	A
40	Home Furlong Orchard		Orchard	—
41	Fish Pond, Bog		Fish Pond Wood	A
42	Palmer's Mead		Palmer's Mead	B
43	Stilcombe Garden	Vineyard 1310 and 1377	Vineyard	A
44	Black Breeches	Blakebridge (a close) 1546	Breeches	A
45	Conygre Garden		Conygre Garden	B
46	Totness		Totness	B
47	Broad Mead	Broadmeade 1672	Broad Mead	A
47a	Mead or Yonder Close	Yorden's Close 1777	Pig's Orchard	A
48	Stibbs Hill	(William Stubbe 1263, Walter Stubbe 1310) 1594	Part of Pigs Orchard	A
49	Mead Orchard		Mead Orchard	B
50	Breach	1777	Breeches	A
51	Lawless	Lawles 1546	Lallis	A
52	Grove Wood		Lyegrove Wood	B
53 53a	Crackham, Crackham Wood	1825	Crackham	A
54	New Leaze	1777	No information	—

S. Catherine—Key to Map 2

Number of field	Name 1490 (Tithe Map)	Other references	Present name	See notes
55 55a 55b	Down Edge, Upper and Lower Down Edge	} 1777	Downage, Upper and Lower Dunnage	A
56	The Down		Crossways	—
57	Bleakmoor, Blakemoor, Holts Down	Blackmore 1594, Blackmoor 1914	Holts Down	A
58	Catherine Field	1925	Catherine Field	B
59	Penny Slait	Pennyslade 1594, Pennys Last 1914	Pennyslait or T. Ground	A
60	Long Acres	1825	Bushy Ground	—
61	Stubby Close	1777	Stubby Close	A
62	Holts Piece		Holts Piece or Tyning	B
63	Powells Land	1825	Bushy Ground	—
64	White Acre			
65	Dollings Tyning	1825	Dollings Tyning	A
66	Swinhill	Swynehill 1594	French Ground	A
67	Tyning or Furlong	Furlong 1777, 1914	Tyning	A
68	Tyning Garden		Prince's Hill	—
69	Tyning or Pit Acre		Pinegar	B
70	The Spy Tyning	Spight Tining 1777	Crossways	A
71	Holts	1777	Holte	A
72	Blackmores	Blackmeres Field 1777	Blackmore Field	A
73	Pointing's Hill Orchard	?Painters Grove 1591, Pontins Hill 1777	Pontins Hill	A

Index